The Pragmatic Turn

The Pragmatic Turn

Richard J. Bernstein

Polity

First published in 2010 by Polity Press
Reprinted in 2010

Polity Press
65 Bridge Street
Cambridge CB2 1UR, UK

Polity Press
350 Main Street
Malden, MA 02148, USA

ISBN-13: 978-0-7456-4907-8 (hardback)
ISBN-13: 978-0-7456-4908-5 (paperback)

A catalogue record for this book is available from the
British Library.

Typeset in 11 on 12.5 pt Baskerville 2
by Toppan Best-set Premedia Limited
Printed and bound in the United States by Odyssey Press Inc.,
Gonic, New Hampshire

For further information on Polity, visit our website:
www.politybooks.com

For Richard and Mary Rorty

Davidson may have been right when he wrote that "a sea change" is occurring in recent philosophical thought – "a change so profound that we may not recognize that it is occurring." If the change of which Davidson spoke is someday recognized as having occurred [then] Peirce, James, and Dewey may cease to be treated as provincial figures. They may be given the place I think they deserve in the story of the West's intellectual progress.

Richard Rorty

Contents

Acknowledgments

I am grateful for permission to use revised versions of my previously published work. "John Dewey's Vision of Radical Democracy," in *The Cambridge Companion to Dewey*, ed. Molly Cochron (Cambridge: Cambridge University Press, 2010); "Hegel and Pragmatism," in *Von der Logik zur Sprache: Stuttgarter Hegel-Kongress, 2005*, ed. R. Bubner and G. Hindrichs (Stuttgart: Kett-Cotta, 2007); "Pragmatism, Objectivity, and Truth," *Philosophical Topics*, 36/1 (Spring 2008); "The Pragmatic Turn: The Entanglement of Fact and Value," in *Hilary Putnam*, ed. Y. Ben-Menahem (Cambridge: Cambridge University Press, 2005); "Rorty's Deep Humanism," *New Literary History*, 39/1 (Winter 2008).

I also want to thank Scott Shushan and Erick Raphael Jiménez who helped in numerous ways to edit the manuscript. Professor Carol Bernstein's perceptive detailed comments and challenging criticisms were, as always, invaluable. Jean van Altena edited my manuscript with great care and excellent judgment. John Thompson has encouraged me at every stage at working on this book.

Preface

When I wrote my dissertation on John Dewey in the 1950s, interest in Dewey and pragmatism seemed to be at an all-time low among academic philosophers. The pragmatists were thought to be passé and to have been displaced by the new linguistic turn in analytic philosophy. I felt then (and continue to believe) that Peirce, James, Dewey, and Mead were really ahead of their time – that they were initiating a sea change in philosophy. Over the years I have explored the works of a variety of thinkers working in Anglo-American and Continental traditions. But it has struck me over and over again that many twentieth- and twenty-first-century philosophers – some of whom had little or no knowledge of the classical pragmatic thinkers – were dealing with similar themes and coming to similar conclusions. In pursuing their distinctive inquiries, they were frequently refining (and, sometimes, challenging) themes prominent in the classical American pragmatists. Gradually, the rationale for this convergence became clear to me. Pragmatism begins with a radical critique of what Peirce called "the spirit of Cartesianism." By this Peirce meant a framework of thinking that had come to dominate much of modern philosophy – where sharp dichotomies are drawn between what is mental and physical, as well as subject and object; where "genuine" knowledge presumably rests upon indubitable foundations; and where we can bracket all prejudices by methodical doubt. This way of thinking introduces a whole series of interrelated problems that preoccupied philosophers: the problem of the external world, the problem of our knowledge of other minds, and the problem of how to correctly represent reality. The pragmatic thinkers called into question the framework in which these traditional problems had been formulated. They rejected what Dewey called the "quest for certainty" and the "spectator theory of knowledge." They sought to develop a comprehensive alternative to Cartesianism – a nonfoundational self-corrective conception of human inquiry based upon an understanding of how human agents are formed by, and actively participate in shaping, normative social practices. And they showed the critical role that philosophy can play in guiding our conduct, enriching our everyday experience, and furthering "creative democracy."

The sharp critique of Cartesianism is also characteristic of two of the most influential philosophers of the twentieth century: Wittgenstein and Heidegger. Neither of them had any serious knowledge of American pragmatism, but in very different ways they were responding to the same deficiencies of modern philosophy that had provoked the pragmatists. It is striking how they (and others influenced by them) came to share many of the same insights of the pragmatists in what Heidegger calls our "being-in-the-world" and Wittgenstein calls "forms of life."

There is a popular belief that, in the mid-twentieth century, the linguistic turn and analytic philosophy displaced pragmatism. But in the past few decades the *continuity* between the classical American pragmatists and much of the best work by analytic philosophers – including Quine, Davidson, and Sellars – has become increasingly evident. Pragmatism began as a distinctive American philosophical movement, but it has had a global reach. This is evident in the influence of pragmatism on post-Second World War German philosophy. Apel, Habermas, Wellmer, Honneth, and Joas have all appropriated and contributed to the development of pragmatic themes. Today there are more and more thinkers all over the world who have come to appreciate the contributions of the classical American pragmatists.

Frequently, academic philosophers speak about the Anglo-American analytic/Continental split, but this unfortunate dichotomy obscures more than it illuminates. Philosophers from both sides of the "split" are discovering how much they can learn from styles of thinking that initially seem so alien. My basic thesis is that, during the past 150 years, philosophers working in different traditions have explored and refined themes that were prominent in the pragmatic movement. In the Prologue, I examine the origins of American pragmatism and set forth my general thesis about the dominance of pragmatic themes in contemporary philosophy. The next three chapters explore central issues in Peirce, James, and Dewey. I then turn to examining the Hegelian influence on pragmatism; the pragmatic understanding of justification, objectivity, and truth; and the role of experience after the linguistic turn. The final chapters deal with three of the most important thinkers shaped by the pragmatic tradition: Hilary Putnam, Jürgen Habermas, and Richard Rorty.

This book is not intended to be a history or survey of pragmatism. I have lived with the pragmatists for more than 50 years, and I want to share what I have learned from them. I believe that my original intuitions about the importance of pragmatism and the sea change it initiated have been fully vindicated. Today, the vigorous creative discussion of pragmatic themes by thinkers all over the world is more widespread than it has ever been in the past.

Prologue

"Isms" in philosophy are notorious, and this is certainly true of "pragmat*ism*." It is fashionable in philosophy to speak about "isms": "materialism," "idealism," "existentialism," "realism," "nominalism," "naturalism," etc. The advantage of this type of talk is that it enables us to label philosophical positions, orientations, and theses that presumably share distinctive characteristics. But there are also dangers, because we may be seduced into thinking that there is an essential hard core to a particular "ism." What is worse, we often use these expressions carelessly, frequently assuming that our hearers and readers have a perfectly clear idea of what we mean. Yet when we closely examine the positions advocated by representatives of these "isms," we discover enormous differences – including conflicting and even contradictory claims. Even the anti-essentialist idiom of "family resemblances" has become a cliché. Not only are differences in a family as striking as any resemblances, but in an actual family, we can typically appeal to common biological factors to *identify* a family. There is nothing comparable to this in philosophy. So it might seem advisable to drop all talk of "isms" in order to avoid confusion, ambiguity, and vagueness. Yet this would also impoverish our ability to understand what we take to be positions and thinkers who, despite significant differences, do share important overlapping features.

These general observations are relevant to pragmatism. In the case of pragmatism, we have the advantage of being able to specify the precise date when the word was first introduced publicly to identify a philosophical position. On 26 August 1898, William James delivered an address before the Philosophical Union of the University of California in Berkeley. Characteristically in his eloquent, gracious, and informal manner, James introduces pragmatism in his talk, "Philosophical Conceptions and Practical Results."

> An occasion like the present would seem to call for an absolutely untechnical discourse. I ought to give a message with a practical outcome and an emotional accompaniment, so to speak, fitted to interest men as men, and yet also not altogether to disappoint philosophers – since philosophers, let them be as queer as they will, still are men in the secret recesses of their hearts, even here in Berkeley. (James 1997, pp. 345–6)[1]

James tells us that "philosophers are after all like poets." They are pathfinders who blaze new trails in the forest. They suggest "a few formulas, a few technical conceptions, a few verbal pointers – which at least define the initial directions of the trail" (James 1997, p. 347). With this initial flourish, he introduces pragmatism.

> I will seek to define with you what seems to be the most likely direction in which to start upon the trail of truth. Years ago this direction was given to me by an American philosopher whose home is in the East, and whose published works, few as they are scattered in periodicals, are no fit expression of his powers. I refer to Mr. Charles S. Peirce, with whose very existence as a philosopher I dare say many of you are unacquainted. He is one of the most original of contemporary thinkers, and the principle of practicalism – or pragmatism, as he called it, when I first heard him enunciate it at Cambridge in the early 70's – is the clue or compass by following which I find myself more and more confirmed in believing we may keep our feet upon the proper trail. (James 1997, p. 348)

This is the first public philosophical introduction of the word "pragmatism," and the first narrative account of the origin of American pragmatism.[2] When James tells us that he heard the principle of pragmatism enunciated in the 1870s, he is referring to the meetings of the Metaphysical Club, an informal discussion group that met in Cambridge, and he specifically refers to Peirce's now famous 1878 paper, "How to Make Our Ideas Clear."[3]

> Peirce's principle, as we may call it, may be expressed in a variety of ways, all of them very simple. In *Popular Science Monthly* for January,

1878, he introduces it as follows: The soul and meaning of thought, he says, can never be made to direct itself toward anything but the production of belief, belief being the demi-cadence which closes a musical phrase in the symphony of our intellectual life. (James 1997, p. 348)[4]

Here is Peirce's own formulation of what has subsequently been called the "pragmatic maxim" – even though Peirce did not use the word "pragmatic" in this article.

> Consider what effects, which might conceivably have practical bearings, we conceive the object of our conception to have. Then our conception of these effects is the whole of our conception of the object. (Peirce 1992, p. 132)

Prior to 1898, neither Peirce nor any of the other thinkers that we today associate with the pragmatic movement had ever mentioned "pragmatism" in their published writings. Yet, after James published his Berkeley address, the word caught on and spread like wildfire. When James published *Pragmatism: A New Name for Some Old Ways of Thinking*, nine years after he delivered his Berkeley address, he wrote the following about "Peirce's principle":

> The term is derived from the same Greek word πρᾶγμα, meaning action, from which our words 'practice' and 'practical' come. It was first introduced into philosophy by Mr. Charles Peirce in 1878. In an article entitled 'How to Make Our Ideas Clear,' ... Mr. Peirce, after pointing out that our beliefs are really rules for action, said that, to develop a thought's meaning, we need only determine what conduct it is fitted to produce: that conduct is for us its sole significance. And the tangible fact at the root of all our thought-distinctions, however subtle, is that there is no one of them so fine as to consist in anything but a possible difference in practice. To attain perfect clearness in our thoughts of an object, then, we need only consider what conceivable effects of a practical kind the object may involved – what sensations we are to expect from it, and what reactions we must prepare. Our conception of these effects, whether immediate or remote, is then for us the whole of our conception of the object, so far as that conception has positive significance at all.
>
> This is the principle of Peirce, the principle of pragmatism. It lay entirely unnoticed by anyone for twenty years, until I ... brought it forward again and made a special application of it to religion. By that date (1898) the times seemed ripe for its reception. The word

'pragmatism' spread, and at present it fairly spots the pages of the philosophic journals. (James 1997, pp. 377–8)

Not only had the word spread, but pragmatism was savagely caricatured and severely criticized. Peirce was so distressed about the popular literary appropriation of "pragmatism" that he disowned the word. In an article entitled "What Pragmatism Is," published in the *Monist* (April 1905), he wrote:

> But at present, the word begins to be met with occasionally in the literary journals where it gets abused in the merciless way that words have to expect when they fall into literary clutches. ... So then, the writer, finding his bantling "pragmatism" so promoted, feels that it is time to kiss his child goodbye and relinquish it to its higher destiny; while to serve the precise purpose of expressing the original definition, he begs to announce the birth of the word "pragmaticism," which is ugly enough to be safe from kidnappers. (Peirce 1998, pp. 334–5)[5]

The confusion about the meaning of pragmatism was so widespread that on the tenth anniversary of James's introduction of the term, Arthur O. Lovejoy set out to distinguish *thirteen* different meanings of pragmatism. With sly irony, Lovejoy wrote:

> In the present year of grace 1908 the term "pragmatism" – if not the doctrine – celebrates its tenth birthday. Before the controversy over the mode of philosophy designated by it enters upon a second decade, it is perhaps not too much to ask that contemporary philosophers should agree to attach some single meaning to the term. ... A complete enumeration of the metamorphoses of so protean an entity is, indeed, perhaps too much to expect: but even after we leave out of the count certain casual expressions of pragmatist writers which they probably would not wish taken too seriously, and also certain mere commonplaces from which scarcely any contemporary philosopher would dissent, there remain at least thirteen pragmatisms: a baker's dozen of contentions which are separate not merely in the sense of being discriminable, but in the sense of being logically independent, so that you may without inconsistency accept any one and reject all the others, or refute one and leave the philosophical standing of the others unimpugned. All of these have generally or frequently been labeled with one name and defended or attacked as if they constituted a single system of thought – sometimes even as if they were severally interchangeable. (Lovejoy 1963, p. 1)

I suspect that today, a hundred years after Lovejoy wrote these words, many philosophers may want to suggest that Lovejoy was far too conservative in discriminating *only* thirteen pragmatisms.

The Cultural Context

In order to bring some clarity to the meaning(s) of pragmatism and the vicissitudes of the movement, I wish to describe briefly the state of philosophy in the United States during the last decades of the nineteenth century – especially after the Civil War. Prior to the Civil War, there is scarcely any evidence of the discipline of philosophy in the United States. Of course, an educated elite existed (primarily clergy) who had some familiarity with the great philosophers of the past, but the institution of an ongoing discipline that we could today identify as philosophy did not exist. Throughout most of the nineteenth century, our colleges were primarily undergraduate teaching institutions preparing young men to become clergy and for citizenship. To speak of undergraduate colleges is already anachronistic, because there was no well-defined graduate education. The idea of a university as an institution dedicated to encouraging scholarly research came into existence only during the last decades of the nineteenth century. But in the period after the Civil War, a remarkable intellectual life flourished. During this time the most creative discussion took place within informal discussion groups. A great center of intellectual life was Cambridge, Massachusetts. The Metaphysical Club was only one of numerous philosophical discussion groups that spontaneously arose. Educated individuals with a great variety of interests (and professions) came together to present papers, discuss texts, and engage in lively debates. Neither Peirce nor James was ever *formally* trained as a philosopher. Peirce, the son of a famous Harvard mathematician, Benjamin Peirce, identified himself as a practicing experimental scientist and a logician. James, who was trained as a medical doctor (but never practiced medicine), initially gained his fame for his work in psychology. They were intellectuals whose interests ranged over the gamut of human affairs. Philosophy, as they practiced it, was not a distinctively demarcated discipline – a *Fach* – but emerged from their reflections on the range of human knowledge and activities. And they

did not hesitate to speculate about the nature of the cosmos. Wilfrid
Sellars tells us: "The aim of philosophy, abstractly formulated, is
to understand how things in the broadest sense of the term hang
together in the broadest possible sense of the term" (Sellars 1963,
p. 1). Peirce and James conceived of, and practiced, philosophical
reflection in this manner.

Cambridge was not the only center of philosophical activity in the
United States during the post-Civil War period. During the nineteenth century a significant number of educated Germans emigrated
to the United States – several of whom rose to prominent positions.
They brought with them a vital interest in German philosophy, especially Kant and Hegel. "Kant clubs" and "Hegel clubs" sprang up in
Missouri and Ohio. Individuals, frequently not associated with any
academic institution, met to discuss and debate philosophical issues.
Few philosophers today are aware of Henry C. Brockmeyer (1826–
1906), a German émigré, lawyer, and lieutenant-governor of Missouri,
who spent many years working on a translation of Hegel's *Logic* – a
translation never published but circulated and recopied by others who
shared Brockmeyer's passion for Hegel. Better known is William T.
Harris, born in New England, who along with Brockmeyer established
the St Louis Philosophical Society. They became known as the "St
Louis Hegelians." Harris, who later was appointed US Commissioner
of Education, founded the *Journal of Speculative Philosophy* in 1867, the
first journal in America dedicated exclusively to philosophical studies.
Harris conceived of the journal as a means for spreading the influence
of Hegel and German idealism in the United States. The early issues
were filled with translations and discussions of German philosophy.
One of Peirce's earliest philosophical publications was an exchange
with Harris about technical issues in Hegel's *Logic* (see Peirce 1984,
pp. 132–59). Some of the most important early articles by Peirce,
James, and Dewey appeared in Harris's journal.

Harris is noteworthy for another reason. When John Dewey was
22, he submitted his first philosophical article to Harris, and hesi-
tantly asked for an assessment of his philosophical ability. Harris's
encouragement played a significant role in Dewey's decision to apply
to the newly founded graduate philosophy program at Johns Hopkins
University. Although Peirce was teaching logic at Johns Hopkins when
Dewey was a graduate student, the major influence on Dewey during
his graduate studies was the neo-Hegelian, G. S. Morris. In Dewey's
own recounting of the development of American pragmatism, he tells

us that the neo-Kantian and Hegelian influences were "very marked in the United States during the last decade of the nineteenth century. I myself, and those who collaborated with me in the exposition of instrumentalism, began by being neo-Kantians, in the same way that Peirce's point of departure was Kantianism and that of James was the empiricism of the British School" (Dewey 1981, p. 52).[6]

Dewey started his teaching career at the University of Minnesota in 1888, but moved to the University of Michigan the following year. At Michigan, he met George H. Mead, who became a lifelong friend and colleague. Mead had studied at Harvard, primarily with the neo-Hegelian Josiah Royce.[7] Mead had also spent some time in Germany studying physiological psychology and attending the lectures of Wilhelm Dilthey. When Dewey was offered the chairmanship of the Department of Philosophy and Psychology at the newly founded University of Chicago in 1894, he brought Mead with him. From their earliest association they exerted a mutual philosophical influence.

The liveliness and fertility of this "classical" period of American pragmatism is due to several factors.[8] These thinkers drew upon a rich diversity of philosophical traditions. Peirce's original source of inspiration was Kant. Peirce also had a sophisticated knowledge of the history of philosophy and science. He was familiar with the subtlety of medieval thought, especially that of Duns Scotus, at a time when philosophers barely paid any attention to this medieval tradition. James appropriated themes from British empiricism and dedicated *Pragmatism* to John Stuart Mill, although he vigorously criticized the static abstractness of the British empiricist conception of experience. Dewey was inspired by the version of Hegelianism that was influential in the United States and England during the last decades of the nineteenth century, although Darwin soon replaced Hegel as Dewey's intellectual hero.[9] Because there was no single dominant philosophical school or tradition in the United States, the pragmatic thinkers enjoyed a freedom in their creative appropriation of philosophical themes. At the time divisions that are now so prominent in academic disciplines and subdisciplines simply did not exist. Consequently, there was an intellectual ease in the way these thinkers spanned the various areas and fields of knowledge and human activity. The more closely one studies these thinkers, the more one realizes how different they were in their temperaments, talents, backgrounds, and interests. With his sophisticated knowledge of mathematics, logic, probability, and the natural sciences, Peirce was certainly the most "tough-minded" of the group. James had remarkable psychological perspicuity and was deeply concerned with the varieties of religious experience throughout his life. James's descriptions of the plurality of human experience display a rare phenomenological subtlety and metaphorical vividness.[10] Consider how Dewey described the difference between Peirce and James:

> Peirce was above all a logician; whereas James was an educator and humanist and wished to force the general public to realize that certain problems, certain philosophic debates, have a real importance for mankind, because the beliefs which they bring into play lead to very different modes of conduct. If this important distinction is not grasped, it is impossible to understand the majority of ambiguities and errors which belong to the later period of the pragmatic movement. (Dewey 1981, p. 46)

James, not Peirce, was the major influence on Dewey during his Chicago years, when he and his colleagues were working out their experimental instrumentalism.[11] Dewey was attracted to the biological motifs in James's *Principles of Psychology*.[12] Dewey's fascination with organic metaphors was already evident in the Hegelian phase of his development, but became dominant with his turn toward Darwin.[13] Darwin's *The Origin of Species* had been published in 1859, the year of Dewey's birth. All the pragmatic thinkers were influenced by Darwin's evolutionary hypotheses.[14] The themes of democracy, education, and social reform became central to Dewey's version of pragmatism. Mead, who shared many of Dewey's interests in philosophy and social reform, was also concerned with the social character and the genesis of language and communication. Mead, more than any other of the pragmatic thinkers, developed a detailed comprehensive social theory of action and language. All of these thinkers were robust naturalists stressing the *continuity* of human beings with the rest of nature, although each of them strongly opposed scientism, reductive naturalism, and mechanical determinism. They argued for the positive role of chance and contingency in the universe. They were skeptical of any attempt to draw a sharp boundary between philosophical reflection and scientific activity. Each of them stressed the need for philosophy to be informed by, and open to, the significance of novel scientific developments. They were critical of the traditional philosophical quest for absolute certainty and of what Dewey labeled the "spectator theory of knowledge." They emphasized the role of *know-how*, *social practices*, and *human agency*.

There is another aspect of the pragmatic thinkers that should be highlighted – their self-understanding that pragmatism was related to important features of American life. (This is especially true of James, Dewey, and Mead, less so of Peirce.) Thus far, I have been stressing how the classical pragmatists were influenced by, and transformed, themes that they appropriated from European philosophy, but they were self-consciously Americans. In "The Development of American Pragmatism," which was originally written for a European audience, Dewey says that the pragmatic movement is a "re-adaptation" of European thought. He vehemently rejects the caricature that pragmatism reflects the worst aspects of American materialism. Speaking of the various philosophical developments in America, Dewey asserts that "they do not aim to glorify the energy and love of action which the new conditions of American life exaggerated. They do not reflect the excessive mercantilism of American life. ... Instrumentalism maintains in opposition to many contrary tendencies in the American environment, that action should be intelligent and reflective, and that thought should occupy a central position in life" (Dewey 1981, p. 56). He also declares:

> It is beyond doubt that the progressive and unstable character of American life and civilization has facilitated the birth of a philosophy which regards the world as being in continuous formation, where there is still place for indeterminism, for the new, and for a real future. But this idea is not exclusively American, although the conditions in American life have aided this idea in becoming self-conscious. (Ibid.)

Peirce was even more emphatic in repudiating the caricature of pragmatism. In "What Pragmatism Is" he presents an imaginary dialogue between a pragmaticist and his questioner.

> *Questioner*: Well, if you choose so to making Doing the Be-all and the End-all of human life, why do you not make meaning to consist simply in doing? ...
>
> *Pragmaticist*: Forcibly put! ... It must be admitted ... that if pragmaticism really made Doing to be the Be-all and the End-all of life, that would be its death. For to say that we live for the mere sake of action, as action, regardless of the thought it carries out, would be

to say that there is no such thing as rational purport. (Peirce 1998, p. 341)

Louis Menand, in *The Metaphysical Club: A Story of Ideas in America*, situates the pragmatic movement in the context of American history. One of Menand's contributions is to show how the origins of pragmatism can, in part, be understood as a critical response to the horrors and excesses of the Civil War. Menand focuses on four individuals: Oliver Wendell Holmes, Jr (a participant in the discussions of the Metaphysical Club), William James, Charles S. Peirce, and John Dewey – although he also discusses many of their contemporaries. Menand makes a bold claim about the influence of these four.

> Their ideas changed the way Americans thought – and continue to think – about education, democracy, liberty, justice, and tolerance. And as a consequence they changed the way Americans live – the way they learn, the way they express themselves, and the way in which they treat people who are different from them. We are still living, to a great extent, in a country these thinkers helped to make. (Menand 2001, p. xi)

What was the bond that tied together these thinkers? Menand's thesis is that they shared a common attitude toward ideas.

> What was that attitude? If we strain out the differences, personal and philosophical, they had with one another, we can say that what these four thinkers had in common was not a group of ideas, but a single idea – an idea about ideas. They all believed that ideas are not "out there" waiting to be discovered, but are tools ... that people devise to cope with the world in which they find themselves. They believed that ideas are produced not by individuals – that ideas are social. They believed that ideas do not develop according to some inner logic of their own, but are entirely dependent, like germs, on human careers and environment. And they believed that since ideas are provisional responses to particular situations, their survival depends not on their immutability but on their adaptability. (Menand 2001, pp. xi–xii)

The Historical Vicissitudes of Pragmatism

Let us return to the history and vicissitudes of the pragmatism in America (see also Bernstein 2006b, pp. 1–14). Originally "pragmatism" was used in a restricted sense – primarily to identify Peirce's theory of meaning and James's extension of Peirce's maxim to characterize truth. Neither Peirce nor James ever used the expression to describe his entire philosophical orientation. Dewey preferred to characterize his philosophy as "experimentalism," or "instrumentalism," and sometimes as "instrumental experimentalism."[15] But gradually "pragmatism" was generalized as a convenient label to refer to this group of diverse thinkers. The expression "pragmatism" is like an accordion; it is sometimes stretched to include a wide diversity of positions and thinkers (not just philosophers) and sometimes restricted to specific doctrines of the original American pragmatists. The truth is that ever since the origins of American pragmatism – and right up to the present – critics and champions of pragmatism have been arguing about what constitutes pragmatism and who is and is not a pragmatist.[16] Rather than attempting to define pragmatism anew, I hope to *show* through my discussion of specific themes what I take to be characteristic of the best of the pragmatic tradition.

Peirce was barely known during his lifetime except by the small circle of his admirers, which included James, Dewey, Royce, and Mead. James was immensely popular – a gifted lecturer who attracted audiences in the hundreds. And during the first decades of the twentieth century, Dewey exerted a powerful influence upon many American progressives, even though his professional philosophical colleagues were critical of his pragmatism, experimentalism, and naturalism. By the 1930s, pragmatism as a vital philosophical movement began to fade from the American scene. The movement seemed to have exhausted its creative potential. William James had characterized pragmatism as a philosophy that is both "tough-minded" and "tender-minded." But increasingly, among academic philosophers, pragmatism was viewed as excessively "tender-minded" – diffuse, fuzzy, and soft at its center. A patronizing attitude toward pragmatism developed. The pragmatists may have had their hearts in the right place, but not their heads. Their vagueness and lack of clarity simply did not meet the high standards of "rigor" required for serious philosophical inquiry.

One cannot overestimate the quiet revolution that was transforming academic philosophy in America. This was, in part, a consequence of the growing influence of the émigré philosophers who had escaped from Europe and joined American philosophy departments: Reichenbach, Carnap, Tarski, Feigl, Hempel, and many others. Several of these philosophers had been associated with the famous Vienna

Circle. They all shared a logical finesse, sophisticated knowledge of the physical sciences, and a commitment to the highest standards of argumentation, which surpassed anything exhibited by the classical pragmatists (with the exception of Peirce). These logical empiricists sought to establish alliances with American philosophers who had been shaped by the pragmatic tradition. From the perspective of the logical empiricists, the pragmatic thinkers were viewed as having seen through a glass darkly what was now seen much more clearly. The *myth* developed (and unfortunately became entrenched) that pragmatism was primarily an anticipation of logical positivism, in particular, the positivist's verifiability criterion of meaning.

Other influences also had a deep impact on the character of philosophy in mid-twentieth-century America. Whereas philosophers from Dewey's and Mead's generation turned to Germany for philosophical inspiration, England – Cambridge, and especially Oxford – became the place where young American philosophers made their intellectual pilgrimage after the Second World War. They were fascinated with the new type of philosophizing initiated by G. E. Moore, Bertrand Russell, Wittgenstein (at least the Wittgenstein filtered by his Anglo-American students), Gilbert Ryle, and J. L. Austin.

After the Second World War, during a period of rapid growth of American universities, academic philosophy in the United States was completely transformed (except for a few pockets of resistance). Virtually every major "respectable" graduate department reshaped itself in the new spirit of tough-minded linguistic analytic philosophy. Philosophers now prided themselves on having made the "linguistic turn."[17] The American pragmatists were marginalized, relegated to the dustbin of history. To the extent that the classical pragmatists were studied, it was primarily by American intellectual historians – not by philosophers. Even though philosophers occasionally paid lip service to the pragmatism, there was a prevailing sense that there really wasn't much that a "serious" philosophy student could learn from the pragmatists. From that time until today, many philosophy students at our most prestigious graduate schools do not even bother to read the works of the classical pragmatists.

The story I have just told about the rise and fall of pragmatism in twentieth-century America is simplified. Nevertheless, some version of it is still the dominant understanding of how philosophy developed in America. For some, the triumph of analytic philosophy is a narrative of progress and technical sophistication. For others, it is a sad story of decline from the speculative spirit of the "golden age" of American philosophy to a thin concern with technical issues that do not really matter to anyone outside the professional circle of like-minded philosophers. But, however one judges what happened, the basic narrative structure of philosophy in America remains the same.

During the past few decades, the philosophical scene has begun to change dramatically. There is a resurgence of pragmatic themes in philosophy throughout the world, and a growing interest in the works of the classical pragmatists. There are the beginnings of a more subtle, complex narrative of the development of philosophy in America that highlights the *continuity* and the *persistence* of the pragmatic legacy. Richard Rorty and Hilary Putnam, both of whom situate their own philosophical approaches within the pragmatic tradition, have played major roles in rethinking and rewriting the history of pragmatism in America. Rorty has argued that such key "analytic" philosophers as W. V. O. Quine, Wilfrid Sellars, and Donald Davidson can and *should* be read as refining basic pragmatic themes anticipated by the classical pragmatic thinkers – especially those that can be found in James and Dewey. In the "Introduction" to *Philosophy and the Mirror of Nature*, Rorty tells us that the central chapter of his book is the one that deals with Sellars and Quine.

> I interpret Sellars's attack on "givenness" and Quine's attack on "necessity" as the crucial steps in undermining the possibility of a "theory of knowledge." The holism and pragmatism common to both philosophers, and which they share with the later Wittgenstein, are the lines of thought within analytic philosophy which I wish to extend. I argue that when extended in a certain way they let us see truth as, in James's phrase, "what is better for us to believe," rather than as "the accurate representation of reality." (Rorty 1979, p. 10)

Rorty interprets Davidson as going beyond Quine and Sellars in furthering the cause of pragmatism. In his introduction to John P. Murphy's *Pragmatism: From Peirce to Davidson*, Rorty writes:

> [W]hat Davidson added to Dewey is a non-representationalist account of knowledge. I have argued elsewhere that the "linguistic turn" in philosophy was sort of a last refuge of representationalism and that the dialectic that leads the later Wittgenstein and Davidson away from a picture theory of language is the same as that which led Dewey away from a spectator theory of knowledge. If no further refuge is found,

then Davidson may have been right when he wrote "a sea change" is occurring in recent philosophical thought – "a change so profound that we may not recognize that it is occurring." If the change of which Davidson spoke is someday recognized as having occurred ... [then] Peirce, James, and Dewey may cease to be treated as provincial figures. They may be given the place I think they deserve in the story of the West's intellectual progress. (Rorty 1990, p. 5)

Regardless of what one thinks of Rorty's own idiosyncratic version of pragmatism, he should be given credit for challenging the standard narrative of the development of twentieth-century philosophy in America. It is superficial and misleading to claim that pragmatism came to an end with the arrival of analytic philosophy. On the contrary, after the linguistic turn, philosophers such as Wittgenstein, Quine, Sellars, and Davidson were able to refine and advance themes that were anticipated by the classical pragmatists. The most original and creative thinking of the best analytic philosophers advances the cause of pragmatism and helps to bring about the sea change that the classical pragmatists initiated.

Rorty has been joined by Hilary Putnam, who, despite his many disputes with Rorty, also stresses the continuity and centrality of pragmatism. In *Realism with a Human Face*, Putnam, whom Rorty once called the leading pragmatist of our time, describes the ideas that he explores as follows:

All of these ideas – that the fact/value dichotomy is untenable, that the fact/convention dichotomy is also untenable, that truth and justification of ideas are closely connected, that the alternative to metaphysical realism is not any form of skepticism, that philosophy is an attempt to achieve the good – are ideas that have long been associated with the American pragmatic tradition. Realizing this has led me (sometimes with the assistance of Ruth Anna Putnam) to make the effort to better understand that tradition from Peirce right up to Quine and Goodman. (Putnam 1990, p. xi)

Before proceeding, I want to emphasize a fundamental point. When Rorty reads the later Wittgenstein, Quine, Sellars, and Davidson as furthering the pragmatist agenda, or when Putnam raises the question "Was Wittgenstein a Pragmatist?," neither is suggesting that the achievements of these philosophers are the result of *direct* influence of the classical pragmatists. There is no evidence that Wittgenstein ever read any of the writings of the classical pragmatists except William James, although it is said that he heard about Peirce from Frank Ramsey. When Quine uses the term "pragmatic" in his famous essay "On What There Is," its meaning owes more to Carnap than to any of the classical pragmatists. Sellars was certainly knowledgeable about the pragmatists, but, like Peirce, he was inspired by Kant. And from Davidson's occasional remarks about pragmatism, it is primarily Rorty's understanding of pragmatism that he has in mind. My fundamental point is that philosophers, starting from the most diverse orientations and without being directly influenced by the classical pragmatists, have been articulating insights and developing theses that are not only congenial with a pragmatic orientation but also *refine* its philosophical import. Cheryl Misak succinctly makes this point in her introduction to *New Pragmatists*.

> It is not of much concern ... whether these philosophers have in fact been influenced by the classical pragmatists or whether they see themselves as part of the pragmatic tradition. What matters is that the best of Peirce, James, and Dewey has resurfaced in deep, interesting and fruitful ways. (Misak 2007, p. 2)

Thus far I have been discussing pragmatism as primarily an American philosophical movement that has its origins in the second half of the nineteenth century and continues in a variety of forms right up to the present. So, despite the conventional story of how analytic philosophy in America displaced pragmatism, we should think of pragmatism as a complex movement that has had a number of tributaries during the past 150 years in America. Pragmatic themes have not been limited to philosophy in North America – they have a much more global significance.

The Global Reach of Pragmatism

Perhaps the most ambitious understanding of pragmatism is that advanced by Robert Brandom. In *Articulating Reasons*, he writes:

> Pragmatism about the norms implicit in cognitive activity came down to us in the first half of the twentieth century from three independent

directions: from the classical American pragmatists, culminating in Dewey; from Heidegger of *Being and Time*; and from Wittgenstein of the *Philosophical Investigations*. In trying to work out how the insights of these traditions (partly common, partly complementary) could be applied to make progress within contemporary philosophy of language and philosophy of mind, however, I found myself driven back to Hegel's original version. For unlike all three of these more recent sorts of social practice theory, Hegel's is a *rationalist* pragmatism. By contrast to their conceptual assimilationism, he gives pride of place to *reasoning* in understanding what it is to say or do something. (Brandom 2000a, p. 34)

At first blush, it may seem excessive to speak of Wittgensteinian, Heideggerian, and Hegelian *pragmatism*. Brandom wants to stress a theme that is central to his own version of pragmatism: conceptual norms are implicit in discursive social practices. In *Making it Explicit*, he works out in great detail a theory of linguistic practices that shows precisely how norms arise within these practices and are made explicit. Linguistic conceptual norms are instituted by social-practical activity – by know-how. Brandom develops an inferential semantics that dovetails with a normative pragmatics. Given this understanding of pragmatism, it makes good sense to see anticipations, insights, and contributions to such a theory of social practices in the classical American pragmatists as well as in Heidegger, Wittgenstein, and Hegel. And it is to his credit that, in *Making it Explicit* (1994) and *Tales of the Mighty Dead* (2002), Brandom provides readings of Hegel, Wittgenstein, and Heidegger to support his interpretation. Although I think it is inflationary to speak of Wittgensteinian, Heideggerian, and Hegelian *pragmatisms*, I endorse the idea that there are identifiable themes in all of these thinkers that are not only compatible with, but also develop in novel ways ideas that are central to the classical American pragmatists. I agree with Brandom that, despite radical differences, Hegel, Wittgenstein, and Heidegger contribute to a richer understanding of the primacy of social practices in all aspects of our lives.

Brandom's comments about the pragmatism of Wittgenstein and Heidegger bring to mind the striking remark by his teacher, Richard Rorty, that the three most important philosophers of the twentieth century are Dewey, Wittgenstein, and Heidegger. "Each tried, in his early years, to find a new way to make philosophy 'foundational' – a new way of formulating an ultimate context for thought. ... Each came to see his earlier effort as self-deceptive. ... They set aside epistemology and metaphysics as possible disciplines" (Rorty 1979, p. 6).[18] They shared much more than a critique of modern philosophy; they opened new vistas and new ways of thinking that Rorty employs in his vision of a post-philosophical pragmatic culture.

Still, one may feel uneasy about making even the more modest claim that there are significant pragmatic themes in Wittgenstein and Heidegger. So let me suggest another perspective for discerning the deep similarities among the American pragmatists, Wittgenstein, and Heidegger. In my chapter on Peirce, I will argue that the origin of American pragmatism lies in a remarkable series of papers that he published in 1868–9 in the *Journal of Speculative Philosophy*.[19] Like so much of Peirce's writing, these articles are brilliant, extremely dense, and occasionally cryptic. In standard accounts of American pragmatism (including James's narrative), Peirce's more popular papers, "The Fixation of Belief" and "How to Make our Ideas Clear" – written a decade later – are cited as inaugurating the pragmatic movement. Yet I believe that these earlier papers, especially the first two – "Questions Concerning Certain Faculties Claimed for Man" and "Some Consequences of Four Incapacities" – are essential for understanding pragmatism, and even for appreciating the significance of his more famous 1878 papers. They provide the necessary background and set an agenda for many of Peirce's subsequent investigations. We hear echoes of these papers in the other classical pragmatists, as well as in the work of Wilfrid Sellars, Hilary Putnam, Richard Rorty, Robert Brandom, Jürgen Habermas, and many others.

Peirce begins the second paper in this series with a succinct summary of his critique of Cartesianism. "Descartes is the father of modern philosophy, and the spirit of Cartesianism – that which principally distinguishes it from the scholasticism which it displaced – may be compendiously stated as follows" (Peirce 1992, p. 28). Peirce then proceeds to list four major contrasts between Cartesianism and the scholasticism that it displaced. These are:

1. a belief that philosophy must begin with universal doubt, as contrasted with scholasticism, which did not question fundamentals;
2. a belief that the ultimate test of certainty is found in individual consciousness, rather than by relying on the testimony of sages;

3. privileging a single thread of inference (depending on inconspicuous premises), rather than appealing to the multiform scholastic argumentation; and finally,
4. Cartesianism fails to explain many things and renders them absolutely inexplicable, whereas scholasticism had its mysteries of faith but attempted to explain all created things.

After listing these contrasts, Peirce makes a striking claim:

> In some, or all of these respects, most modern philosophers have been in effect Cartesians. Now without wishing to return to scholasticism, it seems to me that modern science and modern logic requires us to stand upon a very different platform. (Ibid.)

Peirce's critique of Cartesianism results in four denials:

1. We have no power of Introspection, but all knowledge of the internal world is derived from hypothetical reasoning from our knowledge of external facts.
2. We have no power of Intuition, but every cognition is determined logically by previous cognitions.
3. We have no power of thinking without signs.
4. We have no conception of the absolutely incognizable.

(Peirce 1992, p. 30)

I will be exploring the meaning and consequences of these denials in my chapter on Peirce. Pragmatism begins with a radical critique of Cartesianism. In one fell swoop, Peirce seeks to demolish the interrelated motifs that constitute Cartesianism: the ontological dualism of mind and body; the subjective individualism implicit in the appeal to direct personal verification; the method of universal doubt that is supposed to lead us to incorrigible truths; the conviction that unless we discover firm foundations for knowledge we cannot avoid epistemological skepticism; the belief that knowledge of the world consists of having ideas that correctly represent and correspond to this world; the doctrine that vagueness is "unreal" and that the epistemological endeavor is to know clearly and distinctly a completely determinate reality; and, most fundamentally, that we can break out of language or systems of signs and have direct immediate knowledge of non-linguistic objects. Peirce takes this last claim to be at the core of

Cartesianism, and to be a central dogma of many varieties of modern philosophy. Peirce's attack on Cartesianism is, in effect, a generalized attack on what Wilfrid Sellars calls the Myth of the Given, regardless of what is taken to be the cognitively given – "sense contents, material objects, universals, propositions, real connections, first principles, even givenness itself" (Sellars 1997, p. 14). Peirce is not interested solely in critiquing Cartesianism, but rather, in working out an alternative pragmatic understanding of human beings and their place in the cosmos. We can view the development of pragmatism from Peirce until its recent resurgence as developing and refining this fundamental change of philosophical orientation – this sea change. A unifying theme in all the classical pragmatists as well as their successors is the development of a philosophical orientation that replaces Cartesianism (in all its varieties).

Viewing Peirce's project and the pragmatic movement in this manner enables us to see the plausibility of Brandom speaking of Wittgensteinian and Heideggerian pragmatism. For although their philosophical styles and idioms are strikingly different, Heidegger and the later Wittgenstein can be approached as also engaging in a radical critique of the Cartesianism of modern philosophy. Both of them are critical of epistemological and metaphysical foundationalism; they attack the traditional dualisms that characterize so much of modern philosophy. They contribute to the critique of the Myth of the Given. They argue that subjectivism leads to unavoidable aporias. For very different reasons, both would agree with Peirce's theses that we have no power of immediate intuition and no power of thinking without signs.

Peirce, Wittgenstein, and Heidegger – working in and out of very different traditions – are motivated by a "felt difficulty," a similar problematic. Each of them detects that something is profoundly wrong with Cartesianism, and each of them seeks to rethink a more adequate way of understanding our forms of life and our being-in-the world. They are critical of what Dewey called the "spectator theory of knowledge" and shift our attention to know-how, to how we engage in the world and social practices. Each of them repudiates what Rorty calls "philosophy as the mirror of nature." The similarities and overlaps in their projects are *not* the result of any direct influence. There is no evidence that Heidegger ever read any of the pragmatists or even knew of the existence of Peirce. And although Wittgenstein frequently discusses William James, it was

James's *Principles of Psychology* and the *Varieties of Religious Experience* that fascinated him, not James's explicitly pragmatic writings. With the American pragmatists, Heidegger, and Wittgenstein, we witness a similar dialectic at work in their thinking, a dialectic that starts with the same problematic and thinks through its radical consequences.

When Heidegger introduces his distinction between *Zuhandensein* (readiness-to-hand) and *Vorhandensein* (presence-in-hand) in *Being and Time* and argues for the primacy of readiness-to-hand, he introduces a theme that echoes the pragmatic claims about the primacy of practice and conduct. The readiness-to-hand of a piece of equipment consists in its having a distinctive practical significance like a hammer (Heidegger's famous example). A hammer is the kind of entity that exhibits this sort of being. To take something as a hammer is not simply to perceive it, but to know that it is a piece of equipment used for driving nails (although it can be used for other purposes). And as Heidegger explores the meaning and consequences of *Zuhandensein* and how it is related to *Vorhandensein*, it becomes clear that he is fundamentally altering the way in which we understand our being-in-the-world. Although "being-in-the-world" is not an expression that any of the classical American pragmatists ever used, it beautifully articulates the pragmatic understanding of the transaction that takes place between human organisms and their environment – a transaction that involves know-how and is the basis for knowing-that. When, for example, Axel Honneth tells us that, "according to Heidegger, we do not encounter reality in the stance of a cognitive subject, but rather we practically cope with the world in such a way that it is given to us as a field of practical significance," he is also describing one of the most basic theses of the American pragmatists (Honneth 2008, p. 30).[20] The resonances between Heidegger and the pragmatists can also be detected in Heidegger's exploration of care (*Sorge*), projection (*Entwurf*), and situatedness (*Befindlichheit*).

The literature dealing with the similarities and differences between Heidegger and pragmatism is now quite extensive. In addition to the affinities noted by Brandom and Rorty, one should also mention those emphasized by Hubert Dreyfus and John Haugeland, both of whom have had a significant influence on Anglo-American interpretations of Heidegger.[21] Mark Okrent's *Heidegger's Pragmatism* (1988) is a comprehensive study of pragmatic themes in Heidegger's corpus. There are lively debates and strong disagreements about which aspects of Heidegger's writings are most closely related to pragmatism. Some have argued that we grossly distort Heidegger when we read him through a pragmatic lens. Even if we avoid the "cultural imperialism" that can result from labeling Heidegger a "pragmatist" and focus on shared insights, concerns, and thematic strains in the American pragmatic thinkers and Heidegger, we can see how much they illuminate each other.

Concerning Wittgenstein, let me note that every major post-Wittgensteinian philosopher who has identified with the pragmatic tradition has been attracted to and influenced by the later Wittgenstein. All of them read Wittgenstein as sharing a great deal with pragmatism and as advancing the sophistication of pragmatic themes after the linguistic turn. This is true for Richard Rorty, Hilary Putnam, Wilfrid Sellars, Robert Brandom, Jürgen Habermas, and many others. Indeed, in his *Pragmatism*, based on a series of three lectures, Putnam entitles one of his lectures, "Was Wittgenstein a Pragmatist?" He concludes by declaring that even though Wittgenstein was not in a "strict sense" a "pragmatist," he nevertheless shares "a central – perhaps *the* central – emphasis with pragmatism: the emphasis on the primacy of practice" (Putnam 1995, p. 52).[22]

One of the first philosophers to note the significant commonalities between pragmatism, especially Peirce, and Wittgenstein was Richard Rorty. Rorty begins one of his earliest and most brilliant articles, "Pragmatism, Categories, and Language" (1961), by telling us that "pragmatism is getting respectable again and that the most up-to-date pragmatist is Peirce."[23] Rorty sets out to show that "Peirce's thought envisaged and repudiated in advance, the stages in the development of empiricism, which logical empiricism represented, and that it came to rest in a group of insights and a philosophical mood much like those we find in the *Philosophical Investigations* and in the writings of those influenced by the later Wittgenstein" (Rorty 1961a, pp. 197–8.). Rorty lists five points of convergence between Peirce and Wittgenstein:

1. What Peirce called "nominalism" and what present-day philosophers call "reductionism" are forms of a single error.
2. The error in both cases goes back to "the Protean metaphysical urge to transcend language."
3. Peirce's attempt to give sense to the notion *universalia ante rem* is not the result of succumbing to this urge, but is rather his device for repudiating it as strongly as possible.

4. When Peirce says that "vagueness is real," and when Wittgenstein points to the difference between causal and logical determination, the only differences between what they are saying are verbal (or, to give the cash value of this overworked word, uninteresting).
5. The similarity of their insights about language reflects the fact that the slogans "Don't look for the meaning, look for the use" and "The meaning of a concept is the sum of its possible effects upon conduct" reciprocally support each other.

(Rorty 1961a, p. 198)

Rorty proceeds to show how Peirce and Wittgenstein complement each other. "What I am trying to show is that the closer one brings pragmatism to the writings of the later Wittgenstein and those influenced by him, the more they shed light on each other" (Rorty 1961a, pp. 198–9).[24] I agree entirely with Rorty, and I also think that when we compare Wittgenstein with the other classical pragmatic thinkers, we discover equally illuminating shared insights.[25]

My earlier discussion of the continuity and persistence of the pragmatic tradition in analytic philosophy, and my brief discussion of pragmatic themes in Heidegger and Wittgenstein (the two most influential philosophers of the twentieth century), are intended to provide a very different reading and interpretation of philosophy during the past 150 years. The standard philosophical conventions that divide philosophy into such "schools" as pragmatism, analytic philosophy, and Continental philosophy obscure these common pragmatic themes. Once these ideological blinders are removed, the philosophical investigations of the classical American pragmatists, Heidegger, and Wittgenstein take on a fresh and more exciting character. If we bracket the standard and misleading philosophical classifications and *look* at what these philosophers are actually saying and doing, then a very different panorama emerges. We discover commonalities in what pragmatists, Wittgenstein, and Heidegger are all reacting against, in their critiques of traditional epistemology and metaphysics, and especially in the sea change in philosophical orientation that they seek to bring out. This does not mean that differences among them are any less significant – just as the consequential differences among the individual pragmatists are not less significant than their overlapping agreements. We gain a more nuanced understanding of these differences against the background of what they share.

The German Appropriation of Pragmatic Themes

To justify my thesis about the growing international significance of pragmatism, I want to consider its importance for German intellectual life since the end of the Second World War. During the first half of the twentieth century, German ignorance of pragmatism was – with very few exceptions – matched only by blind prejudice. Just as the cultural, political, and social life in Germany has undergone a radical change since the end of the Second World War, so too this has happened in intellectual life (and the changes here are closely related). German philosophy during the post-Second World War period has been shaped by a threefold concern: to recover and rethink what is "living" in the German philosophical tradition; to engage critically with different contemporary philosophical movements, especially analytic philosophy and pragmatism; and to bring about a transformation of philosophy that would overcome scientism, reductive naturalism, relativism, and historicism.

I shall single out the work of four outstanding German thinkers who have a sophisticated grasp of pragmatism and have also critically appropriated pragmatic themes: Karl-Otto Apel, Jürgen Habermas, Hans Joas, and Axel Honneth. Each of them has argued that the pragmatic thinkers advance contemporary philosophical discussion, and each of them has sought to incorporate and develop pragmatic insights in novel ways. Karl-Otto Apel played a major role in introducing Peirce and pragmatism to a German audience. In 1967 and 1970, he published two volumes of Peirce's writings with extensive introductions. He combined these introductions into a full-scale study of Peirce's philosophical development: *Denkweg von Charles S. Peirce: Eine Einführung in den amerikanischen Pragmatismus*. Translated into English in 1981, *Charles S. Peirce: From Pragmatism to Pragmaticism* is one of the best books written on Peirce in any language (see Bernstein 1981, pp. xix–xxvii). Apel, along with his close colleague Jürgen Habermas, argued that post-Hegelian philosophy has developed three distinctive (and competing) orientations: Marxism, existentialism, and pragmatism.[26] Both Apel and Habermas increasingly came to identify their own philosophical projects with this pragmatic orientation. As Apel tells us, "Peirce finally became important for me primarily as an ally in the systematic undertaking of a 'transformation of (transcendental) philosophy'" (Apel 1981, p. ix). Furthermore, Apel claims that "transcendental semiotic, or transcendental pragmatics, with its insight that the thinking (and by this I mean 'arguing') subject must necessarily conceive of itself as a member of a communication community," can serve as the basis for a final foundation of ethics (ibid., pp. ix–x). Habermas, stimulated by Apel's investigations of pragmatism, argues that a major paradigm shift took place at the end of the nineteenth century – a shift from a philosophy of conscious-ness or subjectivity to a communicative model of action and reason. The classical pragmatists initiated this shift. Habermas conceives of his theory of communicative action as furthering the development of this pragmatic understanding of reciprocal intersubjectivity. In his *Theory of Communicative Action*, Habermas builds on Mead's social understanding of the genesis of human language in order to develop his own normative theory of intersubjectivity. Habermas draws on Peirce in his understanding of truth and justification and on John Dewey in developing his theory of democracy and communicative freedom. The trajectory of Habermas's philosophical development comes increasingly closer to the Kantian strain in pragmatism, so much so that he now identifies himself as a "Kantian pragmatist" (see Habermas 2003). As an engaged democratic intellectual who com-bines sophisticated theoretical analysis with practical, political, and ethical interventions, Habermas has played a role in German society that is comparable to the role that John Dewey played in American society during the first decades of the twentieth century.

Hans Joas, a sociologist by training, is the most perceptive German interpreter of American pragmatism (especially Mead and Dewey). His *Pratische Intersubjectivität: Die Entwicklung des Werkes von George Herbert Mead* (1980), translated as *G. H. Mead: A Contemporary Re-examination of his Thought* (1985), is the finest study of Mead's intel-lectual development. Joas is not exclusively interested in redeeming the importance of Mead, but in showing how Mead contributes to a contemporary philosophical and sociological theory of action. He argues that Mead and the pragmatists provide a more adequate theory of action than Habermas's more "rationalistic" theory. Joas further develops this pragmatic theory of action in his *The Creativity of Action* (1996).

Finally, Axel Honneth draws on the pragmatists at a number of sig-nificant junctures in his comprehensive theory of recognition. Dewey, Honneth argues, provides the resources for developing a theory of radical democracy based upon social cooperation that is superior to contemporary theories that oscillate between republican and procedural understandings of democracy (see Honneth 1998). And recently, in his revival of the concept of reification, Honneth draws upon Dewey to support his thesis that objective thought is rooted in, and emerges out of, nonreflective "qualitative thought" (see Honneth 2008, pp. 36–40). What is especially exciting about this German appropriation of pragmatic themes is the way in which these thinkers draw upon the richness of the pragmatic tradition in order to deal with problems that are at the cutting edge of philosophy today. And there are currently signs that this creative engagement with pragmatic themes is taking place throughout the world.

My Intellectual Journey with Pragmatism

I conclude this Prologue with some personal remarks about my own encounters with the pragmatic thinkers and the journey that I have taken with them.[27] More than 50 years ago, I wrote my dissertation, "John Dewey's Metaphysics of Experience." I was led to Dewey because John E. Smith, an assistant professor of philosophy at Yale, organized an informal reading group to discuss Dewey's *Experience and Nature*. John Smith has been among the most enthusiastic and perceptive interpreters of American philosophy. That informal discussion group – perhaps something like the original Metaphysical Club – was an eye-opener. In the 1950s interest in Dewey and the classical pragmatists was at its lowest point in the twentieth century. Having been an undergraduate at the University of Chicago when Robert Hutchins was still president, I had acquired the prejudice that Dewey was really not worth taking seriously as a philosopher. But the Dewey I encountered in *Experience and Nature* didn't fit the prevailing caricature of Dewey and pragmatism. I was sufficiently stubborn and perverse that I decided to write a dissertation on Dewey at a time when this was extremely unfashionable. Much later, I discovered Oliver Wendell Holmes Jr's wonderful remark about *Experience and Nature*: "Although Dewey's book is incredibly ill-written, it seemed to me ... to have a feeling of intimacy with the universe that I found unequaled. So methought God would have spoken had He been inarticulate but keenly desirous to tell you how it was."[28]

At Yale there was also a great deal of interest in Peirce – inspired, in part, by Paul Weiss, one of the co-editors of Peirce's *Collected Papers*.

Some of my earliest publications dealt with Dewey and Peirce.[29] The study of these thinkers led me back to Kant and Hegel, in order to understand the philosophical background of their ideas. Later I discovered how James, Mead, and Royce contributed to the conversation about pragmatism. Contrary to the conventional bias that the pragmatic thinkers were passé, I had an intuition that they were actually ahead of their time. I felt that the day would come when philosophers would recognize the creativity of these thinkers and "catch up" with their insights.

During the 1950s and 1960s many academic philosophers adopted the "analytic ideology." I have always sharply distinguished this unfortunate ideology from the genuine philosophical contributions of those working in the analytic style. By the "analytic ideology" I mean the presumptuous conviction that the only "game in town" – the only rigorous way of "doing philosophy" – is to work on those problems that were currently being discussed in the latest "respectable" analytic philosophical journals. To the extent that there was any interest in the history of philosophy, it was primarily about the ways in which the "arguments" of past philosophers could be salvaged or reconstructed in order to see how they contributed to the solution or dissolution of contemporary problems. These included the problem of counterfactuals, the mind–body problem, reductionism, the logical character of verification and falsification, the analytic–synthetic distinction, the distinction between conceptual analysis and empirical investigation, reasons and causes, and a few other related problems. These were *the* problems at the cutting edge of philosophy.[30] So-called "Continental" philosophers (and most past philosophers) could be dismissed because they were linguistically confused and failed to meet the "rigorous" criteria for sound philosophical argumentation.

My philosophical interests were always broader and more pluralistic. There is only good and bad philosophical thinking – and there is plenty of both on either side of the Atlantic. I felt then (and still believe) that with a certain amount of hermeneutical generosity and nuanced imagination one can see how philosophers working in different traditions and idioms are struggling with important issues. As I progressed on my own journey, I had the experience of what Yogi Berra once called "déjà vu all over again." The more I explored what initially seemed to be radically different philosophical approaches, the more I discovered significant points of contact with themes central for the classical American pragmatists. Let me illustrate this with a number of thinkers and issues.

I had the good fortune to teach at Yale during the time that Wilfrid Sellars joined the faculty in the late 1950s. The Yale philosophy department was hostile to analytic and linguistic philosophy (even though Carl Hempel and Arthur Pap, with whom I studied, taught at Yale). But my encounter with Sellars was transformative. I attended most of the graduate courses that he taught at Yale. Sellars combined a remarkably sophisticated knowledge of the history of philosophy with a nuanced appreciation of analytic philosophy. He showed that analytic techniques could be employed to elucidate issues central to the great philosophical tradition. When I studied *Empiricism and Philosophy of Mind*, which had been originally published in 1956 just before he came to Yale, I felt that I was rereading Peirce in the "New Way of Words."[31] Sellars's comprehensive critique of the Myth of the Given parallels Peirce's critique of intuitionism. There are striking similarities in their critiques of epistemological foundationalism and "abstractive" theories of concept formation. I was impressed with the rigor, nuance, and insight of Sellars's philosophical vision, which he elaborated in a series of difficult and dense articles. I wrote one of the first critical studies of his work (Bernstein 1966b).

The 1960s were also a time of great political turmoil throughout the United States and the world. I was actively involved in the early Civil Rights movement and the anti-Vietnam War movement. (I spent some time in Mississippi during the summer of 1964.)[32] My political activity was not unrelated to my philosophical interests. I found Dewey appealing because of his steadfast commitment to a radical democracy that involves active participation of *all* citizens. The lack of any serious political philosophy in analytic circles at the time was one of its grave deficiencies. A primary reason for my interest in the tradition of Western Marxism and Hegel was because it provided a richer canvas for dealing philosophically with political issues. Like the Young Hegelians, Dewey also sought a way to integrate theory with *praxis*. In 1971 I published *Praxis and Action* (Bernstein 1971), a book in which I examine how these concepts play themselves out in four traditions: Marxism, existentialism, pragmatism, and analytic philosophy.

The year 1972 was an important one in my personal intellectual journey, for it was the year that I met both Jürgen Habermas and Hannah Arendt. I had been reading the works of Habermas during the 1960s, and when I read *Knowledge and Human Interests*, I experienced a shock of recognition. I felt that it expressed some of my deepest thoughts. Habermas, who had been shaped by the Hegelian–Marxist tradition of the early Frankfurt School, seemed to be moving in a direction that increasingly converged with American pragmatism. And I, who had started with the American pragmatic tradition, sought to enrich it with the insights of the Hegelian–Marxist tradition. In the *Restructuring of Social and Political Theory* (1976), I criticized the positivist legacy in the social sciences and sought to develop a conception of social and political theory that encompassed empirical, interpretive, and critical dimensions. I elaborated a pragmatic understanding of the social and political disciplines that furthered Dewey's hopes for democratic social reform and complemented Habermas's understanding of the critical social sciences. Over the many years of our friendship I have sought to "detranscendentalize" Habermas and bring him closer to the pragmatic spirit of Dewey, and he has attempted to show me the virtues of a "Kantian pragmatism" that still insists on a sharp distinction between theoretical and practical philosophy.

When I first met Hannah Arendt in 1972, I was not much interested in her work; I was actually quite hostile, in part because I thought her interpretations of Hegel and Marx were outrageous. (I still think so!) At our first meeting we spent many hours arguing about Hegel and Marx. I was subsequently invited to participate in a conference dedicated to her work (see Bernstein 1977). This was an opportunity to read her work carefully; it was a great discovery. Arendt provides us with one of the most perceptive, eloquent, and phenomenologically sensitive descriptions of action, politics, and public freedom. Arendt is certainly no pragmatist, but her description of the equality (isonomy) of citizens, the public spaces of tangible freedom, and the "revolutionary spirit" beautifully complements Dewey's understanding of the democratic ethos.[33]

I also want to mention two other thinkers who initially seem quite remote from pragmatism: Hans-Georg Gadamer and Jacques Derrida. I met Gadamer when he first visited the United States in 1968, and we had many encounters in Dubrovnik, Heidelberg, and the United States during his frequent visits. The more I read Gadamer, the more I had a sense of familiarity in the way he characterizes experience (*Erfahrung*). It is similar to Dewey's notion of experience unified by a pervasive qualitative immediacy and funded with meaning. The reason for this similarity gradually became clear. Both

Gadamer and Dewey had been strongly influenced by the dominant role that experience plays in Hegel, especially in the *Phenomenology of Spirit*. Both had reacted against some of the more ambitious claims of Hegel about totality, system, and the Absolute. Furthermore, there are parallels between Gadamer's insistence on the role of prejudice and prejudgment in understanding and Peirce's claim: "We cannot begin with complete doubt. We must begin with all the prejudices which we actually have when we enter upon the study of philosophy" (Peirce 1992, pp. 28–9). When Gadamer elaborates the centrality of *phronēsis* and dialogue for philosophy and hermeneutics, he complements the pragmatic emphasis on practice and dialogue.

In 1983 I published *Beyond Objectivism and Relativism: Science, Hermeneutics, and Praxis*. I coined the phrase "the Cartesian Anxiety" to describe an anxiety that has haunted a good deal of modern and contemporary philosophy (see Bernstein 1983, pp. 16–20). I did not explicitly discuss any of the classical American pragmatists, but the book is informed by a pragmatic sensibility. The pragmatists provide a philosophical orientation that is truly *beyond* the sterile opposition (and oscillation) between objectivism and relativism.

The late 1980s were a time when so-called "postmodernism" seemed to be the rage in many circles. Foucault, Derrida, Lyotard, Deleuze (and other French thinkers) were the "theorists" that excited the imagination of many young intellectuals. At first I found the talk about the novelty of "postmodern" discourse perplexing. For when I examined closely what was being attacked – foundationalism, the metaphysics of presence, grand narratives and systems – I felt that I had seen all this before. This was the starting point for the classical pragmatists in the nineteenth century. A remark that Habermas made about Heidegger, Adorno, and Derrida seemed perfectly apt.

> They all defend themselves as if they were living in the shadow of the "last" philosopher, as did the first generation of Hegelian disciples. They are still battling against the "strong" concepts of theory, truth, and system that have actually belonged to the past for over a century and a half. ... They believe that they have to tear philosophy away from the madness of expounding a theory that has the last word. (Habermas 1987, p. 408)

Their failure, according to Habermas, is not to realize and fully appreciate that the "fallibilist consciousness of the sciences caught up with philosophy too, a long time ago" (ibid.). "Deconstruction" –

contrary to Derrida's intentions – became fetishized into a slogan. In *The New Constellation: The Ethical-Political Horizons of Modernity/ Postmodernity* (1991), I argued that, as the pragmatists showed us, deconstruction is not sufficient; it must be complemented by *reconstruction*.[34]

When I first read Derrida in the 1970s I had a reaction similar to many of his critics. I found his writings infuriating – verbal indulgence without much point. But I persisted in trying to make sense of him. And it was his essay on Levinas, "Violence and Metaphysics," that was a breakthrough. The seriousness, eloquence, and humaneness in his tribute to Levinas didn't fit the then current image of Derrida as engaging in "nihilistic" word play. I discovered that already in his earliest writings Derrida was concerned with the ethical-political issues that were central for the pragmatic thinkers. In a very different philosophical idiom, he has criticized what the pragmatists also rejected. And in his persistent deconstructive musings on "response," "responsibility," "undecidability," and "decision," there are illuminating points of contact with the American pragmatic thinkers.[35]

Throughout my intellectual career, I have sought to articulate and defend the practical consequences of philosophical reflection, and the necessity of reflection for intelligent practice and action. The spirit of critical pragmatic fallibilism represents what is best in the American tradition and has global significance. Yet in the years immediately following 9/11, this open dialogical, fallibilistic orientation was itself under attack. In *The Abuse of Evil: The Corruption of Politics and Religion since 9/11* (2005), I sharply criticized the mentality – all too prevalent – that is drawn to rigid absolutes, a mentality that discourages dialogue, discussion, and debate. The classical American pragmatists believed that once the quest for certainty was exposed, once the craving for absolutes was challenged, once we learned that there is no permanent metaphysical comfort and that we must cope intelligently and imaginatively with unexpected contingencies and dangers, then there would be no going back – no return to a world of simplistic binary oppositions of Good and Evil. But the pragmatists underestimated the appeal of the mentality that they opposed – especially in times of perceived crisis, anxiety, and fear. There is always the threat of regression. This is why I believe that it requires passionate commitment and constant endeavor to make pragmatic fallibilism a living reality in people's everyday lives.

When I teach courses dealing with pragmatism (old and new), I tell my students that it is best to think of the discourse about pragmatism as an open-ended conversation with many loose ends and tangents. I don't mean an "idealized" conversation or dialogue, so frequently described and praised by philosophers. Rather, it is a conversation more like the type that occurs at New York dinner parties where there are misunderstandings, speaking at cross-purposes, conflicts, and contradictions, with personalized voices stressing different points of view (and sometimes talking at the same time). It can seem chaotic, yet somehow the entire conversation is more vital and illuminating than any of the individual voices demanding to be heard. This is what the conversation of pragmatism has been like.[36]

In this final section I have sketched the highlights of my intellectual journey with the pragmatic thinkers and the ways in which my own horizon has been enlarged and enriched by encounters with other thinkers and philosophical traditions. I firmly believe that my original hunch about the significance and relevance of these pragmatic themes has been dramatically vindicated. Philosophers have "caught up" with pragmatism. Today there is much more vigorous, extensive, and illuminating global discussion of the multifaceted aspects of pragmatism than at any time since its origins. The persistence and vitality of pragmatism are emphatically manifest.

1

Charles S. Peirce's Critique
of Cartesianism

In 1868–9 Peirce, who was not quite 30 years old, published a series of ground-breaking articles in the recently founded *Journal of Speculative Philosophy*.[1] These papers preceded by a decade his better-known articles in the *Popular Science Monthly*: "The Fixation of Belief" and "How to Make Our Ideas Clear." If we want to understand Peirce's version of pragmatism and his larger philosophical project, then we must examine closely key themes explored in these earlier papers. In the Prologue, I quoted the opening of his second article: "Descartes is the father of modern philosophy, and the spirit of Cartesianism – that which principally distinguishes it from the scholasticism which it displaced – may be compendiously stated as follows" (Peirce 1992, p. 28). Peirce proceeds to list four contrasts between Cartesianism and scholasticism. He declares that, "without wishing to return to scholasticism, it seems to me that modern science and logic require us to stand upon a different platform from this" (ibid.).

Here I will examine Peirce's explication of his four critical points about the inadequacies of Cartesianism.

1. We cannot begin with complete doubt. We must begin with all the prejudices which we actually have when we enter upon the study of philosophy. These prejudices are not to be dispelled by a maxim, for they are things which it does not occur to us *can* be questioned. ... A person may, if it is true, in the course of his studies, find reason to doubt what he began by believing; but in that case he has a positive reason for it, and not on account of the Cartesian maxim. Let us not

pretend to doubt in philosophy what we do not doubt in our hearts. (Peirce 1992, pp. 28–9)

Peirce speaks about our prejudices when we embark on the study of philosophy, although he argues that *all* inquiry begins with background prejudices. We do not get rid of them by feigned or paper doubt. We must distinguish paper doubt from real doubt – the type for which we have *positive reasons*. Doubt, then, is not a mere psychological state; it is a normative concept insofar as it requires positive reasons.[2] But Peirce also makes a stronger point. He is aware of the negative connotations of the word 'prejudice.' In opposition to Cartesianism and to what Hans-Georg Gadamer calls the "Enlightenment prejudice against prejudice," Peirce insists that all inquiry, including scientific and philosophical inquiry, begins with tacit prejudices and prejudgments.[3] They provide a necessary background and orientation. In the course of a specific inquiry we may come to reject some of these prejudices, but we never escape from having tacit background prejudgments that we do not question. Sorting out which prejudices are to be criticized or rejected is not the beginning point of inquiry, but an end product, an *achievement* of inquiry. Karl Popper, who regarded Peirce as "one of the greatest philosophers of all time" (cited in Peirce 1992, p. xx), forcefully makes the same point. Popper echoes Peirce's critique of Cartesianism when he attacks the search for epistemological origins that has dominated so much of modern philosophy. Like Peirce, Popper argues that this search, which has been characteristic of both rationalist and empiricist strains in modern philosophy, is misguided. When Popper (1963) claims that critical inquiry consists of making bold conjectures and then criticizing, testing, and seeking to refute them, he reaffirms Peirce's own understanding of critical inquiry. Peirce shifts our attention from the origins of ideas and hypotheses to their consequences for our conduct.

Later in his intellectual career, Peirce elaborated a doctrine of "critical commonsensism." Christopher Hookway succinctly summarizes three points that Peirce appropriated from the Scottish philosophy of common sense.

First, justification 'will have to come to a halt somewhere', and rest upon some opinions which are accepted without grounds or justification. Second, the beliefs which provide 'the bedrock of truth' are indubitable, and beyond rational support and criticism. Third, 'they must be regarded as the very truth', and so our reliance upon them does not leave our knowledge without secure foundations. In this spirit, Peirce wrote that 'if you absolutely cannot doubt a proposition ... it is plain that there is no room to desire anything more' (6.498) (Hookway 1985, p. 229)[4]

At first glance, these claims seem to conflict with Peirce's critique of the Cartesian appeal to universal doubt. But Peirce is clarifying and refining his earlier views. There are beliefs that we *take* to be certain and indubitable. Our commonsense view is that there are numerous beliefs that we do not doubt and that provide "the bedrock of truth." But Peirce's commonsensism is a *critical* commonsensism. What is *indubitable* is not to be identified with what is *incorrigible*. As Peirce tells us, "what has been indubitable one day has often been proved on the morrow to be false" (5.514).[5] We never escape from the situation of starting from some beliefs (prejudices and prejudgments) that we *take* to be indubitable. In this sense we can speak of a foundation from which any inquiry begins. Peirce's point is subtle and important. He is an anti-foundationalist when foundationalism is understood as the doctrine that claims that there are basic or incorrigible truths that are not subject to revision. But he is not denying – indeed, he is *affirming* – that all knowing has a foundation in the sense that there are tacitly held beliefs, which we don't doubt and take to be the bedrock of truth. Peirce would certainly endorse Wilfrid Sellars's famous remark: "For empirical knowledge, like its sophisticated extension science, is rational, not because it has a foundation, but because it is a self-correcting enterprise which can put any claim in jeopardy, though not all at once" (Sellars 1997, p. 79). Peirce would add that this is true for any inquiry – including logical, mathematical, and philosophical inquiry. Peirce elaborates his second criticism of Cartesianism thus:

2. The same formalism appears in the Cartesian criterion, which amounts to this: "Whatever I am clearly convinced of, is true." If I really were convinced, I should have done with reasoning, and should require no test of certainty. But thus to make single individuals absolute judges of truth is most pernicious. The result is that metaphysicians will all agree that metaphysics has reached a pitch of certainty far beyond the physical sciences; – only they agree upon nothing else. In sciences in which men come to agreement, when a theory has been broached, it is considered to be on probation until this agreement is

reached. After it has been reached, the question of certainty becomes an idle one, because no one is left who doubts it. We individually cannot reasonably hope to attain the ultimate philosophy which we pursue; we can only seek it, therefore, for the *community* of philosophers. Hence, if disciplined and candid minds carefully examine a theory and refuse to accept it, this ought to create doubts in the mind of the author of the theory itself. (Peirce 1992, p. 29)

There are several points that I want to make about this rich passage.

(a)   I do not think it is completely fair or accurate to say that the Cartesian criterion for truth amounts to the claim "Whatever I am clearly convinced of, is true." Nevertheless, despite valiant attempts by Descartes to specify precisely what he means by "clear and distinct," he does not succeed in providing us with rigorous criteria for distinguishing what *seems* to be clear and distinct from what *really* is clear and distinct. Subjective conviction, like indubitability – no matter how strong and firm – is not a *sufficient* criterion for truth. What we take to be clear and distinct may turn out to be false.

(b)   Peirce's dissatisfaction with the Cartesian understanding of clarity and distinctness is, in part, his motivation for formulating the maxim that was later dubbed the pragmatic maxim. In "How to Make Our Ideas Clear" Peirce declares: "The essence of belief is the establishment of a habit, and different beliefs are distinguished by the different modes of action to which they give rise" (Peirce 1992, pp. 129–30).[6] Peirce distinguishes three grades of clearness; the rule for attaining the third grade is: "Consider what effects, which might conceivably have practical bearings, we conceive the object of our conception to have. Then our conception of these effects is the whole of our conception of the object" (Peirce 1992, p. 132).[7] Later I will comment on the apparently awkward formulation of this maxim and Peirce's subsequent attempts to clarify its meaning. Frankly, I think that the significance of this maxim for understanding pragmatism has been exaggerated. But we should note that Peirce introduces this maxim in order to clarify the *meaning* of concepts and beliefs – not the *truth* of beliefs. The question of truth or falsity cannot be properly raised unless we first clarify the meaning of concepts and beliefs.

(c)   When Peirce declares that "to make single individuals absolute judges of truth is most pernicious," he sets forth what was to become one of the major theses of his philosophical outlook. Peirce relentlessly criticizes the subjectivism that lies at the heart of so much modern epistemology, and he develops an intersubjective (social) understanding of inquiry, knowing, communication, and logic. Jürgen Habermas has argued that at the turn of the twentieth century there was a major paradigm shift from a "philosophy of subjectivity" or a "philosophy of consciousness" to an intersubjective (social) communicative model of understanding human action and rationality. One of the primary sources of this shift is evident in Peirce's early papers. The above passage also anticipates the centrality of the community of inquirers in Peirce's pragmatism. The practices and norms of the critical community of inquirers are the locus for refining, testing, and validating our hypotheses and theories. To say that inquiry is self-correcting is to say that a critical community of inquirers has the intellectual resources for self-correction. Later in the same article, Peirce closely links the concepts of knowing, reality, and community.

> The real, then, is that which sooner or later, information and reasoning would finally result in, and which is therefore independent of the vagaries of me and you. Thus the very origin of the conception of reality shows how this conception essentially involves the notion of a COMMUNITY, without definite limits, and capable of an indefinite increase of knowledge. ... There is nothing, then, to prevent our knowing things as they really are, and it is most likely that we do thus know them in numberless cases, although we can never be absolutely certain of doing so in any special case. (Peirce 1992, p. 52)

This notion of a community of inquirers is also closely linked to Peirce's reflections on the inescapability of prejudices and prejudgments. It is only in and through subjecting our prejudices, hypotheses, and guesses to public criticism by a relevant community of inquirers that we can hope to escape from our limited perspectives, test our beliefs, and bring about the growth of knowledge.[8]

(d) We can also anticipate Peirce's doctrine of fallibilism. Fallibilism means that every knowledge claim – and, more generally, every validity claim – is open to challenge, revision, correction, and even rejection. Fallibilism is not to be confused with epistemological skepticism. Peirce carefully distinguishes between our knowing "things as they are" (which he does not doubt) and being "absolutely certain of doing so in any special case" (which is never completely justified). Fallibilism is entailed by the conception of inquiry as a "self-correcting enterprise which can put any claim in jeopardy, thought not all at once." Epistemological skepticism feeds on the illusion that "genuine" knowledge is incorrigible. If any claim to knowledge may turn out to be false, then, presumably, we are never in a position to say that we "really know" anything. But Peirce's strong thesis is that the very idea of absolute incorrigible knowledge is incoherent and should be abandoned. Any scientist will admit (and should insist) that most of our current hypotheses and theories will need revision in the future. In other words, *strictly speaking*, as they currently stand, they are "false." But it would be absurd to conclude that because we will revise or abandon current hypotheses and theories we do not "really know" anything about the world. We should always seek to test our knowledge claims with the best possible evidence and the strongest arguments, but with an honest sense of human fallibility. F. H. Bradley makes a similar point in his critique of the foundation metaphor.

> We meet here a false doctrine largely due to a misleading metaphor. My known world is taken to be a construction built upon such and such foundations. It is argued, therefore, to be in principle a superstructure which rests upon these supports. You can go on adding to it no doubt, but only so long as the supports remain; and unless they remain, the whole building comes down. But the doctrine, I have to contend, is untenable, and the metaphor ruinously inapplicable. The foundation in truth is provisional merely. In order to begin my construction I take the foundation as absolute – so much certainly is true. But that my construction continues to rest on the beginnings of my knowledge is a conclusion which does not follow. It does not follow that, if these are allowed to be fallible, the whole building collapses. For it is in another sense that my world rests upon the data of perception. (Bradley 1968, p. 209)

Commenting on the importance of "multiform argumentation" in philosophy, Peirce asserts:

> 3. Philosophy ought to imitate the successful sciences in its methods, so far as to proceed only from tangible premises which can be subjected to careful scrutiny, and to trust rather to the multitude and variety of its arguments than to the conclusiveness to any one. Its reasoning should not form a chain which is no stronger than its weakest link, but a cable whose fibres may be ever so slender, provided they are sufficiently numerous and intimately connected. (Peirce 1992, p. 29)

In this forthright statement, Peirce makes one of his most radical pro-
posals about philosophical argumentation. The "chain metaphor" is
closely associated with the "foundation metaphor" and the metaphor
of the "Archimedean point" that Descartes uses in his *Meditations*.
"Archimedes, in order that he might draw the terrestrial globe out
of its place, and transport it elsewhere, demands only that one point
should be fixed and immovable; in the same way I shall have the right
to conceive high hopes if I am happy enough to discover one thing
which is certain and indubitable" (Descartes 1979, vol. 1, p. 149).
There is something enormously seductive about this metaphor. The
dream (some would say, nightmare) of many modern philosophers
has been to discover "one thing which is certain and indubitable,"
or, more generally, to discover those basic truths (what Sellars calls
"self-authenticating episodes") that can serve as an epistemological
foundation (Sellars 1997, p. 73). Then, if we proceed systematically
by a chain of reasoning (inferences), we can build a solid edifice of
knowledge. Suppose, for the sake of argument, we grant that it is
possible to establish such a foundation. Peirce warns that the whole
edifice collapses if there is a single weak link in the chain of inferences. (Consider the many weak links in the *Meditations* as Descartes
moves from *I think, I am,* to the proof of God's existence based on our
idea of God.) Peirce is challenging a profoundly misleading conception of a philosophical system – one that proceeds from presumably
unassailable premises and builds a system by a chain of reasoning.

Peirce's main objection to this chain metaphor is that it fails to
recognize how the sciences proceed. Scientific reasoning is more like a
cable in which there are multiple strands reinforcing each other. Any
one of these strands may be weak, but collectively they can have great
strength. This cable model of multiple argumentation, which has
proved so successful in the sciences, ought to be adopted in philosophical inquiry. This is the practice that Peirce actually follows, and it is
one reason (not the only one) why many of his papers are so dense.
He piles on a great variety of arguments, some of which are stronger
than others. Individually, they do not always support his claims, but
when they are intertwined, they can be extremely forceful.

Finally, Peirce categorically rejects the idea that there are any
"absolutely inexplicable" facts.

> 4. Every unidealistic philosophy supposes some absolutely inexplicable,
> unanalyzable ultimate; in short, something resulting from mediation

itself not susceptible of mediation. Now that anything *is* thus inexplicable can be shown by reasoning from signs. But the only justification of an inference from signs is that the conclusion explains the fact. To suppose the fact absolutely inexplicable, is not to explain it, and hence this supposition is never allowable. (Peirce 1992, p. 29)[9]

Peirce introduces two further themes that stand at the heart of his pragmatism. First, all cognition involves or *presupposes* inferential processes. There is no direct, immediate, intuitive knowledge. And second, these inferential processes involve the use of signs. All thinking and reasoning consists of sign activity. Peirce's critique of Cartesianism anticipates and bears a strong affinity to Wittgenstein's critique of Cartesian themes in his *Philosophical Investigations* and with Sellars's critique of the Myth of the Given in *Empiricism and the Philosophy of Mind*. With some justification we can say that "the linguistic turn" (or, as Peirce would prefer, "the semeiotic turn") begins with Peirce.

Intuitionism

Let us turn to the first essay in the Cognition Series, "Questions Concerning Certain Faculties Claimed for Man," where Peirce criticizes the chief error of Cartesianism: the belief that there is a form of intuitive indubitable knowledge that can serve as a foundation for the sciences. Descartes drew upon the traditional philosophical distinction between two sorts of knowledge, direct and indirect, immediate and inferential. But he gives this distinction a novel twist. The first sort of knowledge consists of intuitions. Intuitive knowledge is conceived of as a two-term (dyadic) relation between a knowing mind and a known truth. A great deal of preliminary investigation may be required to discriminate and isolate these intuitions – to insure that they are clear and distinct – but once this is achieved, then we have direct immediate knowledge; these intuitions are not based upon, nor do they presuppose, any inferential knowledge. On the contrary, they serve as the basis (the premises) for our inferences. The Cartesian version of the distinction between intuitive and inferential knowledge has had a profound influence on subsequent philosophy in both its rationalist and its empiricist strains. For example, in the twentieth century Bertrand Russell distinguished between "knowledge by acquaintance" and "knowledge by description." He characterized "knowledge by acquaintance" as follows: "We have acquaintance with anything of which we are directly aware without the intermediary of any process of inference or any truths" (Russell 1910–11, p. 108).

Peirce directly asks: Do we have such intuitive knowledge? Do we have a faculty or capacity that enables us to have such knowledge? If we have such a capacity, then how do we know it? There are two possibilities. Either we know this intuitively, or we can give reasons to justify that we have such a capacity. Peirce argues: (a) we do not have any grounds for claiming that we know intuitively that we have intuitions; and (b) we do not have good reasons to claim that there *must* be such intuitions. Peirce speaks of a "faculty of intuition," but we can raise the issue in a more straightforward manner. Do we have intuitive knowledge? How do we know this?

Peirce, who admired the intellectual finesse of medieval philosophers, especially Duns Scotus, adopts a procedure common to scholastic thinkers. He raises a question, considers the pros and cons, evaluates them, and then proceeds to answer the question.

Question 1. *Whether by the simple contemplation of a cognition, independently of any previous knowledge and without any reasoning from signs, we are enabled rightly to judge whether the cognition has been determined by a previous cognition or whether it refers immediately to its object.* (Peirce 1992, p. 11)

By 'cognition,' Peirce means anything that can be thought, whether it is a concept, a judgment, or an inference. And he specifies what he means by 'intuition.' "Throughout this paper, the term *intuition* will be taken as signifying a cognition not determined by a previous cognition of the same object and therefore so determined by something outside of consciousness" (Peirce 1992, p. 11). Peirce adds the following footnote to clarify his meaning.

In the middle ages, the term "intuitive cognition" had two principal senses, 1st, as opposed to abstractive cognition, it means knowledge of the present as present, and this is the meaning in Anselm; but 2nd, as no intuitive cognition was allowed to be determined by a previous cognition, it came to be used as the opposite of discursive cognition ... and this is nearly the sense in which I employ it. (Peirce 1992, p. 12n.)

Peirce does not explicitly indicate how he is using the word 'determined,' but from the context it is clear that he is making a distinction between what we might call conceptual determination and the causal determination by which an intuition is presumably "determined by something outside of consciousness."[10] The initial question is whether we have an intuitive power to tell that we have a *genuine* intuition (and not a cognition that is determined by a previous cognition).

> Now, it is plainly one thing to have an intuition and another to know intuitively that it is an intuition, and the question is whether these two things, distinguishable in thought, are, in fact, invariably connected, so that we can always intuitively distinguish between an intuition and a cognition determined by another. ... There is no evidence that we have this faculty, except that we seem to *feel* that we have it. But the weight of that testimony depends entirely on our being supposed to have the power of distinguishing in this feeling whether the feeling be the result of education, old associations, etc., or whether it is an intuitive cognition; or in other words, it depends on presupposing the very matter testified to. Is this feeling infallible? And is the judgment concerning it infallible and so on, *ad infinitum*. (Peirce 1992, p. 12)

Of course, we may think or feel that we intuitively know that we have an intuition. But such thoughts and feelings are eminently fallible. The above argument does not rule out the possibility that we really do have a faculty of intuition. But it does call into question whether we intuitively know that we have intuitions.

What about the other possibility? Can we provide arguments to show that there *must* be intuitions? Peirce now advances a battery of arguments (multiform argumentation) to show (a) why the reasons and evidence offered to support the thesis that there *must* be such a faculty are deficient; and (b) how there is an alternative way of accounting for the "facts" that are presumably explained by intuitions. There is no clear mark that clearly distinguishes an intuition from what is actually the result of an inferential process. This is illustrated by the way in which philosophers "very warmly" dispute these alleged intuitions; disagreements about what are and are not intuitions are notorious. Furthermore, every lawyer knows just how difficult it really is to discern what is presumably directly seen and known "immediately" from what is actually inferred or conditioned by our expectations and interpretations. Peirce also offers a number of arguments developed from perceptual studies to illustrate our inability to sort out what is presumably intuited from what is inferred (consciously or unconsciously). "We have therefore, a variety of facts, all of which are most readily explained on the supposition that we have no intuitive faculty of distinguishing intuitive from mediate cognitions. ... Moreover, no facts require the supposition of the faculty in question" (Peirce 1992, p. 18). In sum, we neither know intuitively that we have intuitions, nor do we have any reason to suppose that there *must* be intuitions.

But a Cartesian may object to this line of reasoning, claiming that by focusing on perceptual knowledge and arguing for the impossibility of distinguishing intuitions from inferred cognitions, Peirce is avoiding the really tough issues. Descartes knows that perception is fallible. Descartes' *cogito*, the exemplar of an incorrigible intuition, is about *thinking* – the awareness of ourselves as thinking beings. This leads directly to Peirce's second question.

Question 2. *Whether we have an intuitive self-consciousness.*

By 'self-consciousness' Peirce means the recognition of "my *private* self," not self-consciousness in general or what Kant calls 'apperception.' "I know that *I* (not merely *the* I) exists. The question is how do I know it, by a special intuitive faculty, or is it determined by previous cognitions" (Peirce 1992, p. 18). On the basis of Peirce's answer to Question 1, we can already say that we do not intuitively know that we have an intuitive self-consciousness. So we need an independent argument to show that there is an intuitive self-consciousness. Peirce argues that coming to an awareness of our self-consciousness is in fact an inferential learning process. He tell us: "At an age at which we know children to be self-conscious, we know that they have been made aware of ignorance and error; and we know them to possess at that age powers of understanding sufficient to enable them to infer from ignorance and error their own existence" (Peirce 1992, p. 20). No Cartesian would be satisfied with this argument. He might accuse Peirce of confusing the empirical question of how children become aware of their private selves with the epistemological status of such knowledge once it is learned. The Cartesian doesn't deny that learning is required in order for me to grasp intuitively my self-consciousness and my own existence. How, then, does Peirce explain that I am more certain of my own existence than of anything else – and that any attempt to doubt my own existence actually affirms it? Peirce meets this objection head-on.

We are more certain of our own existence than any other fact; a premise cannot determine a conclusion to be more certain than it is itself; hence, our own existence cannot be inferred from any other fact. The first premise must be admitted, but the second premise is founded on an exploded theory of logic. A conclusion cannot be more certain than that some one of the facts which support it is true, but it may easily be more certain than any one of those facts. Let us suppose, for example, that a dozen witnesses testify to an occurrence. Then my belief in that occurrence rests on the belief that each of those men is generally to be believed upon oath. Yet the fact testified to is made more certain than any one of those men is generally to be believed. In the same way, to the developed mind of man, his own existence is supported by every other fact, and is, therefore, incomparably more certain than any one of these facts. (Peirce 1992, pp. 20–1)

Peirce concludes by answering Question 2 in the negative: "[T]here is no necessity of supposing an intuitive self-consciousness, since self-consciousness may easily be the result of inference" (Peirce 1992, p. 21). Let us be clear about Peirce's argumentative strategy. His primary objective is to criticize the thesis that we have direct immediate intuitive cognitions. But if he challenges this thesis, then he must, at least, indicate an alternative way of accounting for the "facts" that intuition is supposed to explain. Peirce is *not* denying that there is personal self-consciousness. Rather, he shows that such acknowledgment is not intuitive, but rather the result of complex inferential processes. In this respect, we can say that there is a very close affinity with Hegel's account of self-consciousness in his *Phenomenology of Spirit* as well as with Wittgenstein's reflections on privacy and a private language in the *Philosophical Investigations*. And we find further variations on this pragmatic theme in Mead's account of the social genesis of language, Sellars's account of "privileged access," and Habermas's account of self-consciousness in the context of communicative action and rationality.

In the remainder of the "Questions" paper, Peirce presents other arguments that cast doubt on the idea of "intuitive knowledge." We do not have an intuitive power for distinguishing the subjective element of different types of cognitions. We do not distinguish "dreaming, imagining, conceiving, believing, etc." by intuition (Peirce 1992, p. 21). We do not have an intuitive power of introspection when this is understood to be an immediate intuition of an "internal world."

There is no "knowledge of the internal world not derived from external observation" (Peirce 1992, p. 22).

Thought and Signs

One of the most important claims that Peirce makes in these early papers is that there is no thought without signs, or, more precisely, no thinking without sign activity. At this early stage of his career, Peirce barely sketched his theory of signs, what he later called "semeiotics." He continued to elaborate and refine his theory of signs until the end of his life. But even in these papers, we can detect his core idea: the triadic character of signification. "From the proposition that every thought is a sign, it follows that every thought must address itself to some other, must determine some other, since that is the essence of a sign" (Peirce 1992, p. 24). To elucidate what Peirce means, let us return to the Cartesian understanding of intuition. I have indicated that intuition is a two-termed (dyadic) relation between knower (mind) and a known object. In representational epistemological and semantic accounts of language, attention is focused on the relation between a sign and what it represents. One of Peirce's most original and central claims is that all sign activity is irreducibly triadic: a sign (first term) stands for an object (second term) to an interpretant (third term). This triadic structure is an essential characteristic of both linguistic and nonlinguistic signs.[11] In his theory of signs, Peirce typically speaks about the 'interpretant' rather than the 'interpreter' because he stresses that the interpretant is itself a sign. But if signification involves sign, object, and interpretant, and every interpretant is itself a sign, there is potentially an endless series of signs. What is Peirce driving at in this triadic analysis of sign activity? As W. B. Gallie writes:

> If then, every sign requires an interpretant in the form of a further sign, and admits of such interpretation in a virtually endless number of alternative ways, it follows that there can be no such thing as the (one and only) sign of a given object, and no such thing as the (one and only) interpretant of a given sign. The belief – still all too prevalent among philosophers – that a sign can stand in a simple two-term relation, called its meaning, to its object, is thus seen to rest on a radical misconception of the kind of thing a sign is and of the way in which it

functions. The truth is that a sign can function only as an element in a working systems of signs. (Gallie 1952, p. 125)[12]

As Peirce refines his theory of signs, he makes it clear that the potentially theoretical openness of every sign to further interpretation is compatible with the practical necessity of cutting short potential (endless) interpretation. He also distinguishes different types of interpretant, but it is the "logical interpretant" that is most relevant for understanding inquiry.[13] As Peirce developed his theory of signs, he viewed the pragmatic maxim that he introduced in 1878 as a procedure for determining the logical interpretant of a sign. As I have already noted, the original statement of the maxim is: "Consider what effects, which might conceivably have practical bearings, we conceive the object of our conception to have. Then our conception of these effects is the whole conception of the object" (Peirce 1992, p. 132).[14] At a later date, he comments:

> The employment five times over of derivatives of *concipere* must then have had a purpose. In point of fact it had two. One was to show that I was speaking of meaning in no other sense than that of *intellectual purport*. The other was to avoid all danger of being understood as attempting to explain a concept by percepts, images, schemata, or anything but concepts. I did not, therefore, mean to say that acts, which are more singular than anything, could constitute the purport or adequate proper interpretation, of any symbol. ... Pragmaticism makes thinking to consist in the living inferential metaboly of symbols whose purport lies in the conditional general resolution to act. (5.403 n. 3)

The point of the pragmatic maxim is to relate our concepts and judgments to human conduct. The maxim is intended to single out from "the myriads of forms into which a proposition may be translated ... that form in which the proposition becomes applicable to human conduct" (5.427). When Peirce distinguishes his pragmaticism from other versions of pragmatism, he declares: "To say that I hold the import, or the adequate ultimate interpretation, of a concept contained, not in any deed or deeds that will ever be done, but in a habit of conduct ... is no more to say that I am a pragmaticist" (5.504). We must appreciate the sharp distinction that Peirce draws between action and conduct: action is singular, but conduct is general.[15] Consequently, when we view the pragmatic maxim from the perspective of Peirce's theory of signs, we realize that it is a procedure for clarifying the habits of conduct and the inferential consequences of our concepts and judgments. Such clarification is always provisional – open to new and novel interpretations. Late in his career, Peirce adds one further nuance when he indicates that the logical interpretant is the verbal expression of a habit of conduct.[16]

> The real and living logical conclusion is that habit; the verbal formulation merely expresses it. ... The concept which is a logical interpretant is only imperfectly so. It partakes somewhat of the nature of a verbal definition, and is very inferior to the living definition that grows up in the habit. (5.491)

The Pragmatic Alternative

There is still a major problem that Peirce leaves unresolved in his 1867–8 papers. His primary aim is to criticize Cartesianism and the thesis that we have direct intuitive knowledge – the type of intuition not determined by prior cognitions and one that can serve as an epistemological foundation. He begins to sketch an alternative way of understanding inquiry and knowing. But we need a positive account of what it means to claim that every cognition is determined by a previous cognition. Hegel and his idealist followers also deny that there is intuitive (nonmediated) knowledge and are equally relentless in critiquing epistemological foundationalism. If we relied exclusively on the 1867–8 papers, then we would be hard pressed to answer the question of what is the difference that makes a difference between Peirce's pragmaticism and Hegelian idealism. Peirce states his difference with Hegel when he declares: "The capital error of Hegel which permeates his whole system in every part of it is that he almost altogether ignores the Outward Clash" (Peirce 1992, p. 223). What is this "Outward Clash"? What role does it play in Peirce's version of pragmatism? To answer this question, I want to consider a similar issue that has arisen is contemporary philosophical debates.

Peirce would agree with Donald Davidson's claim that "nothing can count as a reason for holding a belief except another belief" (Davidson 1986, p. 310). He would also agree with Sellars when he argues that all justification takes place within the logical space of giving and asking for reasons. More generally, Sellars's *Empiricism and the Philosophy of Mind* reads like an explication of Peirce in the "new way of words." Peirce might well have written the following:

> Many things have been said to be "given": sense contents, material objects, universals, propositions, real connections, first principles, even givenness itself. And there is a certain way of construing the situations which philosophers analyze in these terms which can be said to be the framework of givenness. This framework has been a common feature of most of the major systems of philosophy, including "dogmatic ratio-nalism" and "skeptical empiricism." (Sellars 1997, p. 14)

John McDowell, who accepts Davidson's thesis about belief and Sellars's critique of the Myth of the Given, notes that there is an "interminable oscillation" between an appeal to a Given that is sup-posed to ground empirical knowledge and a coherentism that is in danger of losing contact with a world that constrains us. Both extremes are unsatisfactory. This oscillation, which McDowell takes to be at the heart of modern philosophy, provokes deep anxieties. McDowell's aim in *Mind and World* is "to propose an account, in a diagnostic spirit, of some characteristic anxieties of modern philosophy – anxieties that centre ... on the relation of mind and world" (McDowell 1996, p. xi). He seeks to provide a "third alternative" that shows how we can "dis-mount from the seesaw" – this "interminable oscillation."

> It can be difficult to accept that the Myth of the Given is a myth. It can seem that if we reject the Given, we merely reopen ourselves to the threat to which the idea of the Given is a response, the threat that our picture does not accommodate any external constraint on our activity in empirical thought and judgement. It can seem that we are retaining a role for spontaneity but refusing to acknowledge any role for recep-tivity, and that is intolerable. If our activity in empirical thought and judgement is to be recognizable as bearing on reality at all, there must be external constraint. There must be a role for receptivity as well as spontaneity, for sensibility as well as understanding. Realizing this, we come under pressure to recoil back into appealing to the Given, only to see all over again that it cannot help. There is a danger of falling into interminable oscillation. (McDowell 1996, pp. 8–9)

Davidson's coherentism represents one of the unsatisfactory extremes in this oscillation. "Davidson recoils from the Myth of the Given all the way to denying experience any justificatory role, and the coherentist upshot is a version of the conception of spontaneity as frictionless, the very thing that makes the idea of the Given so attractive. ... Davidson's picture depicts our empirical thinking as engaged with no rational constraint, but only causal influence, from outside" (McDowell 1996, p. 14). (The same may also be said about Rorty.) McDowell draws a sharp distinction between causal constraint and *rational constraint*. Davidson's blind spot, so McDowell asserts, is his failure to realize that experience (when properly understood and analyzed) is the source of *rational* constraint. Because Davidson thinks that experience can *only* be the source of causal constraint, the worry persists about "whether Davidson's coherentist picture can incorporate thought's bearing on reality." He leaves us with the anxiety that such a picture "leaves our thinking possibly out of touch with a world outside us" (McDowell 1996, pp. 16, 17). We oscillate between some version of the Myth of the Given and a frictionless coherentism that is in danger of losing contact with a world that is independent of us and that *rationally* constrains our empirical beliefs. McDowell argues that the failure to appreciate the way in which the world rationally constrains our thinking is due to a "deep-rooted mental block" against a conception of nature that does justice to "second nature."[17]

We can put the basic issue in a slightly different way. One of the main "dogmas" of contemporary philosophy has been the acceptance of a sharp dichotomy between causal constraint and rational justification; the former ascribed to experience and the latter to reasoning. If one accepts this as an *exclusive* dichotomy, then the interminable oscillation that McDowell describes appears unavoidable and interminable. Why? Because once we abandon the Myth of the Given, the only viable alternative seems to be some version of coherentism or linguistic idealism that has no place for any constraint upon us other than causal constraint. And causal constraint, McDowell argues, does not alleviate the anxiety that our web of beliefs may be frictionless. McDowell's way of getting off this seesaw – or, as he might put it, his therapeutic approach to relieving the anxiety about a "frictionless coherentism" – is to show that the world constrains us, but that this constraint has to be understood as a *rational* constraint. This means that we have to grasp how our "conceptual capacities" permeate experience.

> When we trace the ground for an empirical judgement, the last step takes us to experiences. Experiences already have conceptual content,

so this last step does not take us outside the space of concepts. But it takes us to something in which sensibility – receptivity – is operative, so we need no longer be unnerved by the freedom implicit in the idea that conceptual capacities belong to a faculty of spontaneity. We need not worry that our picture leaves out the external constraint that is required if exercises of our conceptual capacities are to be recognizable as bearing on the world at all. (McDowell 1996, p. 10)

The oscillation that concerns McDowell is also at the center of Peirce's thinking. Like McDowell (and Sellars and Davidson), Peirce categorically rejects the idea of an epistemological Given (intuition) that grounds empirical knowledge. This is the core of his critique of Cartesianism. But Peirce is acutely aware of the temptations of an idealism or coherentism that loses contact with a world that is independent of us and constrains us. This is the point of his remark about the "Outward Clash." Peirce's pragmaticism is a *via media* – a third way – that shows how to avoid the extremes of intuitionism (the Myth of the Given) and idealism (coherentism). Like McDowell, Peirce wants to preserve the central "truth" of the empiricist tradition – that the world constrains what we believe – but he also wants to avoid the confusion between constraint and justification.[18]

When Peirce speaks of the "Outward Clash," he is referring to the category of Secondness in his scheme of Firstness, Secondness, and Thirdness. I examine Peirce's categorical scheme in chapter 6, "Experience after the Linguistic Turn."[19] In this context, I indicate how Peirce's categories of Secondness and Thirdness show us how to avoid the oscillation that McDowell describes. Peirce's categories are intended to designate elements or aspects of phenomena that are distinguishable but not separable. He uses the term 'prescind' as a name for this type of discrimination. For example, when speaking about experience or perception, we can focus our attention on its different aspects. Thirdness includes what Davidson calls beliefs and what Sellars and McDowell call concepts and judgments. Sellars's "logical space of reasons" would be characterized by Peirce as Thirdness. But Secondness is the category that refers to brute constraint, compulsiveness, resistance. It is a dominant feature of experience. Consider some of the ways in which Peirce characterizes Secondness. Secondness is prominent in "the compulsion, the absolute constraint upon us to think otherwise than we have been thinking" (1.336).

> Experience is that determination of belief and cognition generally which the course of life has forced upon man. One may lie about it; but one cannot escape the fact that some things *are* forced upon his cognition. There is an element of brute force, existing whether you opine it exists or not. (2.138)

Peirce carefully distinguishes between *constraint* and epistemic *authority*.[20] What Peirce calls Secondness is not to be identified with causal constraint; it is phenomenologically more primitive than causation.[21] We may be constrained to believe something, but its epistemic authority may be challenged by further inquiry. There is an interplay between Secondness and Thirdness, between brute constraint and epistemic claims. Understanding this interplay enables us to see how Peirce's version of pragmatism avoids the Myth of the Given and the type of frictionless coherentism that ignores the "Outward Clash." Let me illustrate this with reference to Peirce's analysis of perception.

The categories of Secondness and Thirdness enable us to understand properly two different aspects of perceptual judgments: their epistemic status and their insistency. Consider a simple perceptual report when I am looking at the sky on a beautiful sunny day and I report that "I see a cloudless blue sky." I would not be able to make such a report unless I had already mastered what Wittgenstein calls a language game and what Sellars describes as a "battery of concepts." Making such a report requires mastery of the inferences that Peirce designates as Thirdness. But I can also focus on the insistency of this perceptual report. The perceptual judgment is forced upon me in the sense that if I look up (and have normal eyesight), I cannot help seeing that the sky is blue. But the fact that such perceptual judgments are forced upon us does not mean that they are self-authenticating. Even those perceptual judgments that are forced upon us (where there seems no room for doubt) may turn out to be false. "We all know, only too well, how terribly insistent perception may be; and yet, for all that, in its most insistent degrees, it may be utterly false, – that it may not fit into the general mass of experience" (7.647). Peirce, who had a penchant for technical terminology, introduces the expression 'percipuum' to clarify his meaning.

> We know nothing about the percept otherwise than by the testimony of the perceptual judgment, excepting we feel the blow of it, the reaction of it against us, and we see the contents of it arranged into an object, in its totality, – excepting also, of course what the psychologists are

able to make out inferentially. *But the moment we fix our minds upon it and think the least thing about the percept, it is the perceptual judgment that tells us what we so "perceive."* For this and other reasons, I propose to consider the percept as it is immediately interpreted in the perceptual judgment, under the name of the "percipuum." (7.643, emphasis added.)

Just as McDowell argues – using the Kantian terminology of spontaneity and receptivity – that, "even though experience is passive, it draws into operation capacities that genuinely belong to spontaneity," so Peirce argues that perception (the percipuum) involves the conceptual capacities of Thirdness.[22] Although we can discriminate the element of Secondness – the brute compulsion – in perception, this brute compulsion is not a Given. It does not *authenticate* a perceptual judgment. The percipuum is forced upon us. And the percipuum can be analyzed ("prescinded") into the elements designated by Peirce's categorical scheme. The percipuum is *not* a discrete sense datum. It is *not* a self-authenticating episode, which serves as an epistemological foundation of empirical knowledge. It is *not* the Given. It is a judgment forced upon us. When the percipuum appears, we are already at the level of Thirdness; consequently, as a judgment it is eminently fallible; it may turn out to be false. Peirce is disentangling the concept of *brute compulsion* from *epistemic authority*. Both are essential to account for perception and experience. The world does constrain our empirical knowledge, but this constraint (Secondness) is mediated through our perceptual and experiential judgments (Thirdness).[23]

Like Sellars, McDowell, Brandom, and Habermas (among others), Peirce builds upon the Kantian and Hegelian claims about how all thinking and reasoning involves mediation and inference. In Kantian terms, there is no thinking or knowing without spontaneity (understanding). But Peirce seeks to integrate this with what he takes to be the insight and "truth" implicit in the empiricist tradition – that there is a brute compulsion that forces experience upon us and constrains what we can know. And he does this without falling into the trap of the Myth of the Given.[24] Peirce's pragmaticism is a *via media* that avoids the Myth of the Given and a frictionless coherentism, but combines the best insights of the idealist tradition with the best insights of the empiricist tradition.

William James and all subsequent pragmatists acknowledged Peirce as the founder of pragmatism. Typically, this has been taken to mean that Peirce was the first to enunciate the pragmatic maxim in "How to Make Our Ideas Clear." I have been arguing that Peirce is the founder of pragmatism for another reason. His early 1867–8 papers open a way of thinking that goes to the very heart of the matter – profoundly questioning and critiquing the Cartesianism that shaped so much of modern philosophy. They set an agenda that he continued to explore for the rest of his life. They introduced a fallibilistic pragmatism that avoids the Myth of the Given and acknowledges the brute compulsiveness of experience. Peirce opened up a new way of thinking that is still being pursued today in novel and exciting ways by all those who have taken the pragmatic turn. This is the sea change that he helped to initiate.

2

The Ethical Consequences of William James's Pragmatic Pluralism

Since the mid-twentieth century, a specter has haunted philosophy. It is the specter of relativism, and it is a reflection of what I once called "the Cartesian Anxiety." Let me quote how I described this anxiety.

> Reading the *Meditations* as a journey of the soul helps us to appreciate that Descartes' search for a foundation or Archimedean point is more than a device to solve metaphysical and epistemological problems. It is the quest for some fixed point; some stable rock upon which we can secure our lives against the vicissitudes that constantly threaten us. The specter that hovers in the background of this journey is not just radical epistemological skepticism but the dread of madness and chaos where nothing is fixed, where we can neither touch bottom nor support ourselves on the surface. With a chilling clarity Descartes leads us with an apparent and ineluctable necessity to a grand and seductive Either/Or. *Either* there is some support for our being, a fixed foundation for our knowledge, *Or* we cannot escape the forces of darkness that envelop us with madness, with intellectual and moral chaos. (Bernstein 1983, p. 18)

And I go on to say:

> It would be a mistake to think that the Cartesian Anxiety is primarily a religious, metaphysical, epistemological, or moral anxiety. These are only several of the many forms it may assume. In Heideggerian language, it is "ontological" rather than "ontic," for it seems to lie at the very center of our being in the world. Our "god terms" may vary

and be very different from those of Descartes. We may even purge ourselves of the quest for certainty and indubitability. But at the heart of
the objectivist's vision, and what makes sense of his or her passion, is
the belief that there are or must be some fixed, permanent constraints
to which we can appeal and which are secure and stable. At its most
profound level the relativist's message is that there are no such basic
constraints except those that we invent or temporally (and temporarily) accept. Relativists are suspicious of their opponents because,
the relativists claim, all species of objectivism almost inevitably turn
into vulgar or sophisticated forms of ethnocentrism in which some
privileged understanding of rationality is falsely legitimated by claiming for it an unwarranted universality. The primary reason why the
agon between objectivists and relativists has become so intense today
is the growing apprehension that there may be nothing – not God,
reason, philosophy, science, or poetry – that answers to and satisfies
our longing for ultimate constraints, for a stable and reliable rock upon
which we can secure our thought and action. (Bernstein 1983, p. 19)

What do we mean by 'relativism'? Here we face a problem because
many philosophers who have been accused of relativism typically
deny that they are relativists. A good example is Richard Rorty, who
debunks talk of relativism. "'Relativism,'" he tells us, "is the view
that every belief on a certain topic, or perhaps about *any* topic, is as
good as every other. No one holds this view" (Rorty 1982, p. 166). Yet
he has been accused by many, including his fellow pragmatist Hilary
Putnam, of advocating views that lead directly to relativism. I do not
want to try to sort out the various meanings of 'relativism', but I do
want to emphasize that – to use a Wittgensteinian turn of phrase
– there is a picture that holds us captive. It is a picture that Karl
Popper once characterized as the "myth of the framework" (Popper
1974, p. 56). This is the myth that "we are prisoners caught in the
framework of our theories; our past expectations; our language,"
and that we are so locked into these frameworks that we cannot
communicate with those encased in "radically different" frameworks
or paradigms (ibid.).[1] These different frameworks, vocabularies, or
paradigms are incommensurable with each other, and there are no
universal – or even common – standards by which we can evaluate and
adjudicate claims that are made within these alternative frameworks.
Frequently this is the *picture* that one has in mind when one defends
or attacks relativism.

    I have introduced the discussion of pragmatic pluralism by speak-
ing about the Cartesian Anxiety and the "menace" of relativism for

two reasons. First, many critics think that "pluralism" is just a fancy name for relativism. But they are wrong. Second, I will argue that the pragmatic thinkers reject the grand Either/Or of the Cartesian Anxiety. We are not confronted with the alternative of ultimate fixed foundations or a foundationless relativism. *Pragmatic pluralism is not relativism*; it is one of the strongest responses to the picture of relativism suggested by the myth of the framework.

James's Pluralism

I focus on William James's pluralism, and its ethical and cultural consequences. James was one of the first philosophers to dignify the word 'pluralism' when he entitled his book based on lectures delivered at Oxford *A Pluralistic Universe* (1909). But even in his first collection of philosophical essays, *The Will to Believe* (1897), he had declared that "the difference between monism and pluralism is perhaps the most pregnant of all differences in philosophy."

> *Prima facie* the world is a pluralism; as we find it, its unity seems to be that of any collection; and our higher thinking consists chiefly of an effort to redeem it from that first crude form. Postulating more unity than the first experiences yield, we also discover more. But absolute unity, in spite of brilliant dashes in its direction, still remains undiscovered, still remains a *Grenzbegriff*. ... To the very last, there are various "points of view" which the philosopher must distinguish in discussing the world; and what is inwardly clear from one point remains a bare externality and datum to the other. The negative, the alogical, is never wholly banished. Something – call it "fate, chance, freedom, spontaneity, the devil, what you will" – is still wrong and other and outside and unincluded, from *your* point of view, even though you be the greatest of philosophers. (James 1977, pp. 5–6)

James adds that someone who takes the hypothesis that pluralism is "the permanent form of the world is what I call a radical empiricist" (James 1977, p. 5). To understand more fully what James means by pluralism, however, we need to consider the historical and philosophical context in which he elaborated his views. Of all the classical pragmatists, James was the one who felt the deepest affinity with the tradition of British empiricism. He dedicated his *Pragmatism* (1907) to the memory of John Stuart Mill, "from whom I first learned the pragmatic openness of mind and whom my fancy likes to picture as our leader were he alive to-day." James was attracted to the down-to-earth quality of empiricism, its insistence on the appeal to experience as the touchstone of all knowledge, its abhorrence of jargon, and its habit of explaining wholes by parts. Yet James was one of the most acute critics of what he took to be the deficiencies of the empiricist conception of experience.

We can best understand the target of James's critique of the empiricist conception of experience by turning to Hume's account of the mind's perceptions. Hume opens his *Treatise* with the striking claim: "All the perceptions of the human mind resolve themselves into two distinct kinds, which I shall call IMPRESSIONS and IDEAS" (Hume 1978, p. 1). These impressions and ideas can be divided into those that are simple and those that are complex. Our *"simple ideas in their first appearance are deriv'd from simple impressions, which are correspondent to them, and which they exactly represent"* (Hume 1978, p. 4). Ideas are copies of impressions. Hume insists that simple impressions and ideas are distinct and separable from each other. One cannot underestimate the consequences of this starting point for Hume's entire epistemology and philosophy, and for his skeptical analysis of induction, causation, and personal identity. We do not have any direct perception of the connections or relations among these discrete impressions and ideas. They are connected by the principles of association: resemblance, contiguity in time and place, and cause and effect. " 'Tis evident," Hume declares of his account of impressions and ideas. But not so for James! Already in his *Principles of Psychology*, James argues that this account of impressions and ideas is fallacious. We do not begin with impressions and ideas that are distinct and separable. To speak in this way is to substitute a sophisticated abstraction for concrete dynamic experience. James calls this the "intellectualist fallacy," whereby we substitute artificial static constructs for the actual flow of experience. It is an instance of "vicious intellectualism," of what Whitehead felicitously called the "fallacy of misplaced concreteness." In his famous chapter, "The Stream of Thought," in the *Principles of Psychology*, James declares:

> We now begin our study of the mind from within. Most books start with sensations, as the simplest mental facts, and proceed synthetically, constructing each higher stage from below it. But this is abandoning the

empirical method of investigation. No one ever had a simple sensation by itself. Consciousness, from our natal day, is of a teeming multiplicity of objects and relations, and what we call simple sensations are results of discriminative attention, pushed often to a very high degree. It is astonishing what havoc is wrought in psychology by admitting at the outset apparently innocent suppositions that nevertheless contain a flaw. The bad consequences develop themselves later on, and are irremediable, being woven through the whole texture of the work. (James 1981, vol. 1, p. 219)

Or again:

The continuous flow of the mental stream is sacrificed, and in its place an atomism, a brickbat plan of construction, is preached. ... These words are meant to impeach the entire English psychology derived from Locke and Hume, and the entire German psychology derived from Herbart, so far as both treat 'ideas' as separate subjective entities that come and go. (James 1981, vol. 1, p. 195)

In short, James accuses the traditional empiricists of "abandoning the empirical method of investigation." Over and over again, James sought to expose this misguided conception of experience as consisting of the aggregate of discrete units. Positively, he argues that we have *direct* experience of the connections, relations, and transitions within the continuous flow of experience. Subsequently, James's critique of traditional conceptions of experience became even more radical. He challenges the subject–object distinction or consciousness–content distinction that had been so entrenched in modern epistemology. In his 1904 essay "Does 'Consciousness' Exist?" James denied the inner duplicity of subject and object, where we postulate a duality between consciousness and content. "*Experience, I believe, has no inner duplicity: and the separation of it into consciousness and content comes, not by way of subtraction, but by way of addition*" (James 1997, p. 172). Thus one and the same experience – say, of a room – may be at once an element in the reader's personal biography and an element in the physical history of the room in a house. James also departs from many traditional empiricists in that he always emphasized the creative, imaginative, selective dimension of our experienc*ing* – so much so that some commentators have argued that James, despite his barbed comments about Kant and German idealism, was actually influenced by Kant more than he acknowledged.

Whitehead speaks of the historical and philosophical importance of James, and especially the landmark article "Does 'Consciousness' Exist?" "The scientific materialism and the Cartesian ego were both challenged at the same moment, one by science and the other by philosophy, as represented by William James and his psychological antecedents; and the double challenge marks the end of a period which lasted for about two hundred and fifty years" (Whitehead 1959, p. 143).

To fully appreciate how James's radical empiricism contributes to his pluralism, we have to understand that he was seeking a *via media* between the misguided epistemological atomism of the empiricists and the "block universe" monism of the idealists. James's pluralistic radical empiricism was developed in contrast to, and as a reaction against, the varieties of absolutism and monism that he battled with all his life. We frequently forget the dominance of the varieties of absolute idealism in America (and England) during the last decades of the nineteenth century. Although Hegel and German idealism were the source of inspiration, in England, T. H. Green, F. H. Bradley, and Bernard Bosanquet developed their own versions of absolute idealism. In America, the great proponent of a Christianized absolute idealism was Josiah Royce, James's younger colleague at Harvard. James admired and learned from Royce, but he also battled him and the British idealists to the end of his life. He honed his pluralism in reaction to what he took to be the thin, overly intellectualized monism of the absolute idealists. His objections to absolute idealism – especially the Christianized form of Royce – were multifaceted and, at times, almost visceral. He thought that the proponents of absolute idealism did not allow any place for genuine free will, novelty, and chance. They tended to explain away the real evil that exists in the world. Their conception of experience was a distorted reflection of the empiricism that they ruthlessly attacked. Instead of a world of multiple monads – multiple discrete atomic impressions – they opted for one big all-inclusive monad. In part, James's argument for a pragmatic conception of truth was motivated as an alternative to the coherence theory of truth advocated by idealists who basically accepted the Hegelian doctrine that the "truth is the whole." The idealists lacked sensitivity to the varieties of religious experience, and their conception of God was only a threadbare philosophical abstraction. James, who employs a variety of deflationary rhetorical tropes, mocked monistic idealism.

As absolute, then, or *sub specie eternitatis*, or *quatenus infinitus est*, the world repels our sympathy because it has no history. *As such*, the absolute neither acts nor suffers, nor loves nor hates; it has no needs, desires, or aspirations, no failures or successes, friends or enemies, victories or defeats. All such things pertain to the world *qua* relative, in which our finite experiences lie, and whose vicissitudes alone have the power to arouse our interest. What boots it to tell me that the absolute way is the true way, and to exhort me, as Emerson says, to lift mine eye up to its style, and manners of the sky, if the feat is impossible by definition? I am finite once for all, and all the categories of my sympathy are knit up with the finite world *as such*, and with things that have a history. (James 1977, p. 27)

James was fully aware that the type of pluralism that he professed was offensive to many philosophers. He speaks about a deep philosophical impulse that wants something more orderly, more clean-cut, and more systematic. In this respect, James would have found a great ally in the later Wittgenstein, who also sought to cure philosophers of the craving for definitive order. James writes:

It is curious how little countenance radical pluralism has ever had from philosophers. Whether materialistically or spiritually minded, philosophers have always aimed at cleaning up the litter with which the world apparently is filled. They have substituted economical and orderly conceptions for the first sensible tangle; and whether these are morally elevated or only intellectually neat, they were at any rate always aesthetically pure and definite, and aimed at ascribing to the world something clean and intellectual in the way of structure. As compared with all these rationalizing pictures, the pluralistic empiricism which I profess offers but a sorry appearance. It is a turbid, muddled, gothic sort of affair, without sweeping outline and with little pictorial nobility. (James 1977, p. 26)

James, of course, was not advocating that we should leave the world and experience just as we find it. He knows that we cannot give up the search for order, the need to simplify and to discover unities where they may not initially be expected. But even here he challenged the very idea of a single homogeneous unity. Pluralism, in contrast to dogmatic monism, does not deny unity, but directs us to ask what kind of unity we are talking about – to look and see just how much unity we really discover and what kind of unity we mean. "Thus the pragmatic question 'What is the oneness known-as?' 'What practical difference will it make?' saves us from all feverish excitement over it as a principle of sublimity and carries us forward into the stream of experience with a cool head. The stream may indeed reveal far more connexion and union than we now suspect, but we are not entitled on pragmatic principles to claim absolute oneness in any respect in advance" (James 1975a, p. 73).

James's pluralism shapes his understanding of the philosophical task. We can see this by highlighting his reflections on vision and temperament. A motif that runs through *A Pluralistic Universe* is the character of one's philosophical vision. James tells us that "a man's vision is the great fact about him," and that, "if we take the whole history of philosophy, the systems reduce themselves to a few main types which, under all the technical verbiage in which the ingenious intellect of man envelopes them, are just so many visions, modes of feeling the whole push, and seeing the whole drift of life, forced on one by one's total character and experience, and on the whole *preferred* – there is no other true word – as one's best working attitude" (James 1977, pp. 14–15). James also declares: "Any author is easy if you can catch the centre of his vision" (James 1977, p. 44). He stresses the normative significance of vision: "Where there is no vision the people perish. Few professorial philosophers have any vision." But when a philosopher has vision, "one can read him over and over again, and each time bring away a fresh sense of reality" (James 1977, p. 77). When James speaks of vision in this manner, he means one's creative imaginative orientation, one's sense of "feeling the whole push." James's nuanced references to vision deepen our understanding of his pluralism, because there is an irreducible plurality of visions. To use a phrase that Hilary Putnam has popularized, we finite human beings never achieve a "God's-eye" point of view. Our visions are always finite, partial, and incomplete.

James combines sensitivity to imaginative vision with a pragmatic appreciation of the role of argument in articulating a philosophical vision. There is plenty of evidence that James appreciated both the role of argument in philosophy and the brute compulsion of experience – what Peirce calls Secondness. In a passage that anticipates Quine, James stresses that each of us has a stock of well-established opinions and "truths" that may be put under strain when they seem to be contradicted or when we discover facts that do not fit with these opinions. What happens when someone experiences this tension?

He saves as much of it as he can, for in this matter of belief we are all extreme conservatives. So he tries to change first this opinion, and then that (for they resist change very variously), until at last some new idea comes up which he can graft upon the ancient stock with a minimum of disturbance of the latter, some idea that mediates between the stock and the new experience and runs them into one another most felicitously and expediently. (James 1975a, p. 35)

James's Ethical Concern

In all of James's writings about pluralism, one detects a very strong ethical concern. He objects to absolute idealism and monism because he believes that they don't leave room for genuine freedom, novelty, and chance. They overlook the intractable evils that we experience. A pluralistic universe is an open universe, in which there are real possibilities and real contingencies, in which our actions can make a difference for better or worse. A pluralistic universe is open to both tragedy and melioration. Meliorism is "the doctrine that holds up improvement as at least possible" (James 1975a, p. 61). It is a *via media* between optimism and pessimism. Optimism is "the doctrine that thinks the world's salvation is inevitable," and pessimism is "the doctrine that thinks that the world's salvation is impossible" (ibid.).

James is explicit about the ethical consequences of his understanding of pluralism. We can see this in his two remarkable essays "On a Certain Blindness in Human Beings" and "What Makes a Life Significant?" The blindness that James speaks of is "the blindness with which we are all afflicted in regard to the feelings of creatures and people different from ourselves" (James 1997, p. 629). We tend to be egocentric and insensitive to the feelings and opinions of those who are really different. "Hence the stupidity and injustice of our opinions, so far as they deal with the significance of alien lives. Hence the falsity of our judgments, so far as they presume to decide in an absolute way on the value of other persons' conditions or ideals" (James 1997, pp. 629–30). James speaks of a personal experience he had when he was traveling in the mountains of North Carolina, where he passed a number of "coves" – small valleys that had been cleared and planted. James's initial impression was one of unmitigated squalor. "The forest had been destroyed: and what had 'improved' it out of existence was hideous, a sort of ulcer, without a single element of artificial grace to make up for the loss of Nature's beauty" (James 1997, p. 631). He was horrified and wanted to know what sort of people could create so much ugliness.

> Then I said to the mountaineer who was driving me, "What sort of people are they who have to make these new clearings?" "All of us," he replied. "Why, we ain't happy here, unless we are getting one of these coves under cultivation." I instantly felt that I had been losing the whole inward significance of the situation. Because to me the clearings spoke of naught but denudation. I thought that to those whose sturdy arms and obedient axes had made them they could tell no other story. But, when *they* looked on the hideous stumps, what they thought of was personal victory. The chips, the girdled trees, and the vile split rails spoke of honest sweat, persistent toil and final reward. The cabin was a warrant of safety for self and wife and babes. In short, the clearing, which to me was a mere ugly picture on the retina, was to them a symbol redolent with moral memories and sang a very paean of duty, struggle, and success.
>
> I had been as blind to the peculiar ideality of their conditions as they certainly would have been to the ideality of mine, had they had a peep at my strange indoor academic ways of life at Cambridge. (Ibid.)

The story is mundane and folksy, but the moral of this tale has universal significance. Too frequently we are blind and insensitive to what is genuinely different from us, and we are all too quick to scorn and condemn it. There are much more threatening instances of this phenomenon when we come face to face with religious, ethnic, racial, and gender intolerance. We fail to make the effort to see how the world feels and looks from the perspective of those with other life experiences. But we can enlarge our understanding and sympathies to appreciate other points of view, other styles of life, and other horizons. This does *not* mean that when we make a serious effort to understand other points of view we will simply accept them or suspend our critical judgment. James's pluralism is not flabby or sentimental. It calls for a critical engagement with other points of view and with other visions. It is an engaged pluralism.[2] Contrary to the picture of relativism that speaks of incommensurable frameworks and paradigms, James's pluralism demands that we reach out to the points of contact where we can critically engage with each other.

At the beginning of "What Makes Life Significant?" James provides an eloquent and moving summary of his pluralistic vision.

In my previous talk, "On a Certain Blindness," I tried to make you feel how soaked and shot-through life is with values and meanings which we fail to realize because of our external and insensible point of view. The meanings are there for others, but they are not there for us. There lies more than a mere interest of curious speculation in understanding this. It has the most tremendous practical importance. I wish I could convince you of it as I feel it myself. It is the basis of all our tolerance, social, religious, and political. The forgetting of it lies at the root of every stupid and sanguinary mistake that rulers over subject-peoples make. The first thing to learn in intercourse with others is non-interference with their own peculiar ways of being happy, provided those ways do not assume to interfere by violence with ours. No one has insight into all ideals. No one should presume to judge them off-hand. The pretension to dogmatize about them in each other is the root of most human injustices and cruelties, and the trait in human character most likely to make the angels weep. (James 1997, p. 645).

James's Political Interventions

One of the popular myths about James is that he was not really interested in politics, and that his pluralism was essentially apolitical. But James was an engaged intellectual. The political issue that aroused his deepest passions was the war fever that led to the infamous Spanish–American war of 1898. He wrote several passionate articles and public letters protesting imperialism. In a letter to the *Boston Evening Transcript*, dated 1 March 1899, James wrote:

We are now openly engaged in crushing out the sacredest thing in this great human world – the attempt of a people long enslaved to attain to the possession of itself, to organize its laws and government, to be free to follow its internal destinies according to its own ideals. ... Why, then, should we go on? ... We are to be missionaries of civilization and to bear the white man's burden, painful as it often is! ... The individual lives are nothing. Our duty and our destiny call, and civilization must go on! Could there be a more damning indictment of that whole bloated idol termed 'modern civilization' than this amounts to? Civilization is, then, the big hollow, resounding, corrupting, sophisticating, confusing torrent of mere brutal momentum and irrationality that brings forth fruits like this! (James, quoted in Perry 1948, vol. 2, p. 310)

James's anti-imperialism (as well as his anti-monism) is epitomized when he declared: "Damn great Empires! including that of the Absolute. ... Give me individuals and their spheres of activity" (James, quoted in Perry 1948, vol. 2, p. 315).

James was equally outspoken about what he called the "lynching epidemic" of African-Americans in the United States. He was acutely aware of the bloodthirstiness and viciousness that could easily be aroused in a mob. There are those who think that James has a naïve, sentimental picture of human beings. But the following passage about mob psychology and lynching reveals a side of James that sounds more like Freud (or even Nietzsche).

> The average church-going Civilizee realizes, one may say, absolutely nothing of the deeper currents of human nature, or of the aboriginal capacity for murderous excitement which lies sleeping in his own bosom. Religion, custom, law and education have been piling their pressure upon him for centuries mainly with the one intent that his homicidal potentialities should be kept under. The result, achieved with infinite difficulty, is the blessed public peacefulness which until recently we have enjoyed, a regimen in which the usual man forgets that in a practical sense there is any bloodthirstiness about him, and deems it an exceptional passion, only to be read about in newspapers and romances. (James 1987, p. 171)

James called for forceful action to put an end to the anarchy of mob violence. He wanted newspapers to stop playing to mob passions with their lurid descriptions of lynchings. He demanded that officers of the law should do their duty and stand up to mobs. And if this failed, then there should be judicial indictments and convictions of mob leaders. The "lynching epidemic" was an extreme example of the blindness and intolerance that James opposed throughout his life from his pluralistic perspective.

James's Pluralistic Legacy: Horace Kallen and Alain Locke

One way of judging the significance of a thinker is to assess his influence on his students and those who were inspired by him. James had an enormous influence on a younger generation that developed his pluralism in novel ways. They played a key role in reshaping the

intellectual climate in America during the first decades of the twentieth century (see the chapter entitled "Pluralisms," in Menand 2001,
pp. 377–408). W. E. B. Dubois and Alain Locke – two of the most
important African-American intellectuals – studied in the Harvard
philosophy department when James was at the height of his powers.
Horace Kallen, who came from a family of orthodox Jews, considered himself to be one of James's primary philosophical heirs. And
Randolph Bourne, whose Presbyterian family had a long history in
America, wrote to a friend that James represented the most inspiring
modern outlook upon life and reality. These thinkers appropriated
James's pluralistic insights in order to counter the racism, religious
intolerance, and xenophobia that were so prevalent in the United
States during the years leading up to and immediately following the
First World War. It would require a much longer discussion to do
justice to their distinctive contributions; but let me focus briefly on
the pluralism of Horace Kallen and Alain Locke. When James crossed
the Atlantic in 1907 to deliver the lectures that were subsequently
published as *A Pluralistic Universe*, there was an audience of hundreds.
In the audience were two Americans from Harvard, Horace Kallen
and Alain Locke. Kallen and Locke had become friends when Locke
was a student in Santayana's course in Greek philosophy at Harvard.
Kallen had been awarded a Sheldon traveling fellowship to study at
Oxford. Alain Locke was the first African-American to be awarded
a Rhodes fellowship. The Rhodes scholars from the South appealed
to the Rhodes trustees to overturn Locke's award, but they refused.
At Oxford he was shunned by his fellow Americans, although wel-
comed by colonial students. Kallen was outraged by the treatment of
Locke at Oxford and made a public showing of solidarity. The period
just prior to and after the First World War was one of the darkest
periods of anti-immigration and anti-African-American sentiment
in the United States. There was hysteria over immigration, rabid
xenophobia, and violent anti-Semitism and racism. Many of those
who protested this ugly mood were inspired by James's pragmatic
pluralism. They took up the challenge of what America might yet
become – a nation of openness, tolerance, and diversity. In Kallen's
now famous article "Democracy and the Melting Pot," published in
1915, he criticized the metaphor of the melting pot. A melting pot is
something where the elements lose their distinctive individuality and
collective identity and are transformed into a homogeneous mass. In
contrast, Kallen writes:

> At his core no human being, even in a "state of nature," is a mathematical unit of action like "economic man." Behind him in time and tremendously in him in quality are his ancestors; around him in space are his relatives and kin, looking back with him to a remoter common ancestry. In all these he lives and moves and has his being. (Kallen 1996, p. 78)

Kallen wanted different religious and ethnic groups to take pride in their cultural heritage. He envisioned the United States as a nation in which differences would be acknowledged and respected. "What do we will to make of the United States – a unison, singing the old Anglo-Saxon theme 'America,' the America of the New England school, or a harmony, in which that theme shall be dominant, perhaps, among others, but one among many, not the only one?" (Kallen 1996, p. 89). Unison for Kallen is a symbol of leveling and homogeneity; it means the triumph of a cultural monism. Harmony requires different and distinctive voices. Kallen projects a vision of the United States as a democratic community in which "the steady and continuous pressure of inalienable qualities and purposes of human groups more and more dominate the confusion of our common life. ... Its form is that of a Federal republic; its substance a democracy of nationalities, cooperating voluntarily and autonomously in the enterprise of self-realization through the perfection of men according to their kind" (Kallen 1996, p. 92).

Kallen was attracted to musical metaphors: he concludes his article with an extended metaphor of a symphony orchestra.

> As in an orchestra, every type of instrument has its specific timbre and tonality, founded in its substance and form; as every type has its appropriate theme and melody in the whole symphony, so in society each ethnic group is the natural instrument, its spirit and culture are its theme and melody and the harmony and dissonances and discords of them all make the symphony of civilization, with this difference: a musical symphony is written before it is played: in the symphony of civilization the playing is the writing, so that within the limits set by nature they may vary at will, and the range and variety of the harmonies may become wider and richer and more beautiful.
>
> But the primary question is, do the dominant classes in America want such a society? (Kallen 1996, p. 92)

If we take Kallen's analogies and metaphors literally, then there are serious problems. It is not entirely clear how the idea of a "Federal republic," a *political* concept, is to be applied practically to immigrant and ethnic groups. Although he stresses individuality, Kallen does not pay sufficient attention to the many important differences among ethnic and religious groups or the ways in which they change over time. He fails to focus on the conflicts that can arise among different groups. And as John Dewey suggested in a letter to Kallen, the metaphor of a symphony orchestra consisting of different instruments may suggest more fixity than Kallen might have intended. Over the years Kallen modified his views to take account of a greater dynamic flexibility in his vision of cultural pluralism. Like his mentor, William James, he sought to reconcile his plea for cultural pluralism with sensitivity to individual differences.

> Cultures live and grow in and through the individual, and their vitality is a function of individual diversities of interests and associations. Pluralism is the *sine qua non* of their persistence and prosperous growth. But not the absolute pluralism which the concept of the unfaltering and inalterable Monad discloses. On the contrary, the *sine qua non* is fluid, relational pluralism which the living individual encounters in the transactions wherewith he constructs his personal history moving out of groups and into groups, engaging in open or hidden communion with societies of his fellows, every one different from the others, and all teamed together, and struggling to provide and maintain the common means which nourish, assure, enhance the different, and often competing, values they differently cherish. (Kallen 1956, p. 55)

In the same year, (1915), that Kallen published "Democracy and the Melting Pot," Alain Locke delivered a set of five lectures sponsored by the Howard University branch of the NAACP, "Race Contacts and Interracial Relations." They develop an understanding of race that is extremely sophisticated. His views are even closer to the spirit of James's dynamic pluralism than Kallen's. Locke challenges the idea that there is any biological basis for the concept of race. Drawing on the work of Franz Boas, but going beyond Boas, he argues that there are no *fixed* factors – biological, sociological, anthropological, or cultural – that determine race. Jeffrey C. Stewart succinctly states Locke's main thesis.

> Race was not a fixed, biological entity because the physical characteristics of racial groups changed with alterations in social and cultural environment and even varied considerably within groups. ... Race

was simply another word for a social or national group that shared a common history or culture and occupied a geographical region. Race was culture because "every civilization produces its [own] type". ... In a sense, then, Locke was standing racialist theories of culture on their heads: rather than particular races creating Culture, it was culture – social, political, and economic processes – that produced racial character. (Stewart 1992, pp. xxiv–xxv)

Today we would say that Locke was deconstructing the concept of race. He views race as an "ethnic fiction." But this does not mean that it is without powerful practical consequences. On the contrary, it has all too real deleterious consequences. Locke did not, however, draw the conclusion that one should dispense with the concept of race altogether. He shared with W. E. B. Dubois the conviction that African-Americans need a positive idea of race in order to restore a sense of self-esteem and dignity. He set high standards for this positive concept of race as a vehicle for African-Americans to contribute to the literary, artistic, and cultural life of the United States. He developed this thesis in *The New Negro: An Interpretation*. Locke also became one of the leading thinkers of the Harlem Renaissance. Locke's advocacy of African-American artistic and literary culture "showed his pragmatism, just as his rejection of assimilation showed his pluralism. As did William James, Locke saw the world as an open pluriverse in which humanity had the ability to shape its world. Thus, while he drew the outlines of a science of racial interaction, he rejected, again as did James, any determinism, especially racial determinism, which, on the one hand, bound blacks to biology, and on the other, stultified black activism because of the socially unyielding power of racism" (Stewart 1992, p. xxxiii).

The most impressive feature of Locke's reflections on race is his cosmopolitanism. This is reflected in the way in which he examines the concept of race in the context of world history – not just the United States. Long before the term "rooted cosmopolitanism" was coined, Locke advocated a rooted cosmopolitanism for African-Americans. He was not optimistic that we would soon see the end of violent race prejudice, but he expressed a modest hope that we might see its "final stage."

I fancy that we shall have to come [to a] position in race problems [analysis where we] regard some of the reactions of our present situation in America as indicative of a final stage, and welcome them as such, because they seem to be born of the very last effort of society to stem the inevitable when they confront [the reality of progressive change]. But, of course[,] they can only have the sense of jeopardy when they are confronted by an apparent and what may be an actual realization that the fetish of the distinctions is about the only thing that is left. (Locke 1992, p. 58)

Even this modest hope turned out to be overly optimistic in the struggle to overcome race prejudices. Many of the recent discussions of multiculturalism and the politics of identity still have a great deal to learn from the spirit and letter of James's pragmatic pluralism. James was especially insightful about the dangers of reification – the dangers of thinking that groups have fixed identities. He was acutely aware of how identities change, develop, and mutate in the course of history. He was never sentimental about blindly celebrating differences. He was just as concerned with searching for commonalities that can bind us together. He consistently championed those pluralistic perspectives that foster individuality. And in the best pragmatic sense, James insisted that changing historical conditions present new challenges for rethinking a pragmatic pluralistic vision. James's eloquent remarks about vision are self-referential. A man's vision is the great fact about him. "[T]hat is why we can read him over and over again, and each time bring away a fresh sense of reality" (James 1977, p. 77).

3

John Dewey's Vision of Radical Democracy

We tend to forget that the word 'democracy' has had a negative connotation throughout most of its long history. The Greek word *dēmokratia* means rule by the *dēmos*, the populace, the common people. For centuries, there has been a fear that the unchecked rule by the people would be anarchic and turn into tyranny. The Founding Fathers of the United States did not think of themselves as creating a democracy, but rather a new *republic*. The elaborate system of checks and balances, as well as the Bill of Rights, were intended to counter the abuses of unrestrained democracy. Only in the nineteenth century did the word 'democracy' begin to take on a positive connotation, although Alexis de Tocqueville – the most perceptive commentator on American democracy – warned about the many dangers that it confronted. And John Stuart Mill, the great liberal thinker, was worried about the tendency of democratic societies to foster mediocrity. There has always been an undercurrent, even among champions of democracy, that it is neither viable nor desirable to think that a workable democracy can involve the active participation of *all* the people.

Today the word 'democracy' has such a positive aura, and elicits such a powerful emotional response, that we rarely *think* about what we really mean by democracy. A cynic might even claim that 'democracy' is one of those words that can (and has) take(n) on virtually any meaning – ranging from a commitment to free elections and majority rule to an identification with 'free market' capitalism. John Dewey reminds us that even the Soviet Union at the height of Stalinist totalitarianism accused "the traditionally democratic peoples of the West in Europe and America of betraying the cause of democracy and [held] itself up as representing in its politics and principles the fulfillment of the democratic idea now misrepresented and betrayed by peoples who profess democracy but fail to carry it out in practice" (Dewey, *LW* 17: 472).

It is against this background that I want to examine the meaning of democracy in the works of John Dewey. My aim is to retrieve the core of what he means by democracy and to evaluate his contribution from our present perspective. Specifically, I am concerned with what we may still learn from Dewey in our own attempts to understand and foster democratic practices. Among modern philosophers (and even ancient philosophers) Dewey stands out as the thinker for whom democracy is the central theme in virtually all his works. From his earliest writings in the 1880s until his death in 1952, Dewey returned over and over again to the meaning of democracy. The theme of democracy is manifest in his writings on education, science, inquiry, aesthetics, art, metaphysics, nature, and religion.

The Ethics of Democracy

I begin with an examination of Dewey's first explicit essay on democracy, "The Ethics of Democracy," an essay that he wrote when he was 29 and a young professor at the University of Michigan. This review of Sir Henry Maine's critique of democracy in his *Popular Government* provides Dewey with an opportunity to sketch "the ideal of democracy." Despite its arcane language, heavily influenced by the Hegelianism that Dewey learned from his mentor, George Morris, we can already detect several themes that Dewey elaborated, refined, and revised during the rest of his career.

We get a vivid sense of Maine's disdain for democracy from some of the sentences that Dewey quotes. "[Democracy's] legislation is a wild burst of destructive wantonness; an arbitrary overthrow of all existing institutions, followed by a longer period in which its principles put an end to all social and political activity." "There can be no delusion greater than that democracy is a progressive form of government." "The establishment of the masses in power is the blackest omen for all legislation founded on scientific opinion" (Dewey, *EW* 1: 228).

Dewey tells us that Maine's conception of democracy consists of three main points: (1) "democracy is only a form of government"; (2) "government is simply that which has to do with the relation of subject to sovereign, of political superior to inferior"; (3) democracy is that form of government in which the sovereign is the multitude of individuals. Dewey strongly objects to *all* three points and declares that Maine's conception of democracy amounts to little more than the idea of government by "numerical aggregation." The "natural and inevitable" outcome of this notion of democracy is the theory of "Social Contract." Dewey bluntly states: "The essence of the 'Social Contract' theory is not the idea of the formulation of a contract; it is the idea that men are mere individuals, without any social relations *until* they form a contract" (Dewey, *EW* 1: 231). Dewey categorically rejects this notion of the pre-social individual: "The fact is, however, that the theory of the 'social organism,' that theory that men are not isolated non-social atoms, but are men only when in intrinsic relations to men, has wholly superseded the theory of men as an aggregate, as a heap of grains of sand needing some factitious mortar to put them into a semblance of order" (ibid.). If we think of human beings as "non-social units," as "mere multitude," then "the picture drawn of democracy is, in effect, simply an account of anarchy. To define democracy simply as the rule of the many, as sovereignty chopped up into mince meat, is to define it as the abrogation of society, as society dissolved, annihilated" (ibid.). The essential sociality of human beings has both a descriptive and a *normative* significance. Dewey consistently argues that any theory of human beings that fails to acknowledge that human beings "are not isolated non-social atoms" is defective, a misleading abstraction of philosophers. When the normative significance of the distinctive sociality of human beings is fully developed, it leads to the idea of democracy as an ethical form of life. In *The Public and Its Problems* (1927), Dewey tells us that, "regarded as an idea, democracy is not an alternative to other principles of associated life. It is the idea of community life itself. It is the ideal in the only intelligible sense of an ideal: namely, the tendency and movement of some thing which exists carried to its final limit, viewed as completed, perfected" (Dewey, *LW* 2: 328).

Dewey is quite emphatic that democracy is not simply a "form of government" where the majority rules. "But the heart of the matter is found not in the voting nor in counting the votes to see where the majority is formed. It is in the process by which the majority is formed" (Dewey, *EW* 1: 234). Dewey emphasizes two closely related points that characterize his approach to democracy. The first concerns the meaning of democratic sovereignty. Democratic sovereignty does not consist of the numerical aggregate of individuals. If we adopt the conception of society where by the individual and society are reciprocally internally related, then we can understand how "the individual embodies and realizes within himself the spirit and will of the whole organism" (Dewey, *EW* 1: 236). In a democracy *every* individual is a sovereign citizen. Dewey, at this early stage of his career, was influenced not only by the Hegelian idea of the social organism but also by his Congregational Christian background. "And this is the theory, often crudely expressed, but none the less true in substance, that every citizen is a sovereign, the American theory, a doctrine which in grandeur has but one equal in history, and that its fellow, namely, that every man is a priest of God" (Dewey, *EW* 1: 237). Consequently, it is a serious mistake to suggest, as Maine does, that democracy, like all forms of government, consists of two classes, "one of governors, one of governed." "Government does not mean one class or side of society set over against the other. The government is not made up of those who hold office, or sit in the legislature. It consists of every member of political society" (Dewey, *EW* 1: 238). This is the true meaning of the democratic idea that government derives its powers from the consent of the people.

The second point that Dewey emphasizes for a correct understanding of democracy is that democracy is primarily an *ethical way of life*.

> To say that democracy is *only* a form of government is like saying that a home is a more or less geometrical arrangement of bricks and mortar; that a church is a building with pews, pulpit and spire. It is true; they certainly are so much. But it is false; they are infinitely more. Democracy, like any other polity, has been finely termed the memory of an historic past, the consciousness of a living present, the ideal of a coming future. Democracy, in a word, is social, that is to say, an ethical conception, and upon its ethical significance is based its significance as governmental. Democracy is a form of government only because it is a form of moral and spiritual association. (Dewey, *EW* 1: 240)

When Dewey speaks of democracy as ethical, he is drawing upon the rich Hegelian understanding of *Sittlichkeit* and the Greek understanding of *ethos* as the customs, norms, attitudes, sentiments, and aspirations that characterize the life of a people. Throughout his life, Dewey argued that without a vital democratic *ethos* or culture, political democracy becomes hollow and meaningless. Democracy as a form of government is an outgrowth of, and is dependent upon, this living *ethos*. "A government springs from a vast mass of sentiments, many vague, some defined, of instincts, of aspirations, of ideas, of hopes and fears, of purposes. It is their reflex and incorporation; their projection and outgrowth" (ibid.).

But what is distinctive about the democratic *ethos*? What distinguishes the democratic *ethos* from the aristocratic *ethos*? To highlight the difference, Dewey gives a brief sketch of Plato's *Republic*, "the most perfect picture of the aristocratic ideal which history affords. The few best, the aristoi; these know and are fitted to rule, but they are to rule not in their own interests but in that of society as a whole, and therefore, in that of every individual in society. They do not bear rule *over* others; they show them what they can best do, and guide them in doing it" (Dewey, *EW* 1: 242). Consequently, Plato's ideal republic is also a form of moral and spiritual association in which the "development of man's nature ... brings him into complete harmony with the universe of spiritual relations, or in Platonic language, the state (*polis*)." But "according to Plato (and the aristocratic idea everywhere), the multitude is incapable of forming such an ideal and attempting to reach it" (Dewey, *EW* 1: 241).

Democracy is distinguished from all forms of aristocracy because it is based on the conviction that *every* human being is capable of personal responsibility and individual initiative. "There is individualism in democracy which there is not in aristocracy; but it is an ethical, not a numerical individualism; it is an individualism of freedom, of responsibility, of initiative to and for the ethical ideal, not an individualism of lawlessness" (Dewey, *EW* 1: 243–4). Dewey calls this ethical individualism *personality* – personality is not something ontologically given but rather an *achievement*. In a democratic society every sovereign citizen is capable of achieving personality.

The point that Dewey stresses in this early article goes beyond a critique of the classic aristocratic ideal. Throughout his career, Dewey was critical of what came to be called "democratic elitism" or "democratic realism." Democratic realists adopt a version of the aristocratic argument. They claim that in the contemporary world, in which individuals can be so effectively manipulated by mass media and the problems of society have become so complex, a viable democracy requires the "wisdom" of an intelligentsia, who, like Plato's *aristoi*, "rule not in their own interests but in that of society as a whole." But Dewey was always deeply suspicious of those who advocated that a viable democracy requires a special class of intelligentsia which has the responsibility to make "wise" democratic decisions. This became the central issue in Dewey's famous dispute with Walter Lippmann, an issue that Dewey confronted in *The Public and Its Problems*.

Democratic Faith

Dewey certainly recognizes that there is a positive role for expert knowledge in a democratic society. He always emphasized the importance of social inquiry for advancing social reform. But ultimately, democratic citizens must judge and decide; not the experts. This stands at the core of Dewey's democratic faith. Robert B. Westbrook eloquently summarizes this democratic faith when he speaks of Dewey's "belief that democracy as an ethical ideal calls upon men and women to build communities in which the necessary opportunities and resources are available for every individual to realize fully his or her particular capacities and powers through participation in political, social, and cultural life" (Westbrook 1991, p. xv). Dewey never wavered in his democratic faith. Fifty years after he published "The Ethics of Democracy," on the occasion of his eightieth birthday, he reiterated that the democratic ideal rests on a "faith in the capacity of human beings for intelligent judgment and action if the proper conditions are furnished" (Dewey, *LW* 14: 227). We can see clearly the continuity between Dewey's earliest formulation of the meaning of democracy and what he affirms in "Creative Democracy – The Task before Us."

> Democracy is a way of life controlled by a working faith in the possibilities of human nature. Belief in the Common Man is a familiar article in the democratic creed. The belief is without basis and significance save as it means faith in the possibilities of human nature is exhibited in every human being irrespective of race, color, sex, birth and family, of material or cultural wealth. This faith may be enacted in statutes, but it is only on paper unless it is put in force in the attitudes which human beings display to one another in all the incidents and relations of daily life. (Dewey, *LW* 14: 226)

Dewey does not hesitate to speak about his democratic faith, but this faith is not a blind faith or a vapid optimism. It is a reflective, intelligent faith that is based on his understanding of human beings and their potentialities (for good and evil). When challenged by his critics, Dewey did not hesitate to defend this democratic faith.

> I have been accused more than once and from opposed quarters of an undue, a utopian faith in the possibilities of intelligence and in education as a correlate of intelligence. At all events, I did not invent this faith. I acquired it from my surroundings as far as those surroundings were animated by the democratic spirit. For what is the faith in democracy in the role of consultation, of conference, of persuasion, of discussion, in the formation of public opinion, which in the long run is self-corrective, except faith in the capacity of the intelligence of the common man to respond with commonsense to the free play of facts and ideas which are secured by effective guarantees of free inquiry, free assembly and free communication? (Dewey, *LW* 14: 227)

I have discussed "The Ethics of Democracy" in some detail because, despite the abstractness of Dewey's argument and the vagueness of such key concepts as "social organism" and "personality," many of the major themes in his understanding of democracy are already sketched there. Furthermore, it sets an agenda for the problems that Dewey was yet to confront – problems concerning the relation of "really existing democracy" to the ethical ideal of democracy, the role of conflict within democratic societies, and the means by which we can approximate the democratic ideal. "The Ethics of Democracy," with its reliance on organic metaphors and spiritual references to Christianity, was written when Dewey was still very much isolated from the dynamic changes that were taking place in America's urban culture. When Dewey moved to Chicago in 1894, he was fully exposed to the human consequences of rapid industrialization, labor strife, and the practical problems that arose from the influx of immigrant populations. To appreciate how Dewey developed his ideas about democracy, we need to grasp the practical problem that became his primary concern. Dewey sharply criticized the abuses of a laissez-faire mentality, the fetish of individualism, and the "pseudo-liberalism" that had become so dominant during the last decades of nineteenth century in America. He believed that the greatest dangers to democracy are *internal* ones, which arise when the democratic *ethos* and democratic practices are undermined. He was scornful of "moralism" – the belief that genuine social reform could be achieved simply by calling for individual moral reform. He felt that liberalism, which had once served radical ends, was being used to justify the status quo and to block social reform. The turn toward *praxis* that shaped the Young Hegelians and the early Marx also shaped Dewey's outlook. But Dewey was never tempted by the idea of a violent revolution. He advocated social reform by democratic means.

Democracy is Radical

In a late essay, "Democracy Is Radical," Dewey reiterated what he had consistently advocated: "*The fundamental principle of democracy is that the ends of freedom and individuality for all can be attained only by the means that accord with those ends.*" He also affirmed:

> *The end of democracy is a radical end. For it is an end that has not been adequately realized in any country at any time.* It is radical because it requires great change in existing social institutions, economic, legal and cultural. A democratic liberalism that does not recognize these things in thought and action is not awake to its own meaning and to what that meaning demands. (Dewey, *LW* 11: 298–9)

This ideal of radical democracy is not an impossible "utopian" ideal – or even a regulative principle in the Kantian sense that can never, in principle, be realized. Rather, it is an end-in-view that can guide our actions *here and now*. It is an ideal that serves as a critical standard for evaluating the deficiencies of "really existing" democracies and serves also as a guide for concrete action. Alan Ryan beautifully captures the spirit of Dewey when he concludes his study of Dewey by telling us that

> Dewey was a visionary. That was his appeal. He was a curious visionary, because he did not speak of a distant goal or a city not built with hands. He was a visionary about the here and now, about the potentiality of the modern world, modern society, modern man, and thus, as it happened, America and the Americans of the twentieth century. (Ryan 1995, p. 369)

One of the clearest and most forceful statements of Dewey's belief that democratic means are integral to democratic ends is found in his response to Leon Trotsky. In 1937, at the age of 78, Dewey agreed to serve as chairman of the Commission of Inquiry that was formed to hear and evaluate the charges made against Trotsky and his son by Stalin. At the time Trotsky was living in exile in Mexico at the home of Diego Rivera. When Dewey agreed to chair the Commission, Communists and Popular Front sympathizers vilified him. Threats were made against his life. Friends and family urged him not to go to Mexico. Nevertheless, Dewey made the arduous trip to Mexico City, where the inquiry was held. His sense of justice and decency demanded that he participate in the investigation of the charges brought against Trotsky. Dewey's willingness to set aside his intellectual work – he was working on *Logic: The Theory of Inquiry* when he was asked to chair the Commission – was consistent with the way in which he always lived his life. "But I have given my life to the work of education, which I have conceived to be that of public enlightenment in the interests of society. If I finally accepted the responsible post I now occupy, it was because I realized that to act otherwise would be false to my life work" (Dewey, *LW* 11: 309). The Commission provided an opportunity to expose the horrors of Stalinist terror and the scandal of the Moscow purges.

When Dewey first visited the Soviet Union in 1928, he was enthusiastic about the prospects for freedom and education, but subsequently he expressed his bitter disappointment. Reflecting on what he learned from the Inquiry and his encounter with Trotsky, he wrote:

> The great lesson for all American radicals and for all sympathizers with the U.S.S.R. is that they must go back and reconsider the whole question of the means of bringing about social changes and of truly democratic methods of approach to social progress. ... The dictatorship of the proletariat had led to and, I am convinced, always must lead to a dictatorship over the proletariat and the party. I see no reason to believe that something similar would not happen in every country in which an attempt is made to establish a Communist government. (Dewey, *LW* 11: 331)

After the Commission exonerated Trotsky, he published an article, "Their Morals and Ours," in the *New International*, in which he set forth his commitment to "the liberating morality of the proletariat" which "deduces a rule of conduct from the law as of the development of society, thus primarily from the class struggle, the law of all laws." Dewey was invited to respond, and he did so vigorously.[1] He sharply criticized Trotsky for claiming that "the end justifies the means," and for abandoning the principle of the interdependence of means and ends. He strongly objected to the idea that democratic ends can be achieved by nondemocratic means. It is fraudulent and ultimately incoherent to claim that democratic ends can be achieved by violent nondemocratic means. "Democratic ends" are never fixed or static; they are dynamic and integral to democratic processes. Democratic means are *constitutive* of democratic ends-in-view. Furthermore, there are always unintended consequences of our actions; consequently, a democratic *ethos* demands flexibility and the acknowledgment of our fallibility about both means and ends. Dewey claims that Trotsky, who attempts to avoid one kind of absolutism, actually plunges us "into another kind of absolutism" (Dewey, *LW* 13: 354).[2]

The Failures of Democracy

Dewey was realistic about the failures and limitations of democracy in the United States. The history of the United States is a history not only of democratic aspirations and achievements, but of brutality, violence, and bigotry. His concluding remarks in "The Need for a Recovery of Philosophy" (1917) have an uncanny contemporary resonance:

> We pride ourselves upon being realistic, desiring a hard-hearted cognizance of facts, and devoted to mastering the means of life. We pride ourselves upon a practical idealism, a lively and easily moved faith in the possibilities as yet unrealized, in willingness to make sacrifice in their realization. Idealism easily becomes a sanction of waste and carelessness, and realism a sanction of legal formalism in behalf of things that are – the rights of the possessor. We thus tend to combine a loose and ineffective optimism with assent to the doctrine of take who take can: a deification of power. All peoples at all times have been narrowly realistic in practice and have employed idealization to cover in sentiment and theory their brutalities. But never, perhaps, has the tendency been so dangerous and so tempting as with ourselves. Faith in the power of intelligence to imagine a future which is the projection of

the desirable in the present, and to invent the instrumentalities of its realization, is our salvation. And it is a faith which must be nurtured and made articulate: surely a sufficiently large task for our philosophy. (Dewey, *MW* 10: 48)[3]

Dewey was also alarmed by the growth of a corporate mentality in America. What he wrote in 1930 seems even more threatening today.

> The business mind, having its own conversation and language, its own interests, its own intimate groupings in which men of this mind, in their collective capacity, determine the tone of society at large as well as the government of industrial society, and have more political influence than the government itself. ... We now have, although without formal or legal status, a mental and moral corporateness for which history affords no parallel. (Dewey, *LW* 5: 61)[4]

When in the 1920s Walter Lippmann criticized the very idea of an informed citizen and described the way in which mass media can distort public opinion, Dewey agreed with his diagnosis. Dewey himself spoke of the "eclipse of the public." "[The] Public seems to be lost; it is certainly bewildered." But unlike Lippmann, who argued that the best hope for American democracy was the leadership that "disinterested experts" might provide, Dewey claimed that the cure for the ills of democracy was a more radical and committed democracy.

> The old saying that the cure for the ills of democracy is more democracy is not apt if it means that the evils may be remedied by introducing more machinery of the same kind as that which already exists, or by refining and perfecting that machinery. But the phrase may also indicate the need of returning to the idea itself, of clarifying and deepening our apprehension of it, and of employing our sense of its meaning to criticize and remake its political manifestations. (Dewey, *LW* 2: 325)

If democracy is to be made a living everyday reality, then our task now is "to re-create by deliberate and determined endeavor the kind of democracy which in its origin ... was largely the product of a fortunate combination of men and circumstances" (Dewey, *LW* 14: 225). We can no longer act as if democracy takes place when individuals go to the polls to vote. Democracy is a personal way of individual life and it becomes a concrete reality only when it is practiced in our everyday lives.

Thomas Jefferson was one of Dewey's heroes because his understanding of democracy is moral through and through: in its foundations, its methods, and its ends. Jefferson thought that the transformation of America from an agricultural society to an industrial one would pose a serious threat to democracy. But Dewey claimed that industrialization is not the problem, but rather the "dislocation and unsettlement of local communities." Dewey admired Jefferson because he so clearly recognized the need for active citizen participation in local communities to keep the democratic promise alive. Jefferson called these little republics "wards." Jefferson "was impressed, practically as well as theoretically, with the effectiveness of the New England town meeting, and wished to see something of the sort made an organic part of the governing process of the whole country" (Dewey, *LW* 14: 217). Consequently, we must find new ways to revitalize local communities and foster the development of *multiple* publics where citizens can engage in debate and deliberation together.

Beyond Communitarianism and Liberalism

Among current debates in democratic political theory is the debate between communitarians and liberals. Communitarians typically defend the centrality of vital communities in which we find our political identity. Michael J. Sandel, who was one of the first to advance a communitarian critique of the liberalism developed by John Rawls, distinguishes between instrumental, sentimental, and a strong constitutive sense of community. "On this strong view to say that the members of a society are bound by a sense of community is not to say that a great many of them profess communitarian sentiments and pursue communitarian aims, but rather that they conceive their identity – the subject and not just the object of their feelings and aspirations – as defined to some extent by the community of which they are a part" (Sandel 1982, p. 147). Liberals are wary of this strong sense of community, because they fear that it all too easily leads to an infringement of individual rights and liberties. Where does Dewey stand in this opposition between communitarians and liberals? There are passages in Dewey's writings that appear to place him in both camps – especially if they are quoted out of context. But Dewey would have viewed this as a *false* opposition. Like communitarians, Dewey stresses that democracy requires public spaces and communities in which citizens can participate as equals and engage in collective deliberation. In *The Public and Its Problems*, he declared: "Unless local communal life can be restored, the public cannot adequately solve its most urgent problem: to find and identify itself" (Dewey, *LW* 2: 370). But Dewey never thought that democratic communal life was incompatible with liberalism. Liberalism is not a fixed or static doctrine. It is a dynamic changing tradition that has served different purposes at different times in its development. In the eighteenth century, liberalism placed primary emphasis on individual liberty and religious confessional freedom. This liberalism was effective in sweeping away innumerable abuses. In the nineteenth century, liberal ideas were extended to economic interests. Liberal ideas include a "strenuous demand for liberty of mind – the freedom of thought and its expression in speech, writing, print and assemblage. The earlier interest in confessional freedom was generalized, and thereby deepened and broadened" (Dewey, *LW* 11: 290). But something else also happened. Liberalism ossified: it degenerated into "pseudo-liberalism." It turned into a rationalization for unbridled laissez-faire entrepreneurship. Furthermore, this "pseudo-liberalism" conceived of "the individual as something given, complete in itself, and of liberty as a ready-made possession of the individual, which only needed the removal of external restrictions in order to manifest itself" (ibid.). In 1935, in the middle of the Depression, Dewey called for a new liberalism that would be truly radical.

> Liberalism must now become radical, meaning by "radical" perception of the necessity of thorough-going changes in the set-up of institutions and corresponding activity to bring the changes to pass. For the gulf between what the actual situation makes possible and the actual state of affairs is so great that it cannot be bridged by piecemeal policies undertaken *ad hoc*. The process of producing the changes will be, in any case, a gradual one. But "reforms" that deal now with this abuse and now with that without having a social goal based on an inclusive plan, differ entirely from effort at re-forming, in its literal sense, the institutional scheme of things. The liberals of more than a century ago were denounced in their time as subversive radicals, and only when the new economic order was established did they become apologists for the status quo, or else content with social patchwork. If radicalism is defined as perception of the need for radical change, then today any liberalism which is not also radicalism is irrelevant and doomed. (Dewey, *LW* 11: 41)

This passage expresses Dewey's hopes for a radical turn in the liberal tradition, a radical turn that is not only compatible with, but also requires a vital local community life. But for all its stirring rhetoric, and despite Dewey's persistent demands to deal with concrete problems and to specify the means for achieving ends-in-view, Dewey never specified those "thorough-going changes in the set-up of institutions," nor did he specify the "corresponding activity to bring the changes to pass." I will return to this weakness in Dewey's conception of radical liberalism at the end of this chapter, but I want to emphasize that Dewey's vision of democracy incorporates both communitarian and liberal insights. He rejects the claim that these two emphases are incompatible with each other. On the contrary, they are mutually interdependent. The democratic communities that Dewey envisioned encourage individual initiative, personal responsibility, protection of rights, and active citizen participation.

The Role of Conflict in Democratic Politics

I suggested earlier that "The Ethics of Democracy" not only introduces some of the central themes of Dewey's vision of democracy, but also exposes serious problems that he was yet to confront. One of the most serious is the role of conflict within a democratic polity. The excessive reliance on the concept of "social organism" obscures this problem, because it emphasizes the harmony of the individual and the social organism. Dewey tells us: "In conception, at least, democracy approaches the ideal of social organization; that in which individual and society are organic to each other." "The whole lives truly in every member. ... The organism manifests itself as what truly is, an ideal or spiritual life, and a unity of *will*" (Dewey, *EW* 1: 237). Not only is this notion of the social organism problematic; it also has consequences that are anti-democratic. It fails to do justice to a feature of democracy that Dewey came to realize is at the heart of vibrant democracies – conflict and struggle.

When Dewey moved to Chicago, he arrived during the bitter conflict of the famous Pullman strike. Dewey followed the strike closely, and his sympathies were clearly with the striking workers. He came to appreciate the important functional role of conflicts that take place within a democratic society. Robert B. Westbrook notes that Dewey believed "the elimination of conflict to be 'a hopeless and self-contradictory ideal' for social life, like individual life, entailed an ongoing reconstruction of conflict-ridden, 'disintegrating coordinations.' This view of conflict as an inevitable and potentially functional aspect of social life distinguished Dewey from reformers, including his friend Jane Addams, who regarded it as unnecessary and thoroughly dysfunctional" (Westbrook 1991, p. 80). But Dewey also dissociated himself from those who advocated versions of social Darwinism, which falsely claimed that the ruthless "struggle for existence" is the governing principle of all human life. Conflict is not just "ineliminable" in democratic politics; it is *essential* for the achievement of social reform and justice. No longer does Dewey speak of democracy as an ideal organic unity of the individual and society. New conflicts will always break out. The key point is how one *responds* to conflict. And this requires imagination, intelligence, and a commitment to solve concrete problems. Dewey might well have endorsed the following eloquent description of democratic politics.

> Democratic politics is an encounter among people with differing interests, perspectives, and opinions – an encounter in which they reconsider and mutually revise opinions and interests, both individual and common. It happens always in a context of conflict, imperfect knowledge, and uncertainty, but where community action is necessary. The resolutions achieved are always more or less temporary, subject to reconsideration, and rarely unanimous. What matters is not unanimity but discourse. The substantive common interest is only discovered or created in democratic political struggle, and it remains contested as much as shared. Far from being inimical to democracy, conflict – handled in democratic ways, with openness and persuasion – is what makes democracy work, what makes for mutual revision of opinions and interests. (Pitkin and Shumer 1982, pp. 47–8)

Once again we see how Dewey develops a *via media* between extremes. Many political theorists stress the agonistic aspect of democratic politics – the way in which democracy requires and thrives on conflict. And there are those who emphasize the deliberative features of democracy – the need for discourse, deliberation, and persuasion. But both are required for a healthy democratic polity. Champions of agonistic politics are suspicious of talk of "community," "harmony," "consensus," "deliberation," and the "common good." They think that these "soothing" expressions harbor oppressive power and sup-press the voices of those who are disenfranchised. "Consensus" means the death of democratic politics. But too frequently these defenders of "agonistic" politics do not face up to the dangers of agonism when it is carried to its extreme. Agonism – as Hegel reminds us – can lead to a life-and-death struggle in which one seeks not only to defeat an opponent but to annihilate him. The primary issue, as I have indi-cated, is always how we *respond* to conflict. And here is where Dewey emphasizes the "role of consultation, of conference, of persuasion, of discussion in the formation of public opinion" (Dewey, *LW* 14: 227). This is the practical issue that any living democracy confronts. One must do more than protect the rights of minorities and dissenters; one must work toward developing a culture in which plurality and dif-ference of opinion are encouraged. Dewey emphasized that without creative conflict there is the danger of complacency and stagnation. But a democracy degenerates into a sheer contest of wills and a naked power struggle if there is not a serious attempt to engage in deliberation and public debate – if there is not a serious attempt to establish shared communal values in which there is reciprocal trust and respect.

There is another important respect in which Dewey departs from those who advocate what has been called "deliberative democracy." Some versions of "deliberative democracy" tend to exaggerate the role of rational persuasion in democratic politics. There is a tendency to overemphasize the role and potential power of rational argumenta-tion. Dewey was never happy with the way in which philosophers and political theorists characterized reason – especially when they sharply distinguished reason from emotion, desire, and passion. He preferred to speak about intelligence and intelligent action. Intelligence is not the name of a special faculty. Rather, it designates a cluster of habits and dispositions that includes attentiveness to details, imagination, and passionate commitment. What is most essential for Dewey is the *embodiment* of intelligence in everyday practices.

Democracy, Social Cooperation, and Education

Axel Honneth has argued that Dewey's conception of radical democ-racy is superior to two of the prevailing models currently discussed. "In his endeavor to justify principles of an expanded democracy Dewey, in contrast to republicanism and to democratic proceduralism, takes his orientation not from the model of communicative consultation but from the model of social cooperation. In brief: because Dewey wishes to understand democracy as a reflexive form of community cooperation, he is able to bring together the two opposing positions of current democratic theory." "Dewey's theory of democracy contains an answer that opens up a third avenue between the false option of an over ethicized republicanism and an empty proceduralism" (Honneth 1998, p. 765). Dewey understands "democratic ethical life as the outcome of the experience that all members of the society could have if they related to one another cooperatively through a just organizing of the division of labor" (Honneth 1998, p. 780).[5]

Ever since the "linguistic turn" there has been a tendency for democratic theorists to focus almost exclusively on speech acts and linguistic procedures for adjudicating differences. But Dewey's vision of radical democracy is much thicker. It is not limited to deliberation or what has been called public reason; it encompasses and presupposes the full range of human experience. Democracy requires a robust democratic culture in which the attitudes, emotions, and habits that constitute a democratic *ethos* are embodied.

From this perspective we can appreciate Dewey's lifelong interest in education, especially education of the young. The great hope for nurturing individuals who will be sensitive to social injustice and for developing the flexible habits of intelligence required for social reform is democratic public education. Already in "My Pedagogic Creed" (1897) Dewey insisted that "education is the fundamental method of social reform" and that "it is the business of every one interested in education to insist upon the school as the primary and the most effective interest in social progress and reform in order that society may be awakened to realize what the school stands for." Contrary to many distorted interpretations of Dewey's views on education, he was a sharp and persistent critic of sentimentalism. "[N]ext to deadness and dullness, formalism and routine, our education is threatened with no greater evil than sentimentalism. ... this sentimentalism is the necessary result of the attempt to divorce feeling from action" (Dewey, *EW* 5: 93).

Many of the points that I have been stressing about his vision of radical democracy are epitomized in the final paragraph of his essay "Creative democracy."

Democracy as compared with other ways of life is the sole way of living which believes wholeheartedly in the process of experience as end and as means; as that which is capable of generating science which is the sole dependable authority for the direction of further experience and which releases emotions, needs and desires so as to call into being things that have not existed in the past. For every way of life that fails in its democracy limits the contacts, the exchanges, the communications, the interactions by which experience is steadied while it is also enlarged and enriched. The task of this release and enrichment is one that has to be carried on day by day. Since it is one that can have no end till experience itself comes to an end, the task of democracy is forever that of creation of a freer and more humane experience in which all share and to which all contribute. (Dewey, *LW* 14: 229–30)

Dewey's Contemporary Relevance

For all the attractiveness of Dewey's vision of radical democracy, he can be criticized on a number of counts. There is too little emphasis on institutional analysis – on what sorts of institutions are required for a flourishing democracy. Perhaps the most serious weakness is the one that I mentioned earlier. Dewey declared that radical liberalism requires "a social goal based on an inclusive plan." But Dewey never spelled out the details of such an "inclusive plan." More seriously, although he always emphasized the need for fundamental economic changes in furthering the realization of radical democracy, he never indicated in detail what these should be. And at times, Dewey fails to appreciate the powerful forces that resist the political and educational reforms that he called for. But these criticisms need to be tempered by the fact that Dewey was the leading social reformer of his time. He worked closely with Jane Addams at Hull House in Chicago. He helped to found the American Civil Liberties Union, the New School for Social Research, the American Federation of Teachers, and many other progressive voluntary organizations. He was a staunch defender of freedom of speech and civil rights; he led campaigns to defend the rights of Maxim Gorky and Bertrand Russell. Although he strongly identified with the American democratic tradition, his interests were international. He advised government officials, national groups, and educators in Japan, China, Turkey, Mexico, and South Africa. All these activities were informed by his radical democratic vision. Dewey was a "rooted cosmopolitan."[6] He strongly identified with an American Jeffersonian and Emersonian tradition. But there was nothing parochial about his vision of radical democracy. In both theory and practice he was deeply involved in encouraging democratic practices throughout the world. He was a thoroughly engaged democratic public intellectual. But Dewey also had a profound understanding of the fragility of democracy. Unless we constantly work at incorporating a democratic ethos into our everyday lives, democracy can all too easily become hollow and meaningless.

Today, in academic circles, there are lively debates about democratic theory. But unfortunately, these debates are mostly limited to other academics. Dewey had the rare ability to reach beyond the academy, to speak to a wide audience of citizens and to the concerns of common people. I do not think that we can turn to Dewey for solutions to the problems and threats to democracy in our time. Dewey would be the first to insist that new conflicts and problems require new approaches. But Dewey's vision of a radical democracy as "a personal way of individual life in which we open ourselves to the fullness of communication" can still inspire us in our own endeavors to rethink and revitalize "really existing democracies." Creative democracy is still the task before us!

4

Hegel and Pragmatism

I want to consider three moments in the history of philosophy in the United States when Hegel became a source of philosophical inspiration and discussion: the latter part of the nineteenth century, the mid-twentieth century, and the present time. Each of these moments is directly or indirectly related to pragmatism. In the Prologue I indicated that the second half of the nineteenth century in America witnessed a strong interest in German philosophy, especially in Kant, Hegel, and, more generally, the tradition of German idealism. The early issues of the *Journal of Speculative Philosophy* (founded in 1867) were filled with articles about, and translations of, Fichte, Schelling, and Hegel. In the opening article of the first issue, W. T. Harris declared: "He, then, who would ascend into the thought of the best thinkers the world has seen, must spare no pains to elevate his thinking to pure thought. The completest discipline for this may be found in Hegel's *Logic*" (Harris 1867, p. 6). In Great Britain too, a version of idealism was flourishing. T. H. Green, F. H. Bradley, and Bernard Bosanquet were among the most prominent of the British idealists who advocated a form of absolutism – a single coherent system in which everything is internally related.[1] They were all sharp critics of traditional British empiricism. We sometimes forget that both Bertrand Russell and G. E. Moore, considered to be two of the most important founders of analytic philosophy, were originally defenders of idealism. In America, the great proponent of absolute idealism was the charismatic Harvard philosopher Josiah Royce. Absolute idealism flourished in both the United States and England. The influence of absolute idealism had been so strong at the turn of the twentieth century that when William James was invited to give the Hibbert Lectures at Oxford in 1907, he declared in a passage that I have previously quoted:

> Fortunately, our age seems to be growing philosophical again – still in the ashes live the wonted fires. Oxford, long the seed-bed, for the English world, of the idealism inspired by Kant and Hegel, has recently become the nursery of a very different way of thinking. Even non-philosophers have begun to take an interest in a controversy over what is known as pluralism or humanism. It looks a little as if the ancient English empiricism, so long put out of fashion here by nobler sounding Germanic formulas, might be re-pluming itself and getting ready for a stronger flight than ever. (James 1977, p. 7)

I will briefly describe the significance of Hegel for Dewey, Peirce and James. I begin with Dewey because Hegel had the greatest influence on his thinking.

Dewey's Early Hegelianism

In his autobiographical sketch (1930), Dewey tells us that as an under-graduate at the University of Vermont, he was "subconsciously ... led to desire a world and life that would have the same properties as had the human organism" (Dewey 1981, p. 2). At that time Dewey had not yet discovered Hegel.[2] But when he entered the graduate program in philosophy at Johns Hopkins, he came under the dominant influence of G. S. Morris – an enthusiast for Hegel and idealism.

> While it was impossible that a young and impressionable student unacquainted with any system of thought that satisfied his head and heart, should not have been deeply affected, to the point of at least a temporary conversion, by the enthusiastic and scholarly devotion of Mr. Morris, this effect was far from being the only source of my own "Hegelianism". The 'eighties and 'nineties were a time of new ferment in English thought; the reaction against atomic individualism and sen-sationalistic empiricism was in full swing. It was the time of Thomas Hill Green, of the two Cairds, of Wallace, of the appearance of the *Essays in Philosophical Criticism*, co-operatively produced by a younger

group under the leadership of the late Lord Haldane. This movement was at the time the vital and constructive one in philosophy. (Dewey 1981, p. 6)

What did the young Dewey find so attractive in Hegel? It was not Hegel's claims about the Absolute, or the unfolding of the categories in the *Logic*, or the grand sweep of Hegel's narrative of the West, or even the technical details of Hegel's dialectic. It was the sense of life, the dynamism, and especially the vision of organic inter-related reality that Dewey found so appealing. What Dewey wrote about his teacher, G. H. Morris, might just as well have been said about himself.

> I should say that he was at once strangely indifferent to and strangely preoccupied with the dialectic of Hegel. Its purely technical aspects did not interest him. But he derived from it an abiding sense of what he was wont to term the organic relationship of subject and object, intelligence and the world. ... His adherence to Hegel (I feel quite sure) was because Hegel had demonstrated to him, in a great variety of fields of experience, the supreme reality of this principle of living unity maintaining itself through the medium of differences and distinctions. (Cited in Wenley 1917, pp. 136–7)

But Dewey's most revealing remark about Hegel's inspiration is the following:

> There were, however, also "subjective" reasons for the appeal that Hegel's thought made to me; it supplied a demand for unification that was doubtless an intense emotional craving, and yet was a hunger that only an intellectualized subject-matter could satisfy. It is more than difficult, it is impossible, to recover that early mood. But the sense of divisions and separations that were, I suppose, borne in upon me as a consequence of a heritage of New England culture, divisions by way of isolation of self from the world, of soul from body, of nature from God, brought a painful oppression – or, rather, they were an inward lac-eration. My earlier philosophic study [prior to his discovery of Hegel] – had been intellectual gymnastic. Hegel's synthesis of subject and object, matter and spirit, the divine and the human, was, however, no mere intellectual formula; it operated as an immense release, a libera-tion. Hegel's treatment of human culture, of institutions and the arts, involved the same dissolution of hard-and-fast dividing walls, and had a special attraction for me. (Dewey 1981, p. 7)

Despite these heady attractions, Dewey gradually drifted away from Hegel. Darwin replaced Hegel as a source of inspiration for the organic, dynamic, changing character of life. But the "subjective" factors that originally attracted Dewey to Hegel stayed with him throughout his life and deeply marked his own experimentalist version of pragmatism. Dewey, in effect, naturalized Hegel. Dewey's concept of experience as a transaction that spans space and time, involving both undergoing and activity, shows the Hegelian influence. Subject and object are understood as *functional* distinctions within the dynamics of a unified developing experience. Like Hegel, Dewey is critical of all dualisms and the fixed dichotomies that have plagued philosophy, including mind and body as well as nature and experience. Dewey's hostility to the merely formal and static was inspired by Hegel. Dewey, like Hegel, was alert to the role of conflicts in experience: how they are be overcome in the course of experience, and how new conflicts break out. Typically he approaches philosophical problems in a Hegelian manner by delineating opposing extremes, showing what is *false* about them, indicating how we can preserve the *truth* implicit in them, and passing beyond these extremes to a more comprehensive resolution. Like Hegel, Dewey believed that philosophy must be approached in it historical context.

Peirce's Ambivalence toward Hegel

Peirce's original philosophical source of inspiration was Kant – and not Kant as interpreted through Hegelian spectacles. Peirce detested what Hegel and the Hegelians took to be the character of logic. He even criticized Dewey severely for the pernicious influence of Hegelianism on his early "logical" studies. The latter are better characterized as "natural history" than normative logic.[3] But eventually Peirce came to recognize the affinity between his pragmaticism and Hegelian absolute idealism.

> The truth is that pragmaticism is closely allied to Hegelian absolute idealism, from which it is sundered by its vigorous denial that the third category (which Hegel degrades to a mere stage of thinking) suffices to make the world, or even so much as self-sufficient. Had Hegel, instead of regarding the first two stages with his smile of contempt,

held on to them as independent or distinct elements of a triune Reality, pragmaticists might have looked upon him as the great vindicator of their truth. (5.436)

Peirce is referring to his categorial scheme of Firstness, Secondness, and Thirdness, which he takes to be basic for any adequate philosophical understanding of phenomena, logic, signification, experience, and reality. Writing to Lady Welby in 1904, Peirce declares:

> I was long ago (1867) led, after only three or four years' study, to throw all ideas into the three classes of Firstness, of Secondness, and of Thirdness. This sort of notion is as distasteful to me as to anybody; and for years, I endeavored to pooh-pooh and refute it; but it long ago conquered me completely. Disagreeable as it is to attribute such meaning to numbers, and to a triad above all, it is true as it is disagreeable. (8.328)

Peirce, of course, recognizes the affinity between his threefold categorical scheme and Hegel's penchant for triads. But he claims that Hegel viewed these categories as mere stages of *thinking*. He failed to appreciate that the categories designate elements that have an independence that is *not* reducible to thinking.[4] I have explored one crucial aspect of this difference – the role of Secondness in Peirce's analysis of experience, perception, and inquiry.[5] Peirce's critique of intuitionism – the core of the Cartesianism that he sought to displace – complements Hegel's critique of the very idea of pure (unmediated) immediacy.

James: Hegel's "Abominable Habits of Speech"

James, the great popularizer of "pragmatism," had a deep aversion to German philosophy, and rarely resisted an opportunity to ridicule what he took to be its misguided pretentiousness. James's real enemy was not so much Hegel, but rather the version of idealism advocated by British idealists and by his Harvard colleague Josiah Royce. Unfortunately, Royce is scarcely read today – except by specialists. Yet Royce is the American philosopher who exhibited the most sensitive understanding of Hegel and German idealism. In this late work,

Royce also noted the convergence of Hegelian and pragmatic themes developed by Peirce.

James spent two chapters of *A Pluralistic Universe* explaining what is wrong with "monistic idealism," and lamenting the pernicious influence of Hegel. Pluralism, as James understood it, is a radical alternative to any form of Hegelianism. James deplored Hegel's "abominable habits of speech," "his passion for the slipshod in the way of sentences, his unprincipled playing fast and loose with terms; his dreadful vocabulary." "All these things make his present-day readers wish to tear their hair – or his – out of desperation" (James 1977, p. 44). "The only thing that is certain is that whatever you may say of [Hegel's] procedure, someone will accuse you of misunderstanding it." In short, Hegel epitomized precisely what philosophers should avoid: vicious intellectualism, abstract monism, cultivated obscurity, and long grandiloquent pretentious sentences that sound profound, but are really quite vacuous. Summing up his criticism of monistic idealism, James declares:

> The prestige of the absolute has rather crumbled in our hands. The logical proofs of it miss fire: the portraits which its best court-painters show of it are featureless and foggy in the extreme; and, apart from the cold comfort of assuring us that with *it* all is well, and that to see that all is well with us also we need only rise to its eternal point of view, it yields us no relief whatever. It introduces, on the contrary, into philosophy and theology certain poisonous difficulties of which but for its intrusion we never should have heard. (James 1977, p. 63)

Yet, for all his disdain of Hegel and absolute idealism, James tells us that Hegel was "a naively observant man" who "plants himself in the empirical flux of things and gets the impression of what happens" (James 1977, p. 44). He extols Hegel for his keen awareness of the quality of the world as alive, and as involving a dialectic movement in things. He singles out Hegel's revolutionary achievement: "Concepts were not in his eyes the static self-contained things that previous logicians had supposed, but were germinative, and passed beyond themselves into each other by what he called their immanent dialectic" (James 1977, p. 46). The category of negation is Hegel's most original stroke. "Merely as a reporter of certain empirical aspects of the actual, Hegel is great and true" (James 1977, p. 49). James displays a rare ability to understand sympathetically those whom he most bitterly opposes. His portrait is based on Hegel's *Logic*, a primary Hegelian text for the British idealists. If James had discussed Hegel's *Phenomenology of Spirit*, he might have found even more direct support for the aspects of Hegel's thinking that he singles out for praise – the dynamic living quality of experience and reality.

Nevertheless, James's devastating caricature of Hegel helped to suppress any serious interest in Hegel. Many Anglo-American philosophers today would still endorse James's portrait of Hegel. Ironically, Hegel, who had been a source of inspiration for Dewey, was killed off by James's popular version of pragmatism. It is too mild to say that serious interest in Hegel in the United States waned during the next 50 years. It was completely moribund – and this is just the way that most philosophers in America thought it should be.

The Revival of Interest in Hegel

Beginning in the 1950s, and in subsequent decades, the situation slowly changed. When I was a graduate student in the 1950s, the question was frequently asked, "Do you do philosophy? Or do you do the history of philosophy?" The presumption was that there was little of genuine philosophical interest to be found in turning to the history of philosophy – except to show how confused and misguided past philosophers had been. At best, we might recast some of the occasional insights of past philosophers in the new way of words. By this criterion, Hegel was not even worthy of being read. For many analytic philosophers, Hegel was an exemplar of the type of vacuous speculation that every respectable analytic thinker should avoid. But gradually – at least among a marginal group – there were signs of a growing interest in Hegel. There were three primary reasons for this. The first was clearly political. With the emergence of the New Left, there was a search for an intellectual basis that could serve to motivate and legitimate the call for social justice and radical democratic action. The early "humanistic" Marx was being rediscovered. And it soon became evident that Marx led one back to Hegel. This was the time when Left students in America were discovering the rich Marxist tradition of Lukács, Gramsci, and the Frankfurt School. Initially, Hegel was read through the spectacles of Western Marxism, Hegel seen through the eyes of Adorno and Marcuse. When I wrote

Praxis and Action during the late 1960s and argued that Marxism, existentialism, pragmatism, and analytic philosophy were movements that arose out of, or in reaction to, Hegel, there were scarcely any philosophers in the United States who took Hegel seriously. Although the New Left stimulated commentaries and new translations of Marx and Hegel, it still did not influence the mainstream academic philosophy taught in graduate schools.

There was a second source of the interest in Hegel. No respectable philosopher of the time could completely ignore the analytic orientations that were emerging during the 1950s and 1960s. But there was a group that found the limited scope of analytic philosophy stifling. They were searching for an alternative, a way in which one could take on board the new insights and achievements of the linguistic turn, but also broaden philosophical discourse – to show how philosophy could still deal with the range of human culture and experience instead of focusing exclusively on a narrow set of technical issues. I would place Charles Taylor, Alasdair MacIntyre, Richard Rorty, and myself in this group. One of the consequences of the growing interest in Hegel at mid-century was the production of new translations, commentaries, and serious discussions of Hegel's work. I do not think it is an exaggeration to say that, in the 1950s, one could count on one hand the number of books published in America that dealt with Hegel – and these were of uneven quality. But today, 50 years later, there are good reasons to say that the Hegelian *Geist* has moved to America, where we find some of the most creative and thought-provoking Hegelian scholarship.

A third source of the renewed interest in Hegel that also had its origins in the 1950s was so subterranean as to be almost totally neglected. Nevertheless, it is this underground current that has come to shape some of the most original philosophical inquiry today. I am thinking here of the work of Wilfrid Sellars.

Sellars: "Incipient *Meditations Hegeliènnes*"

A philosopher comes alive and speaks to us from the past when his work becomes a fertile source for dealing with current philosophical problems, when his work can be engaged in novel ways. Otherwise, paying homage to the tradition is a way of embalming it. This is what

I see happening in the United States today with regard to Hegel. To demonstrate this, I shall return to Sellars, who leads us *back* to Peirce and *forward* to the recent contributions of John McDowell and Robert Brandom. I shall also take a side-glance at Richard Rorty, who was also influenced by Sellars and was Brandom's teacher. Rorty was also one of the first to take note of this Hegelian turn.

Initially, the German philosopher who comes to mind when we think of Sellars is Kant, not Hegel. Like that of Peirce, Sellars's philosophy can be understood as variations on Kantian themes. But a careful reading of his work, especially his classic monograph *Empiricism and the Philosophy of Mind*, reveals how close his orientation is to the opening sections of Hegel's *Phenomenology*. Sellars's critique of the Myth of the Given reads as if it were a translation of the opening sections of the *Phenomenology* into what Sellars called the "new way of words." Sellars, who has a sophisticated knowledge of the history of philosophy, introduces his critique of the Given with an allusion to Hegel's critique of immediacy. If we translate Sellars back into Hegel's idiom, we can say that the critique of the Given rejects the claim that there is immediate knowledge that doesn't involve any conceptual mediation – a type of direct intuitive knowledge that *allegedly* serves as the foundation for all inferential knowledge. Put this way, Sellars's monograph calls to mind those early articles of Peirce that appeared in the *Journal of Speculative Philosophy*. Peirce anticipates many of the arguments developed by Sellars.[6] Peirce, like Sellars, argues that once we give up the Myth of the Given, we are led to a nonfoundational, fallibilistic, intersubjective understanding of concept formation and inference. This also entails a rejection of representationalist semantics and requires a more holistic understanding of meaning and inference. The appropriation and critique of Kant by Peirce and Sellars reflect the very spirit of Hegel. Richard Rorty was one of the first to suggest that Sellars was leading us from Kant to Hegel.

Let me be a bit more specific. I am not suggesting that Hegel directly influenced either Peirce or Sellars in their critiques of the Myth of the Given. Rather, I am claiming something that is more important and interesting. Just as Hegel detected a dialectical instability in the key Kantian dichotomies and distinctions – for example, between sensibility and understanding, receptivity and spontaneity – so both Sellars and Peirce were alert to this dialectical instability – and the need to pass beyond it. If we think of Hegel as introducing a philosophical line of argument that has its own integrity, then we can say that both Peirce and Sellars share this critical mode of thinking.[7] Without denying the "truth" of empiricism – that in our empirical and scientific knowledge, we are subject to a brute compulsion – Peirce and Sellars challenge the very idea that there is (or can be) any knowledge "below" the level of concepts, "below" what Kant and Hegel call *Verstand* (understanding). There is no "pure" receptive knowledge that does not *always already* involve what Kant calls spontaneity. There is no immediate knowledge or knowledge by acquaintance when this is understood to be a type of immediate *self-authenticating* episode that can presumably serve as an epistemic foundation for inferential knowledge. Both argue that a major confusion in the classical empiricist tradition was to confuse brute compulsion (Peirce's Secondness) with epistemic justification (Peirce's Thirdness). Russell's understanding of "knowledge by acquaintance," one of the targets of Sellars's critique of the Given, exemplifies what Hegel had already criticized in the opening dialectical critique of "Sense Certainty" in his *Phenomenology*. Both Peirce and Sellars swerve away from some of the excesses of Hegel. Both seek to develop a fallibilistic communal understanding of inquiry that is compatible with the "truth" implicit in the empiricist tradition – where experience serves to check the validity of our knowledge claims.

During his creative years at the University of Minnesota, Yale, and the University of Pittsburgh, Sellars had his dedicated admirers. But his philosophical contributions were overshadowed by those of Quine and Davidson. In the past few decades, primarily as a result of the publications of John McDowell and Robert Brandom, there is a much greater appreciation of the fecundity of Sellars's work. McDowell and Brandom, known as the "Pittsburgh Hegelians," have acknowledged the influence of Sellars on their own philosophical investigations, and they have also been explicit about this Hegelian turn. I suspect that many of John McDowell's former Oxford colleagues thought it was a joke when he declared, in the preface to *Mind and World*, "one way that I would like to conceive this work is as a prolegomenon to the reading of [Hegel's *Phenomenology of Spirit*]." But it is no joke, and McDowell is extremely insightful about Hegel. In the same preface (written before the publication of Brandom's *Making It Explicit*), he also acknowledges "the substantial marks of Brandom's influence" – and especially his "eye-opening seminar on Hegel's *Phenomenology of Spirit*," which McDowell attended in 1990 (McDowell 1996, p. ix). In *Articulating Reasons*, Brandom affirms that his philosophical work represents a continuation of this Hegelian line of thinking. He tells us, "My teacher Richard Rorty has described the enterprise to which this volume is a contribution as an extension of Sellars's; to make possible a further transition from a *kantian* to a *hegelian* approach to thought and action" (Brandom 2000a, p. 32). Brandom explains what he means:

> First, I am interested in the divide between *nature* and *culture*. In this context we can identify the realm of the cultural with activities that either consist in the application of concepts in judgment and action or that presuppose such capacities. The *Geisteswissenschaften* have as their proper aim the study of concept use and things made possible by it – activities of which only concept users are capable. One of my principal goals is to present and explore the consequences of a particular sort of principle of demarcation for the realm of culture, so understood. Although of course cultural activities arise within the framework of a natural world, I am most concerned with what is made possible by the emergence of the peculiar constellation of conceptually articulated comportments that Hegel called "Geist." Cultural products and activities become explicit as such only by the use of normative vocabulary that is in principle not reducible to the vocabulary of the natural sciences. ... The study of natures itself has a history, and its own nature, if any, must be approached through the study of that history. This is a picture and an aspiration that we owe to Hegel. (Brandom 2000a, p. 33)

Brandom also stresses a second dimension of Hegelian influence – what he calls Hegel's *"pragmatism* about conceptual norms." I will shortly explain what Brandom means by this and how it brings us back to the pragmatism of Peirce.

The "Pittsburgh Hegelians": McDowell and Brandom

McDowell's references to Hegel are sparse, but they are revealing. At a crucial stage in the development of his argument in *Mind and World* he writes:

> It is central to Absolute Idealism to reject that the conceptual realm has an outer boundary, and we have arrived at a point from which we could start to domesticate the rhetoric of that philosophy. Consider, for

instance, this remark of Hegel's: "In thinking, I *am free*, because I am not in an *other*." This expresses exactly the image I have been using, in which the conceptual is unbounded; there is nothing outside it. The point is the same as the point of that remark of Wittgenstein's. ... We – and our meaning – do not stop anywhere short of the fact. (McDowell 1996, p. 44)

This is a central thesis of *Mind and World*. In his attempt to escape from the oscillating seesaw such that we *either* fall victim to some form of the Myth of the Given *or* slip into an unsatisfying "frictionless" coherentism, McDowell argues that the conceptual realm is unbounded and that the world imposes *rational* constraints upon us. At first glance (and some would say, even after a second or third glance), many of his critics fail to see what is the difference that makes a difference between what he is advocating and the coherentism that he criticizes and rejects.[8] McDowell seeks to show – in his Wittgensteinian mode of therapeutic reflection – that the philosophical anxiety resulting from this oscillating seesaw is alleviated once we realize that the conceptual realm is unbounded and does not cut us off from reality. On the contrary, it is precisely *because of* this unboundedness that we can achieve knowledge and access to a reality that is independent of us. Reality is not located "outside" the conceptual realm. McDowell succinctly states his main point thus:

> In a particular experience in which one is not misled, what one takes in is *that things are thus and so*. *That things are thus and so* is the content of the experience and it can also be the content of a judgement if the subject decides to take the experience at face value. So it is a conceptual content. But *that things are thus and so* is also, if one is not misled, an aspect of the layout of the world: it is how things are. (McDowell 1996, p. 26)

McDowell takes this to be a gloss on the Wittgensteinian remark: "When we say, and *mean*, that such-and-such is the case, we – and our meaning – do not stop anywhere short of the fact; but we mean: this – is – so" (cited in McDowell 1996, p. 27). When we unpack McDowell's meaning, it sheds light on his project as well as on Hegel's. McDowell is aware of the popular view that Hegelian idealism, with its emphasis on mind (*Geist*), thought (*Denken*), and concept (*Begriff*), fails to do justice to a reality and a world that is "outside of" and independent of mind and thought. This caricature of Hegel is based on the presupposition that the distinction between what is "inside the mind" and "outside the mind," or what is "inside" the conceptual realm and "outside" this realm, is itself unproblematic. Presumably idealism is the philosophical position that tells us that there is nothing that is "outside the mind." McDowell correctly realizes that this is a caricature; Hegel's idealism involves a total rejection of this entrenched dichotomy of what is "inside" and "outside" the conceptual realm. Hegel (like McDowell) categorically rejects this misleading picture. McDowell's Hegelian claim is that a proper understanding of what it means to affirm the unboundedness of the conceptual shows us that it is precisely *because of* this unboundedness that we can come to know of a reality that is independent of us. What McDowell says about Wittgenstein is just as true of Hegel.

> [T]here is no ontological gap between the sort of thing one can mean, or generally the sort of thing one can think, and the sort of thing that can be the case. When one thinks truly, what one thinks *is* what is the case. So since the world is everything that is the case ... there is no gap between thought, as such, and the world. Of course thought can be distanced from the world by being false, but there is no distance from the world implicit in the very idea of thought. (McDowell 1996, p. 27)

A second related feature of McDowell's philosophical investigations that bears a strong affinity with Hegel is his critique of what he calls the "disenchanted" conception of nature, which has dominated so much of modern philosophy. He seeks to recover the idea of "second nature." McDowell draws upon Aristotle's ethical writings rather than Hegel to explain what he means. But we should not forget how much Hegel himself is indebted to Aristotle. Furthermore, Hegel also argued that the "truth" of nature is spirit. McDowell's basic point is that as long as we operate with a conception of nature that is completely disenchanted, and a conception of naturalism that is essentially reductionist, we cannot avoid the philosophical anxieties and aporias of a bifurcation of nature and freedom. We need to rethink the concept of nature in a manner that is compatible with idea of a human *second nature*. In this way we avoid both reductionism and dualism, both of which McDowell takes to be philosophically unacceptable. We open the way to a more adequate conception of nature that is compatible with the *sui generis* character of spontaneity. McDowell gives an eloquent description of the type of integration that he envisions when he writes:

> We need to recapture the Aristotelian idea that a normal mature
> human being is a rational animal, but without losing the Kantian idea
> that rationality operates freely in its own sphere. The Kantian idea
> is reflected in the contrast between the organization of the space of
> reasons and the structure of the realm of natural law. Modern natu-
> ralism is forgetful of second nature; if we try to preserve the Kantian
> thought that reason is autonomous within the framework of that kind
> of naturalism, we disconnect our rationality from our animal being,
> which is what gives us a foothold in nature. ... If we want to combine
> avoiding the problems with a more substantial acknowledgement of
> them, we need to see ourselves as animals whose natural being is
> permeated with rationality, even though rationality is appropriately
> conceived in Kantian terms. (McDowell 1996, p. 85)[9]

We should not forget that Hegel himself sought to integrate Aristotle
with Kant in a manner that is very similar to the way in which
McDowell characterizes this need for a genuine synthesis.

McDowell merely sketches what this rethinking of the concept
of nature requires. There are many hurdles that need to be overcome
to carry this out successfully.[10] In this context, I shall limit myself
to the observation that this project bears a strong affinity with
post-Kantian idealism. Fichte, Schelling, and Hegel all felt that
Kant had left us in an intolerable position insofar as he introduced
what seemed to be a categorical dichotomy between the realm
of nature and the realm of freedom. They all felt, as the later Kant
came to realize in the *Critique of Judgment*, that this chasm had to be
bridged. They all rejected what McDowell calls "bald naturalism,"
which in their vocabularies was identical with "naturalism." They
would all agree with McDowell when he affirms that spontaneity is
sui generis (McDowell 1996, p. 76). And each, in his distinctive manner,
sought to rethink the concept of nature in a way that shows how it
is continuous with the higher reaches of rationality and thought. I
do not want to suggest that the German idealists were successful in
carrying out this project, just as I do not think that McDowell thus far
has provided more than hints about how this is to be done. Actually,
the type of naturalism that McDowell proposes has an even closer
affinity with the nonreductive emergent naturalism of Peirce, James,
and Dewey.

I cannot explore the rich and multifarious ways in which we see
the traces of Hegel in Brandom – or the differences between him and
McDowell. But I do want to pick up one major strand in his appro-

priation of Hegel – what Brandom calls "Hegel's pragmatism." Like Peirce, Sellars, and McDowell, Brandom's starting point is Kant. His philosophical reflections begin with Kant's insights about normativity and rationality. He tells us:

> One of Kant's great insights is that judgments and actions are to be distinguished from the responses of merely natural creatures by their distinctive *normative* status, as things we are in a distinctive sense *responsible* for. He understood *concepts* as the norms that determine just what we have made ourselves responsible for, what we have committed ourselves to and what would entitle us to it, by the particular acts of judging and acting. (Brandom 2000a, p. 33)

This is Brandom's starting point, but he thinks that there are many hard questions about normativity that are not adequately accounted for by Kant. He goes on to tell us:

> Kant, however, punted many hard questions about the nature and origins of this normativity, of the bindingness of concepts, out of the familiar phenomenal realm of experience into the noumenal realm. Hegel brought these issues back to earth by understanding *normative* statuses as *social* statuses – by developing a view according to which ... *all transcendental constitution is social institution*. The background against which the conceptual activity of making things explicit is intelligible is taken to be implicitly normative essentially *social* practice. (Brandom 2000a, pp. 33–4)[11]

This is a succinct statement of Brandom's philosophical project – one that he pursues with analytic finesse and systematic thoroughness. Carrying it out requires the development of a concept of discursive social practices that enables us to do full justice to the normativity implicit in these social practices. Brandom characterizes Hegel's pragmatism as "a *rationalist* pragmatism" (Brandom 2000a, p. 34). He thinks that Hegel's pragmatism is richer and more fertile than the pragmatism that one finds in Peirce, James, and Dewey, or even the "pragmatism" of the early Heidegger and the later Wittgenstein. I strongly disagree with Brandom's assessment of the American pragmatic tradition.[12] He fails to recognize that Peirce's pragmaticism is a normative pragmatism that is based upon an inferential semantics. We also find in Peirce an anticipation of Brandom's inferential semantics, and his all-important distinction between what is implicit and what is explicit in social practices. For example, Peirce tells us that all reasoning involves inferential "leading" or "guiding" principles.

> That which determines us, from given premises, to draw one inference rather than another, is some habit of mind. ... The particular habit of mind which governs this or that inference may be formulated in a proposition whose truth depends on the validity of the inferences which the habit determines; and such a formula is called a *guiding principle* of inference. (5.367)

I am not suggesting that everything of importance in Brandom is already to be found in Peirce. But I do want to affirm that being sensitive to anticipations, similar dialectical moves, and closely related argumentative strategies, enables us to detect continuities in the pragmatic tradition. Specifically, it enables us to become more reflective about the Hegelian motifs in a pragmatic tradition that reaches back to Peirce and encompasses the philosophical contributions of Dewey, Sellars, McDowell, and Brandom. It opens us to a rethinking of the course of philosophy in the United States during the past 150 years. Sellars, McDowell, and Brandom are solidly grounded in analytic philosophy, but their philosophical investigations cut across the divide between Anglo-American and Continental philosophy.

I agree with Richard Rorty when he writes, in his introduction to Sellars's *Empiricism and Philosophy of Mind*, that the "prope-Hegelianism" of Sellars and Brandom "suggest that the Sellars–Brandom 'social practice' approach to the traditional topics of analytic philosophy might help reconnect that philosophical tradition with the so-called 'Continental' tradition" (Rorty 1997a, p. 11).

> Philosophers in non-anglophone countries typically think quite hard about Hegel, whereas the rather skimpy training in the history of philosophy which most analytic philosophers receive often tempts them to skip straight from Kant to Frege. It is agreeable to imagine a future in which the tiresome 'analytic–Continental split' is looked back upon as an unfortunate, temporary breakdown of communication – a future in which Sellars and Habermas, Davidson and Gadamer, Putnam and Derrida, Rawls and Foucault, are seen as fellow-travelers on the same journey, fellow-citizens of what Michael Oakeshott called a *civitas pelegrina*. (Rorty 1997a, pp. 11–12)

Rorty's suggestion about the future of philosophy is consistent with the thesis that I have been advocating throughout this book. If we concentrate on the vital and varied development of pragmatic themes during the past 150 years, if we are sensitive to the ways in which pragmatic thinkers have detranscendentalized Kant and incorporated Hegelian motifs, then those standard "tiresome" classifications – "analytic–Continental" – actually *obscure* the pragmatic sea change that has been taken place in philosophy.

5

Pragmatism, Objectivity, and Truth

We philosophers are frequently disinclined to admit how great a role intuition and temperament play in our philosophical disputes. By 'intuitions' I mean something like our 'hunches,' our pre-analytic sense of the way things are, rather than something that is immediately or directly known. We think that any philosophical thesis that we propose must take account of our intuitions – or at least our primary intuitions when there is a clash. But whatever role they may play in initiating and guiding our philosophical inquiries, what really count "officially" are the force and the validity of the reasons we advance to support and justify our claims. Our intuitions, moreover, are closely related to our temperaments. Many philosophers have been scandalized by the remarks of William James about the significance of temperament in philosophical disputes.

> The history of philosophy is to a great extent that of a certain clash of human temperaments. Undignified as such a treatment may seem to some of my colleagues, I shall have to take account of this clash and explain a good many divergences of philosophers by it. Of whatever temperament a professional philosopher is, he tries, when philosophizing, to sink the fact of this temperament. Temperament is no conventionally recognized reason, so he urges impersonal reasons only for his conclusions. Yet his temperament really gives him a stronger bias than any of his more strictly objective premises. It loads the evidence for him one way or the other, making a more sentimental or more hardhearted view of the universe, just as this fact or that principle

would. He trusts his temperament. Wanting a universe that suits it, he believes in any representation of the universe that does suit it. He feels men of the opposite temper to be out of key with the world's character, and in his heart he considers them incompetent and "not in it," in the philosophic business, even though they may far excel him in dialectical ability. (James 1975a, p. 11)[1]

There are those who (mis)read this as licensing the worst sort of subjectivism, but I think that James is both extremely perceptive and forthrightly honest. Let me illustrate James's point with regard to the much-debated topic of objectivity. There are philosophers who think that there is a reality "out there" that is independent of any of our subjective beliefs. They argue that we may never fully come to know this reality, but to the extent that we do, we achieve objective knowledge. Our knowledge corresponds to this reality, to the objective facts. Now this intuition may lead a philosopher to defend a variety of positions – to advocate a form of realism, to defend a correspondence theory of truth, to argue that objective facts must be sharply distinguished from anything that is subjective, etc. If anyone denies the intuition that underlies these philosophical positions, she must be mistaken, or – to use James's phrase, "incompetent and 'not in it.'" So, for example, a philosopher who takes this "realistic" intuition to be primary will be incredulous when she comes across the following statement by Richard Rorty: "Since 'truths' and 'facts' are pretty nearly equivalent notions, I think it is important to get rid of both. So I still want to defend the claim that there were no truths before human beings began using language: for all true sentences S, it was true back then that S, but there were no 'worldly items' – no facts, no truths – of the sort that Brandom believes in" (Rorty 2000a, p. 184). For the defender of "realistic intuitions" Rorty is just being perverse. How can anyone deny that there are plenty of objective facts that made up the world before humans came along? Why, we may wonder, is Rorty maintaining such a perverse and counterintuitive thesis?

The Correspondence Theory of Truth?

I have begun with these informal reflections about intuition and temperament because I am convinced that the clash of intuitions and temperaments underlies and motivates many of the contemporary disputes about truth, justification, realism, and objectivity. But let me come closer to my subject and be somewhat more technical. If we look back at the past 50 years, many of the traditional understandings of theories of truth, reality, and objectivity have been subjected to severe criticism. The notion of correspondence or agreement does "work" in many straightforward cases; this is part of its charm and appeal. If I say it is now raining outside and you deny it, we may go outside to look. And if we see that the sun is shining and there is no sign of rain, then I realize that I was mistaken. If I am more "highfalutin" and have been around philosophers, I might say that my assertion that it is raining does not correspond to the objective facts. We may even say that there is a direct comparison between my statement and the reality to which it refers. "Correspondence" or "agreement" works in such straightforward, noncontroversial instances, but things get much more confusing and messier when we are dealing with more complicated cases of philosophical, scientific, mathematical, or historical assertions. Here we can't simply look and see; rather, we are required to give reasons to support our claims about what is objectively true. The very meaning and criteria for determining what does and does not correspond to objective reality aren't at all clear. Albrecht Wellmer gives a succinct summary of why the idea of "correspondence" becomes so problematic.

> We try to decide the question whether something is so, as one says it is, with reasons (where in many cases the reasons that are at our disposal are not sufficient for bringing about such a decision). At this point it becomes clear that the idea of a "correspondence" between a statement and reality (or between a statement and a fact) suggests a misleading picture: namely, it suggests the picture of a relation of agreement – ascertainable from some standpoint (which cannot be ours, but perhaps that of God) – between statements or beliefs and a piece of reality or the things themselves. If, however, one detaches the idea of agreement between what one says and what is (really) the case from the way we justify or deny assertions or beliefs with reasons – or by calling on perceptions – then this idea becomes something completely incomprehensible. For how then should one think of such agreement between statements (thoughts, convictions, etc.) and reality – two totally incommensurable relata: how and what should be tested here as agreement – and who should carry out such a test? A correspondence concept of truth ... becomes either incomprehensible or metaphysical, or both at the same time, if we seek to think of the

idea of "just like," i.e., "agreement," independently of our justificatory praxis. (Wellmer 2004, p. 95)

Wellmer summarizes some of the key objections to theories of correspondence or agreement when we think that what makes an assertion or statement true is its correspondence with objective facts. Despite the many important differences among Wittgenstein, Quine, Davidson, Sellars, Rorty, McDowell, Brandom (and many others), they all contribute to undermining our confidence in any of the traditional correspondence theories. Or if our philosophical tastes are more Continental, we can read Heidegger, Foucault, Derrida, Deleuze, Habermas, and Apel as contributing to the demise of this approach to truth and objectivity.

But now we come closer to the heart of the problem. If we affirm that there is a close relation between our understanding of truth and objectivity and our "justificatory praxis," what precisely is it? And here we confront an "interminable oscillation" that is provoked by a clash of intuitions and temperaments. There are those who believe that whatever difficulties we may discover with traditional correspondence or agreement theories, no philosophical theory is acceptable that fails to do justice to the intuition that there is an objective reality "out there," and that what we count as genuine knowledge must somehow correctly represent this objective reality. But there are those who argue that this way of posing the problem leads to dead-ends and aporias. If we are to give a proper account of objectivity, we must give up on any and all forms of representationalism; we must appeal to intersubjective (or better social) justificatory practices. Then the pendulum swings back, because the champions of objectivist or realist intuitions claim that any attempt to link objectivity and/or truth to social practices willy-nilly leads us to 'bad relativism.' By 'bad relativism,' I mean the sort of relativism that claims that there is really no truth (except truth for me or my group), no objective facts, and no universal validity claims.[2] Can we get off this seesaw? Is it really the case that if we link objectivity to our social justificatory practices we are ineluctably led to 'bad relativism'? I do not think so; nor have philosophers who have been inspired by a pragmatic approach to the relevant issues. But the mention of 'pragmatism' has its own problems, for this is a term that encompasses a variety of different and conflicting positions. The most controversial pragmatist (or neo-pragmatist) of our time, Richard Rorty, spent decades denying that he is a relativist, and yet his fellow pragmatist, Hilary Putnam, kept arguing that Rorty's views lead straight to "bad relativism." Rorty, as we have seen, not only wants to get rid of "truths" and "facts," but he thinks we can dispense with "objectivity" altogether in favor of "solidarity." John McDowell offers a succinct summary of why Rorty is so hostile toward the very idea of objectivity.

> What Rorty takes to parallel authoritarian religion is the very idea that in everyday and scientific investigation we submit to standards constituted by the things themselves, the reality that is supposed to be the topic of the investigation. Accepting that idea, Rorty suggests, is casting the world in the role of the non-human Other before which we are to humble ourselves. Full human maturity would require us to acknowledge authority only if the acknowledgement does not involve abasing ourselves before something non-human. The only authority that meets this requirement is that of human consensus. If we conceive inquiry and judgment in terms of making ourselves answerable to the world, as opposed to being answerable to our fellows, we are merely postponing the completion of a humanism whose achievement begins with discarding authoritarian religion. (McDowell 2000, p. 110)[3]

A Pragmatic Account of Objectivity

Yet most pragmatists – including the classical pragmatists Peirce, James, Dewey, and Mead, as well as such contemporaries as Hilary Putnam, Cheryl J. Misak, Jeffrey Stout, Bjorn Ramberg, Robert Brandom, and the "Kantian pragmatist" Jürgen Habermas – do think that it is possible to give a pragmatic account of objectivity that (a) links objectivity to our justificatory social practices; (b) does not identify justification with truth, and (c) avoids the self-defeating aporias of bad relativism and conventionalism. In the remainder of this chapter, I shall consider some of the approaches to relevant issues in order to clear the way for a robust pragmatic conception of objectivity.[4]

I have spoken of linking the concept of justificatory praxis with truth and objectivity, but this linkage is not to be thought of as identification, or as dispensing with truth and objectivity in favor of justification. It is frequently said that pragmatists – following John Dewey – substitute the justificatory concept of warranted assertibility for truth. Actually, when Dewey introduces the expression 'warranted assertibility' he does so as an alternative to the terms 'belief' and 'knowledge' rather than 'truth.'[5] And even Rorty admits that there is a role for what he calls the "cautionary" role of truth that is distinct from justification.[6]

Let us consider Peirce's classic characterization of truth in his essay "How to Make Our Ideas Clear": "The opinion which is fated to be ultimately agreed to by all who investigate is what we mean by truth, and the object represented by the opinion is the real" (Peirce 1992, p. 139).[7] A decade earlier, Peirce had already sought to establish the internal relations among inquiry, community, reality, and objectivity.

> The real, then, is that which, sooner or later, information and reasoning would finally result in, and which is therefore independent of the vagaries of me and you. Thus the very origin of the conception of reality shows that this conception essentially involves the notion of a COMMUNITY, without definite limits, and capable of an increase of knowledge. And so those two series of cognitions – the real and the unreal – consist of those which, at a time sufficiently future, the community will always continue to reaffirm; and of those which, under the same conditions, will ever after be denied. Now a proposition whose falsity can never be discovered, and the error of which therefore is absolutely incognizable, contains, upon our principle, absolutely no error. Consequently, that which is thought in these cognitions is the real as it really is. There is nothing, then, to prevent our knowing outward things as they really are, and it is most likely that we do thus know them in numberless cases, although we can never be absolutely certain of doing so in any special case. (Peirce 1992, p. 52)

Peirce does not doubt that that there are real things that are independent of our thought and that constrain our opinions. But he challenges the claim that we can have direct, immediate, intuitive knowledge of what is real. All such knowledge involves or *presupposes* inferential processes.

> All human thought and opinion contains an arbitrary, accidental element, dependent on the limitations of circumstances, power, and bent of the individual; an element of error, in short. But human opinion universally tends in the long run to a definite form, which is the truth. Let any human being have enough information and exert enough thought upon any question, and the result will be that he will arrive

at a certain definite conclusion, which is the same that any other mind will reach under sufficiently favorable circumstances. ... The arbitrary will or other individual peculiarities of a sufficiently large number of minds may postpone the general agreement in that opinion indefinitely; but it cannot affect what the character of that opinion shall be when it is reached. This final opinion, then, is independent, not indeed of thought in general, but of all that is arbitrary and individual in thought; is quite independent of how you, or I, or any number of men think. (Peirce 1992, p. 89)

These claims have several attractive features, especially if we focus on the spirit of these remarks. Although Peirce notes the importance of a community – a community of inquirers – he does not claim that an actually achieved consensus is the measure of truth and reality. He speaks of a community without definite limits. We are not cut off from the reality that we seek to know. Peirce is not a skeptic. There is nothing that prevents us from knowing "outward things as they really are." But this is not achieved by any test of correspondence or agreement; it is the product of critical inquiry. These passages also indicate Peirce's fallibilism. We can achieve knowledge of reality, although we are never "in any special case" warranted in claiming that we know this with *absolute certainty*.

But if we take Peirce's remarks about truth, community, reality, and knowledge literally, then there are serious problems. Peirce seems to assume that "ideally" there will a consensus of scientific inquirers and a convergence of beliefs, but Putnam and others have seriously questioned whether such an assumption is warranted.[8] Furthermore, there are difficulties concerning the meaning of the "end of inquiry." Peirce, in his mature philosophy, made it perfectly clear that he was not speaking about a datable time in the future when inquiry ends, but rather about the end of inquiry as a regulative ideal. But even this revision creates its own problems. The idea of inquiry itself is essentially a normative concept, but can we really specify *now* the norms that will govern future inquiry? Cheryl Misak, who is perhaps the strongest defender of a Peircian conception of truth, reality, and objectivity, acknowledges the difficulties with Peirce's formulation. She offers an alternative formulation of the notion of a true belief that takes account of Peirce's revisions, one that is also intended to defuse some of the obvious objections: "A true belief is one that would withstand doubt, were we to inquire as far as we fruitfully could on the matter. A true belief is such that no matter how much further we were to investigate and debate, that belief would not be overturned by recalcitrant experience and argument." Misak's formulation "does not require the pragmatist to attempt the doomed task of saying just what is meant by the hypothetical end of inquiry, cognitively ideal conditions, or perfect evidence, whatever these might be. Any attempt at articulating such notions will have to face the objection that it is a mere glorification of what we presently take to be good" (Misak 2007, pp. 49–50).[9]

Ideal Justification and Truth

I want to consider the objection that truth as ideal justification is a "mere glorification of what we presently take to be good," because this is related to the important distinction between justification and truth. Wellmer points out that Putnam, Habermas, and Apel – all of whom are sympathetic to a pragmatic conception of truth and objectivity – seek to show that although truth is internally connected to justification, we can still sharply distinguish between them.

> The basic idea common to all three philosophers is as follows: if truth is internally connected with justification and nevertheless not the same as justification (here and now), then further conditions must be stated in such a way that an assertion or conviction justified under such conditions would be necessarily true. Truth would, therefore, be maintained as an "epistemic" concept – internally connected with the concept of justification – and nevertheless the simple equation of the predicates "is true" and "is justified" would be avoided. The conditions in question would have to be ideal conditions, and the basic idea is that an assertion or conviction justified under such ideal conditions would be necessarily true – whereas the "necessarily" should give expression to a conceptual necessity. Putnam, Habermas, and Apel want to say that this is how we understand the concept of truth (or this is how we ought to understand it). (Wellmer 2004, p. 97)[10]

But here's the rub: Can we really specify now, even counterfactually, what constitutes these "ideal conditions"? We frequently do say that if, at some future date, we reject what we now take to be fully justified, we will do so because we have good reasons. But are we able to specify now what are or will count as "good reasons" or even the criteria of what constitutes good reasons? Even without any future reference, we philosophers are always arguing about what are and are not good reasons to justify our claims. When we engage in a philosophical argument with an opponent, the primary issue is frequently about who has offered the best reasons to support her thesis. It is an illusion to think that there are ahistorical determinate standards to which we can appeal that will sharply distinguish once and for all what "really" are good or better reasons. What counts as "good reasons" is essentially contested. If we look back over the history of science from Aristotle to the present – or even from the beginnings of modern science to the present – we discover that standards of argumentation and justification have changed in ways that no scientist or philosopher might have anticipated. So although I am not denying that we may have a vague notion of "ideal" epistemic conditions, too frequently this turns out to be empty rhetoric or "a glorification of what we presently consider to be good."[11] So the question now becomes whether it is possible, to use Wellmer's apt phrase, to speak about "pragmatism without regulative ideas."

Wellmer thinks that we can, and he adopts a line of thinking that bears a strong similarity to the way in which Brandom deals with objectivity. But before examining this approach, let us review what we have learned. I began with a discussion of the intuition of those who think that there is an objective real world "out there" that is independent of us: that is, independent of our subjective opinions and prejudices. An adequate theory of truth (and justification) must do justice to this intuition. This is what typically informs the thinking of those who want to defend a correspondence theory of truth, representationalism (epistemic or semantic), or what has been called "metaphysical realism." But during the past 50 years or so, powerful arguments have been advanced from a variety of perspectives that expose all sorts of difficulties in these doctrines. Davidson succinctly tells us that "there are no interesting and appropriate entities available which, by being somehow related to sentences, can explain why the true ones are true and the others not. There is good reason, then, to be skeptical about the importance of the correspondence theory of truth" (Davidson 2000, p. 66). The failure of correspondence theories of truth helps to feed the opposing intuition that it is really our justificatory inferential social practices that are primary, and that any adequate conception of reality, objectivity, and truth must begin with this insight. But it is immediately obvious that we cannot merely appeal to our current *de facto* justifications or practices of justification, because, even with the best intentions and the most rigorous standards of justification, what is justified today may turn out to be false – not a correct account of what is the objective reality. And there appears to be a legitimate sense in which we can speak of truths that may never be justified. The challenge that critics raise against pragmatism is that, willy-nilly, it ends up in "bad relativism" or in an unsatisfactory conventionalism. Jerry Fodor, a fierce critic of pragmatist approaches to mind and language, puts this sort of criticism in a nutshell when he says: "First the pragmatist theory of concepts, then the theory theory of concepts, then holism, then relativism. So it goes" (Fodor 1994, p. 111).

We have examined various strategies for answering this criticism, and although each may help to defuse some of the objections of the critics of pragmatism, none of those that we have considered thus far is completely satisfactory. No one could accuse Peirce of being a relativist or a conventionalist, but even sympathetic critics have highlighted difficulties with Peirce's conception of the hypothetical end of inquiry. Addressing these difficulties leads to different strategies – for example, the approach adopted by Misak or the one adopted by Putnam, Habermas, and Apel. Misak's reformulation of Peirce's account of a true belief avoids any reference to a hypothetical end of inquiry or ideal conditions, but the price she pays is that we are never in a position to assert that any of our current beliefs are actually true. If we take her reformulation literally, we cannot even speak about any actual "true beliefs," because any of our current beliefs may be overturned in the future by "recalcitrant experience and argument." We can only speak of "true beliefs" in a subjunctive mode – what would not be overturned by future experience and argument, what would withstand doubt. Are there any criteria (even fuzzy ones) for determining when inquiry has "fruitfully" been carried far enough? We can also understand the motivation for Putnam, Habermas, and Apel to introduce a sharp distinction between actual existing discursive practices of justification and the ideal conditions for justification that would enable one to characterize truth as rational acceptability under epistemically ideal conditions. We can appreciate why these three philosophers insist that ideal conditions are not some distant utopian goal but are pragmatically effective (as counterfactuals) on the level of everyday communication and argumentation. Yet, the various attempts to spell out these ideal conditions amount to little more than a promissory note – little more than a glorification of what we now take to be the best standards of justification.[12] So let me return to the issue of whether it is really possible to defend a pragmatic theory of justification, truth, and objectivity that does justice to these various difficulties.

Truth and Justification without Regulative Ideals

Wellmer affirms that although there is a difference between 'truth' and 'justification,' there is also an internal connection. In making this general point, he basically agrees with Putnam, Habermas, and Apel, but thinks that this internal connection must be approached in a different way. He also disagrees with Rorty – who originally sought to dispense altogether with the notion of truth, but later sought to trivialize it, conceding that it plays a cautionary role.[13] Wellmer argues that we can explicate a normatively meaningful concept of truth without an appeal to regulative ideas. To appreciate his strategy, I shall return to Peirce's claim about the fundamental role of community in his characterization of inquiry and reality. How are we to understand this notion of community? More generally, how are we to characterize the intersubjective or social character of inquiry and discursive practices?[14] We should remember that Peirce placed so much stress on the communal nature of inquiry because he believed that it is only in and through communal interaction and criticism that we find the corrective to our prejudices and idiosyncratic perspectives. In a late letter to Lady Welby he writes:

> Unless truth be recognized as *public*, – as that of which *any* person would come to be convinced if he carried his inquiry, his sincere search for immovable belief, far enough, – then there will be nothing to prevent each one of us from adopting an utterly futile belief of his own which all the rest will disbelieve. Each one will set himself up as a little prophet; that is, a little "crank," a half-witted victim of his own narrowness.
>
> But if Truth be something public, it must mean that the acceptance of which as a basis of conduct any person you please would ultimately come if he pursued his inquiries far enough; – yes every rational being,

however prejudiced he might be at the outset. (Peirce and Welby 1977, p. 73)[15]

Although Wellmer does not cite Peirce in this context, he, in effect, seeks to explicate how we are to understand the public character of justificatory practices – practices that involve asking, offering, defending, and criticizing reasons. This is what Wilfrid Sellars calls "the logical space of reasons." Wellmer claims that the internal connection between truth and justification can be explained by the following two theses: "(a) The truth conditions of statements are only given to us as conditions of justifiability and assertibility, respectively. (b) Assertions (and in general, convictions) are, according to their meaning – as validity claims – internally related to justification in a normative sense." To justify an assertion, that 'p,' means to justify it as true. Wellmer tells us that "we must take into account the perspective of the first person (a speaker) has of himself or herself and the first person's perspective on another speaker" (Wellmer 2004, p. 101). When I justify my assertion, I justify it as true, but it certainly doesn't follow that I recognize that the justifications of assertions of my dialogue partner are true – especially when they conflict with what I have claimed to justify. It would seem that this is just the type of consideration that leads thinkers such as Putnam, Habermas, and Apel to distinguish actual justification from ideal justification. So where is the advance here? It is at this point that Wellmer makes a crucial move. "The error of all considerations of this kind [those that appeal to justification under ideal conditions] lies in the fact that they do not take seriously the constitutive difference between a first person's perspective on herself and her perspective (as that of a 'second person' or interpreter) on other speakers, and instead attempt to take on a 'metaperspective'; that is precisely what I called 'metaphysical'" (ibid.). How does this difference of perspectives advance the argument? Let us follow Wellmer's reasoning. "If I make an assertion – hold a belief with reasons – then I understand it, with reasons, as true. That is the internal connection between truth and justification." But if another person makes an assertion, I may well understand her reasons, but it doesn't follow that I consider her assertion to be true. "With reference to another person, however, his or her ways of reasoning are not necessarily sound from my perspective, and the corresponding convictions are not necessarily true. This should not mean that I exclude myself from the sphere of fallible beings, because the same goes for every other speaker from an I-perspective" (Wellmer 2004, p. 102). But even if we acknowledge the difference of perspectives, it still isn't clear what follows. Wellmer tells us:

> What I hold as reasoned truth deserves agreement: truth is transsubjective. And if I argue for my conviction, I wish to bring about, with reasons, such an agreement. In this sense a rational consensus is the telos of argumentation. But "rational" here means precisely reasoned, and that means: similarly reasoned for all those taking part. We can offer no criteria for rational consensus other than this: that precisely all those taking part are similarly persuaded by good reasons. Since, however, what "good reasons" are can only be shown in that they compel us towards agreement, a consensus can never be the criterion that what we have before us are good reasons. The concept of a "good reason" is attached, in an irreducible way, to the perspective of the one "persuaded" by good reasons. One cannot describe from a meta-perspective which "qualities" reasons must have in order to be really good reasons. To call reasons "good" is not the ascription of an "objective" quality; rather it is the adoption of an attitude with normative consequences. (Wellmer 2004, pp. 102–3)

Wellmer draws the conclusion that the transsubjective space of truth can be constituted only by way of the difference of perspectives. Consensus and dissensus are equiprimordial. "And now this means that truth, as encompassing various perspectives, is essentially controversial" (Wellmer 2004, p. 103).

What are we to make of this attempt to develop a pragmatic view of justification and truth without regulative ideas? It strikes me that there is a fatal flaw because of a crucial ambiguity. When Wellmer tells us that "what good reasons are can only be shown in that they compel us towards agreement," or that "the concept of a 'good reason' is attached, in an irreducible way, to the perspective of the one persuaded by good reasons," the precise meaning and force of 'compels' and 'persuaded' is not clear. Does he mean that in fact one is actually compelled and persuaded? Or does he mean that one *ought* to be compelled and persuaded? Clearly we may be factually compelled and persuaded by all sorts of considerations that are not good reasons. And unfortunately, all too often, "good reasons" do not, in fact, compel and persuade. But if what is meant is that one *ought* to be compelled and that one *ought* to be persuaded by good reasons – regardless of whether we are speaking from my first-person perspective or the first-person perspective of someone else – then this opens up a Pandora's box of problems. We have to ask, What justifies this 'ought'? So it looks as if Wellmer is begging the key question. Nevertheless, I do think that he is on to something that can advance our understanding. His argument, although sketchy and condensed, bears a strong resemblance to the way in which Brandom deals with objectivity.[16] Specifically, Wellmer's insight is related to the way in which Brandom distinguishes between I–thou and I–we relations.

Brandom's Contribution

I cannot do justice to Brandom's complex and intricate pragmatic account of discursive justificatory practices, truth claims, and objectivity. His discussion of objectivity appears only at the end of chapter 8 in *Making It Explicit*, after more than 500 pages of densely textured argument – and what he has to say about objectivity largely depends on what has come before. I will limit myself to a few key points. Brandom leaves us with many issues that need further clarification, but he opens one of the most promising lines of inquiry for giving a strong pragmatic account of justification, truth, and objectivity – one that avoids both relativism and conventionalism. As I read Brandom, I see him – to use a Hegelian turn of phrase – drawing out the 'truth' implicit in the various attempts to articulate a pragmatic conception of justification, truth, sociality, and objectivity, and to reject what is misleading or mistaken.[17] Let me give an informal statement of what Brandom seeks to show before turning to some details. Since the time when Charles Morris introduced his distinctions of syntax, semantics, and pragmatics, it has become a virtual dogma that there is a clear hierarchical ordering among these three disciplines. First comes syntax, then semantics, and finally pragmatics; pragmatics is dependent on semantics, and semantics is dependent on syntax. Brandom radically challenges this dogma and turns things upside down. His basic thesis is that pragmatics has explanatory primacy; that is, we can give an adequate account of semantics only from the perspective of a properly developed normative pragmatics. Brandom is well aware of the ambitiousness of his project – how it calls into question the dominant understanding of semantics. "The semantic explanatory strategy, which takes inference as its basic concept, contrasts with the one that has been dominant since the Enlightenment, which takes representation as its basic concept" (Brandom 1994, p. xvi). A major challenge of an inferential approach to semantics is to show that it can account for the representational dimension of semantic content. Stating Brandom's project from a more traditional pragmatic perspective means the primacy of practice – *knowing how* to do something is the basis for *knowing that*. Consequently, the challenge Brandom faces is to develop a rich enough understanding of social discursive inferential practices that can do all the work that he claims it can do. He seeks to do this with an elaborate theory of deontic scorekeeping that highlights the role of human commitments and entitlements. These commitments and entitlements are themselves the products of human activity that generate norms. "Mastering this sort of norm-instituting social practice is a kind of practical know-how – a matter of keeping deontic score by keeping track of one's own and others' commitments and entitlements to those commitments, and altering that score in systematic ways based on performances each practitioner produces. The norms that govern the use of linguistic expressions are implicit in these deontic scorekeeping practices" (Brandom 1994, p. xiv).[18]

Even on the basis of this preliminary sketch, we can see why critics of Brandom have been so skeptical about the details of his project and about the project overall. If one really takes human social practices to be primary, how is one ever going to escape from relativism and conventionalism? How is one ever going to be able to give a plausible account of meaning, truth, and objectivity? To quote the title of Rorty's sympathetic discussion of Brandom, "What do you do when they call you a 'relativist'?" Throughout the book, Brandom is acutely aware of these sorts of objections, as well as the objections of those who will say (and have said) that for all its elaborateness, his normative pragmatics amounts to little more than a linguistic idealism that loses contact with a real objective world that is "out there."[19] There are critics who accuse Brandom of being "guilty" of the sin that is presumably characteristic of all Hegelians – losing contact with a real objective world. Brandom designs his project in order to anticipate and answer these objections. In his preface he informs us:

> The most essential bit is Chapter 8, for that is where the representational dimension of discursive practice is explained in terms of interaction of the social and inferential articulation of the communication

of reasons for belief and action. It is this interaction that is appealed to there also to make intelligible how objective norms come to apply to the essentially social statuses – paradigmatically the doxastic and practical propositionally contentful commitments to beliefs and intentions – and so underwrite such fundamental practices as assessing the truth of beliefs and the success of actions. (Brandom 1994, p. xxiii)

It takes some hard work to master Brandom's intricate and distinctive idiom, but his main point is clear – his pragmatic approach can link justification, truth, and objectivity and explain them through a proper understanding of the dynamics of discursive inferential practices.[20] So how does he do this?

Let us go back to the point where Wellmer's appeal to different perspectives relates to Brandom's distinction between I–we and I–thou sociality. By an 'I–we sociality,' Brandom means an understanding of intersubjectivity that focuses on the contrast between an individual and the community. From this perspective the community is privileged. Objective correctness is identified with the "privileged" voice of the community. Brandom categorically rejects this understanding of intersubjectivity. It is the notion that lies behind all forms of conventionalism and those consensus theories that take "the community" as being the final arbitrator of what is true and objective.

In contrast to this mistaken conception of intersubjectivity, Brandom opts for a Davidsonian understanding of intersubjectivity, an I–thou sociality "that focuses on the relation between commitments undertaken by a scorekeeper interpreting others and the commitments attributed by the scorekeeper to those others" (Brandom 1994, p. 599).[21] This understanding of intersubjectivity is fundamental for his account of objectivity. According to the I–thou construal (in contrast to I–we), there is no *privileged* perspective. Or we might say that each perspective is temporarily "locally privileged in that it incorporates a structural distinction between objectively correct applications of concepts and applications that are merely subjectively taken to be correct" (Brandom 1994, p. 600). Objectivity then consists "in a kind of perspectival form, rather than in a nonperspectival or cross-perspectival content. What is shared by all discursive practices is that there is a difference between what is objectively correct in the way of concept application and what is merely taken to be so, not what it is – the structure, not the content." And what is most crucial is the "symmetry of the state and attitude between ascriber and the one to whom a commitment is ascribed" (ibid.). To put Brandom's point in my own words, he is telling us that built into the very structure of social discursive practices is a distinction between what is "merely" subjective and what is objective, what seems to be so and what really is so.

The point that Wellmer makes about the error of moving from the different participants' perspectives to a privileged "metaperspectival" point of view is similar to Brandom's claim when he says:

> [T]here is no bird's eye view above the fray of competing claims from which those that deserve to prevail can be identified, nor from which even necessary and sufficient conditions for such desserts can be formulated. The status of any such principles as probative is always itself at issue in the same way as the status of any particular factual claim. (Brandom 1994, p. 601)

Rorty, citing this same passage, suggests that philosophers who view relativism with "fear and loathing" (like Putnam and Habermas) will accuse Brandom of giving up on rationality by making inquiry seem to be a mere power struggle – "the fray of competing claims" (Rorty 1997b, p. 175). But Brandom points out that "there is no danger of discursive practice coming to appear as a 'mere power struggle' because the 'fray of competing claims' is a rational fray, one in which the things we are talking about exert rational constraint on our entitlement to the claims we make." Brandom also distances himself from Rorty, who, at times, views all talk about universal validity "with fear and loathing," and hyperventilates whenever anyone speaks about "context-transcending truth claims" or "getting things right." Brandom tells us that his "account of discursive practice makes sense of commitments to getting things right, and funds a sense of 'right' that is attitude-transcendent in the sense of swinging free of the contents of any and all actual or possible attitudes – though not of the very possibility of contentful attitudes" (Brandom 1997a, p. 201).[22]

There are some important aspects of Brandom's account of objectivity that I have not discussed, such as the role of *de re* and *de dicto* ascriptions of propositional attitudes, but I think I have said enough to convey the gist of his line of thinking.[23] I do not want to suggest that Brandom's account of objectivity is unproblematic; but he opens up one of the most promising ways of dealing with the relevant issues and shows how one can develop a robust pragmatic understanding of justification, truth, intersubjectivity, and objectivity.[24] I also think that we can view the several attempts since the time of Peirce to develop a pragmatic understanding of inquiry, justification, truth, sociality, and objectivity – which include some false starts and cul-de-sacs – as a progressive narrative. It is a narrative in which hypotheses are proposed, difficulties are located, and new strategies are developed to meet these difficulties. The cumulative effect of this progressive narrative is to enrich and texture a robust pragmatism.

Realist Intuitions?

I return now to my initial remarks about intuition and temperament. I am not optimistic that anyone who holds steadfastly to strong "realistic intuitions" will ever be satisfied with any version of a pragmatic account. Rorty is right when he suggests that anyone of this temperament will immediately seize on Brandom's claim that objectivity "is a kind of perspectival form, rather than a non-perspectival content," and "that readers who are accustomed to using 'relativist' as a term of abuse are going to insist that being a relativist consists precisely in denying the existence of nonperspectival content" (Rorty 1998b, p. 133). Brandom's critics, and more generally those critics of pragmatism who hold fast to their strong "realistic intuitions," want something much more substantial and nonperspectival. They want acknowledgment of a hard-core reality that is not "contaminated" by human subjectivity or perspective. Here I think that four comments are appropriate.

1. Critics of pragmatism argue that the trouble with pragmatists is that, at best, they come up with only "soft" objectivity rather than really "hard" objectivity. But here the tables can be turned, and we can ask the canonical pragmatic question, what is the difference here that really makes a difference? What really is the difference between the type of objectivity that we humans can achieve and the presumably super-hard objectivity? I suggest – in a Wittgensteinian spirit – that this "super-hard objectivity" really turns out to be a diaphanous illusion.
2. Appeal to competing intuitions and temperaments may be the beginning of philosophical dispute, but nothing is finally resolved

by simply appealing to them. The difficult work consists in developing arguments based on these intuitions, and answering objections to the theses that one advances. I have tried to show that one can develop a pragmatic conception of justification, truth, intersubjectivity, and objectivity that avoids appealing to the final end of inquiry, ideal conditions of justification, and does not lead to "bad relativism" or conventionalism.

3. Rorty distinguishes two different attitudes that we can take toward intuitions: (a) an ecumenical attitude where we try to harmonize intuitions and to accommodate as many of these as possible; and (b) a more revolutionary stance where by we are fully prepared to turn a deaf ear to what our opponents claim to be their primary intuitions. Sometimes, it is necessary to say, "so much the worse for your old intuitions; start working up some new ones." It is desirable to be ecumenical as long as it is reasonable. (This is always a matter of judgment.) As reasonable disputants, we ought to try to do justice to those strongly held intuitions of our opponents. But if someone "digs in" obstinately and is unable to come up with reasonable arguments to support their intuitions, then it is fair game to say "so much the worse for your old intuitions."[25]

4. If James is right (as I think he is), it is unrealistic and undesirable to think that we will ever escape from some form of the clash of intuitions and temperaments. This pluralistic clash energizes philosophical speculation and enlivens philosophical debate. Sometimes it is just the slings and arrows that we feel from those who oppose us that drive us to a more subtle articulation of a philosophical orientation. This is the way in which I think it is best to view the development of pragmatism from Peirce to Brandom and Habermas. And as any good pragmatist knows, nobody has the final word.

6

Experience after the Linguistic Turn

In 1953, in an article entitled "Logical Positivism, Language, and the Reconstruction of Metaphysics," Gustav Bergmann set out to describe the new style of philosophizing, which he characterized as the "linguistic turn." Speaking of philosophers primarily influenced by logical positivism, he tells us: "They all accept the linguistic turn Wittgenstein initiated in the *Tractatus*. To be sure, they interpret and develop it in their several ways, hence the disagreements; yet they are under its spell" (Bergmann 1953, p. 63). In 1964, explaining why philosophers *should* make the linguistic turn, he amplifies his remarks:

All linguistic philosophers talk about the world by means of talking about a suitable language. This is the linguistic turn, the fundamental gambit as to method, on which ordinary and ideal language philosophers (OLP, ILP) agree. Equally fundamentally, they disagree on what is in this sense a "language" and what makes it "suitable." Clearly one may execute the turn. The question is why one should. I shall mention three reasons.

First. Words are used either ordinarily (commonsensically) or philosophically. On this distinction, above all, the method rests. The prelinguistic philosophers did not make it. Yet they use words philosophically. *Prima facie* such uses are unintelligible. They require commonsensical explication. The method insists that we provide it. ... *Second.* Much of the paradox, absurdity, and opacity of prelinguistic philosophy stems from failure to distinguish between speaking and speaking about speaking. Such failure, or confusion, is harder to avoid than one may think. The method is the safest way of avoiding it. *Third.*

Some things any conceivable language merely shows. Not that these things are literally "ineffable"; rather, the proper (and safe) way of speaking about them is to speak about (the syntax and interpretation of a) language. (Bergmann 1964, p. 177)[1]

In 1967 Richard Rorty canonized the phrase "The Linguistic Turn," as the title of his classic anthology.

The purpose of this present volume is to provide materials for reflection on the most recent philosophical revolution, that of linguistic philosophy. I shall mean by "linguistic philosophy" the view that philosophical problems are problems which may be solved (or dissolved) either by reforming language, or by understanding more about the language we presently use. This view is considered by many as the most important philosophical discovery of our time, and indeed, of the ages. (Rorty 1967, p. 3)

In his magisterial introduction to *The Linguistic Turn*, Rorty surveys the varieties of linguistic philosophy that were prevalent at the time, in order to elucidate their metaphilosophical presuppositions. A careful reading of his introduction discloses Rorty's own ambivalence. On the one hand, he speaks of progress in philosophy "as movement toward a contemporary consensus." On the other hand, he also tells us that in the past every revolution in philosophy has failed and that there are reasons to believe that this will also be the fate of the linguistic turn. Even if we think of the linguistic turn with reference to those philosophers who are roughly classified as "analytic," not only is there disagreement, but their varying conceptions of language are all over the place. The more carefully one examines what Bergmann, Carnap, Ryle, Black, Austin, Strawson, Wittgenstein, Quine, Sellars, Davidson, and others mean by language and the linguistic turn, the more difficult it becomes to speak even about family resemblances. But this is not the end of the confusion about the linguistic turn. The phrase "the linguistic turn" has been used to characterize Habermas's theory of communicative action and discourse theory of ethics, Heidegger's late philosophy, Gadamer's ontological hermeneutics, Derrida's deconstruction, and Foucault's discourse theory. Furthermore, the term has been taken up by thinkers across the humanistic and social science disciplines – and it has been hotly debated. One of the most controversial discussions among historians and feminists has been about whether the so-called linguistic turn displaces the direct appeal to experience. As the intellectual historian Martin Jay comments, "In fact, the unlamented 'demise of experience' became in some quarters almost conventional wisdom" (Jay 2005, p. 3). One commentator tells us that the expression "the linguistic turn" became "a catch-all phrase for divergent critiques of established historical paradigms, narratives, and chronologies, encompassing not only poststructural-ist linguistic criticism, linguistic theory, and philosophy but also cultural and symbolic anthropology, new historicism and gender theory" (Canning 1994, p. 369).[2]

Rorty has played a major role in furthering the linguistic turn in the revival of pragmatism. But this has also been a mixed blessing. There are still many thinkers who take Rorty's idiosyncratic version of pragmatism as canonical – and what is worse, they accept his tendentious readings of the classical pragmatists as authoritative. Although he frequently expresses his ambivalence about the linguistic turn, Rorty has also been its champion. In *The Linguistic Turn* he doesn't hesitate to speak about the progress achieved by the linguistic turn, which he calls "the most recent philosophical revolution." Despite his sustained and relentless critique of the varieties of epistemological and semantic representationalism, Rorty favors the replacement of representationalism by the idea of alternative *incommensurable vocabularies*.[3] Unfortunately, Rorty bears a primary (but not exclusive) responsibility for denigrating the significance of the concept of experience in pragmatism – and he has been vigorously attacked for this.[4]

In "Dewey's Metaphysics" (1977) Rorty takes Dewey to task for wanting to create a metaphysical system. He agrees with Santayana's critique of Dewey that the very idea of a "naturalistic metaphysics" is a contradiction in terms. Rorty cites Dewey's remark, written near the end of his life, about a proposed new edition of *Experience and Nature* in which he spoke about "changing the title as well as the subject matter from *Nature and Experience* [*sic*] to *Nature and Culture*." In a letter to his friend Arthur Bentley, Dewey wrote: "I was dumb not to have seen the need for such a shift when the old text was written. I was still hopeful that the philosophic word 'Experience' could be redeemed by being returned to its idiomatic usages – which was a piece of historic folly, the hope I mean."[5] Rorty not only mocks and dismisses a metaphysics of experience; he asserts that we are better off if we simply drop any reference to 'experience' – a term that he thinks is excessively vague and confusing. Dewey, he tells us, never succeeded in developing a coherent notion of experience that would allow him to combine Hegel's historicism with a Darwinian naturalism. The tenor of Rorty's critique of Dewey is evident in the following passage:

> What Kant had called "the constitution of the empirical world by synthesis of intuitions under concepts," Dewey wanted to call "interactions in which both extra-organic things and organisms partake." But he wanted this harmless sounding naturalistic phrase to have the same generality, and to accomplish the same epistemological feats, which Kant's talk of the "constitution of objects" had performed. He wanted phrases like "transaction with the environment" and "adaptations to conditions" to be simultaneously naturalistic and transcendental – to be common-sensical remarks about human perception and knowledge viewed as a psychologist views it and also to be expressions of "generic traits of existence." So he blew up notions like "transaction" and "situation" until they sounded as mysterious as "prime matter" or "thing-in-itself." (Rorty 1977, p. 84).

Rorty is just as dismissive of James's many references to 'experience' – a word that appears in almost every text that James ever wrote. In short, Rorty's pragmatism is a pragmatism *without* experience. And frankly, I agree with those who have strongly argued that to eliminate experience from pragmatism (old or new) is to eviscerate pragmatism, to leave us with a gutless shadow of pragmatism.[6]

Frequently the appeal to experience by the classical American pragmatists does function like a *deus ex machina* that is supposed to solve (or dissolve) all sorts of knotty philosophical problems. It would be a fruitless task to try to develop an overarching theory that encompasses *all* the meanings and uses of experience by the classical American pragmatists. (It would be equally hopeless to try to encompass the multifarious meanings and uses of 'language' and the 'linguistic turn' into a single coherent theory or narrative.) But this should not dissuade us from recovering what is insightful and still relevant in the reflections on experience by the classical American pragmatists. They certainly took experience to be central to their philosophical visions – and if we want to do justice to their way of thinking, we must understand why experience played such a central role for them. But the primary issue is a philosophical one. I argue that the fashionable and apparently well-entrenched dichotomy between experience and the linguistic turn is just the sort of dichotomy that pragmatists ought to reject. This dichotomy – this either/or – is at once obfuscating and sterile. I shall elucidate the contributions to our concept(s) of experience in the works of Peirce, James, and Dewey. And I shall also indicate briefly George H. Mead's contribution to understanding language. Finally – and most important – I shall argue that *after* the linguistic turn, a pragmatic orientation demands a thoughtful and nuanced understanding of the meaning and significance of experience. An enriched pragmatism can integrate the linguistic turn with a subtle appreciation of the role and varieties of experience.

Peirce: Three Categorial Aspects of Experience

One of the features of Peirce's philosophy that has not had an enduring philosophical influence – with the exception of Peirce scholars – is his categorial scheme of Firstness, Secondness, and Thirdness. There are several reasons for this neglect. Many of Peirce's claims about meaning, truth, inference, inquiry, and community can be restated without any reference to his categorial scheme. Despite the fact that the appeal to categories has played an essential role in philosophy from Aristotle through Kant to Hegel, most twentieth-century philosophers have been wary of appealing to categorial schemes. Furthermore, to identify categories with ordinal numbers seems excessively formal and almost empty. One may wonder whether such a categorial scheme can provide any philosophical illumination. Finally, Peirce employs his categorial scheme in different domains (logic, semiotics, phenomenology, and metaphysics), and in ways that are not always consistent. Yet I believe that Peirce's categorical scheme of Firstness, Secondness, and Thirdness – especially as developed in his mature philosophy – is a powerful heuristic device for grasping what he means by experience.

Consider one of Peirce's typical statements about phenomenology and the categories:

> Phenomenology is that branch of science which is treated in Hegel's *Phenomenologie des Geistes* (a work far too inaccurate to be recommended to mature scholars, though perhaps the most profound ever written) in which the author makes out what are the elements, or, if you please, the kinds of elements, that are invariably present in whatever is, in any

sense in mind. According to the present writer these *universal categories* are three. Since all three are invariably present, a pure idea of any one, absolutely distinct from the others, is impossible; indeed, anything like a satisfactorily clear examination of them is a work of long and active meditation. They may be termed *Firstness*, *Secondness*, and *Thirdness*.

Firstness is that which is such as it is positively and regardless of anything else.

Secondness is that which is as it is in a second something's being as it is, regardless of any third.

Thirdness is that whose being consists in bringing about a Secondness. (Peirce 1998, p. 267)

This passage calls for several comments. When Peirce claims that these elements are invariably present in whatever is in any sense "in mind," he doesn't mean that the categories are "merely" mental. They are elements of all phenomena. It would have been better if he had said that these are elements "we are aware of," to avoid any suggestion that they are "merely" *in* the mind. The categories are intended to designate features or aspects of all phenomena. These features are *distinguishable*, but not *separable* from each other. All of these elements are always present together, so it is impossible to have a "pure idea" of any one of them. Sometimes Peirce uses the technical term 'precision' to describe the mode of discrimination that "arises from *attention to* one element and *neglect of* the other" (Peirce 1992, p. 2). Moreover, the above statements about these categories are so abstract that, taken alone, they are not very helpful for understanding the meaning or importance of these categories. So let us turn to some of Peirce's examples of Firstness, Secondness, and Thirdness. (I focus primarily on Secondness because it is the category most relevant for grasping what Peirce takes to be distinctive about experience.)

To illustrate Firstness, Peirce tells us to "look at anything red."

That redness is positively what it is. Contrast may heighten our consciousness of it; but the redness is not relative to anything; it is absolute, or positive. If one imagines or remembers red, his imagination will be either vivid or dim; but that will not, in the least, affect the quality of the redness, which may be brilliant or dull, in either case. ... The quality in itself has no vividness or dimness. In itself, then, it cannot be consciousness. It is, indeed, in itself a mere possibility. ... Possibility, the mode of being of Firstness, is the embryo of being. It is not nothing. It is not existence. (Peirce 1998, p. 268)

Initially, one might think that Peirce is merely reiterating the traditional doctrine of our awareness of secondary qualities. But to jump to this inference would be a serious mistake. This becomes immediately evident when Peirce goes on to say:

> We not only have an immediate acquaintance with Firstness in the qualities of feelings and sensations, but we attribute it to outward things. We think that a piece of iron has a quality in it that a piece of brass has not, which consists in the steadily continuing *possibility* of its being attracted by a magnet. In fact, it seems undeniable that there really are such possibilities, and that, though they are not existences, they are not *nothing*. They are possibilities, and nothing more. (Peirce 1998, p. 269)

For Peirce there is Firstness, or a qualitative aspect, of *every* phenomenon. Look at the range of examples that Peirce uses to illustrate what he means by Firstness or quality: "the scarlet of your royal liveries, the quality itself, independently of its being perceived or remembered" (8.329); "the quality of the emotion upon contemplating a fine mathematical demonstration, and the quality of feeling of love" (1.304); "a vague, unobjectified, still less subjectified, sense of redness, or of salt taste, or of an ache, or of grief or joy, or of a prolonged musical note" (1.303). Qualities, then, are not subjective feelings that are somehow locked up in the privacy of our minds (even though a feeling may have its own distinctive quality). "The tragedy of King Lear has its Firstness, its flavor *sui generis*" (1.531).[7]

When Peirce says that we have "immediate acquaintance with Firstness," he is *not* saying that we have immediate or *direct knowledge* of these qualities. We can speak of knowledge or our epistemic awareness *only* when we introduce the category of Thirdness. Of course, we know that we have an awareness of Firstness, but this "knowledge that" is not to be identified or confused with our awareness of qualities. For Peirce there is no direct immediate intuitive *knowledge* of anything. (He emphatically rejects the Myth of the Given.)

We should note that in the above passages, Peirce several times states that Firstness is *not existence*. This provides a clue to how Peirce understands Secondness, the category that he thinks is the easiest to comprehend of the three categories.

> Of the three, Secondness is the easiest to comprehend, being the element that the rough-and-tumble of the world renders most promi-

nent. We talk of *hard* facts. That hardness, that compulsiveness of experience, is Secondness. A door is slightly ajar. You try to open it. Something prevents. You put your shoulder against it, and experience a sense of effort and a sense of resistance. These are not two forms of consciousness; they are two aspects of one two-sided consciousness. It is inconceivable that there should be any effort without resistance, or any resistance without a contrary effort. This double-sided consciousness is Secondness. All consciousness, all being awake, consists in a sense of reaction between *ego* and *non-ego*. (Peirce 1998, p. 268)

Once again, we must not think that Secondness is *merely* subjective. "We not only thus experience Secondness, but we attribute it to outward things: which we regard as so many individual objects, or quasi-selves, reacting on one another" (ibid.). Existence itself is Secondness. "The existent is that which reacts against other things" (8.191). We can see why Peirce uses ordinal numbers to name his categories. Firstness is monadic, and Secondness is dyadic – it always involves doubleness.

Secondness is the category that brings out the feature of experience that Peirce most wants to emphasize. Experience involves bruteness, constraint, "over-and-againstness." Experience is our great teacher. And experience takes place by a series of surprises. "It is by surprises that experience teaches all she deigns to teach us" (Peirce 1998, p. 154). This element of surprise is essential in any experimentation, for we learn the most from surprises – and disappointments.

> In all the works on pedagogy that ever I read ... I don't remember that anyone has advocated a system of teaching by practical jokes, mostly cruel. That, however, describes the method of our great teacher, Experience. She says,
>
> > Open your mouth and shut your eyes
> > And I'll give you something to make you wise;
>
> And thereupon she keeps her promise, and seems to take her pay in the fun of tormenting us. (Ibid.)

We grasp why experience is categorized as Secondness when Peirce writes: "I ask you whether at that instant of surprise there is not a double consciousness, on the one hand of an Ego, which is simply the expected idea suddenly broken off, on the other hand of the Non-ego, which is the Strange Intruder, in his abrupt entrance" (ibid.).

Let us turn to Thirdness. Although all three categories are intended to discriminate or prescind elements or aspects of every phenomenon, some of Peirce's most original thinking concerns Thirdness. This category is labeled "Thirdness" because everything that it designates involves triadic relations. Habits, laws, rules, inferences, intentions, practices, conduct, concepts, "would-be's" (subjunctive conditionals), and especially signs are all classified as Thirdness. One of Peirce's favorite examples of Thirdness is "giving."

> A gives B to C. This does not consist of A's throwing B away and its accidentally hitting C. ... If that were all, it would not be a genuine triadic relation, but merely one dyadic relation followed by another. There need be no motion of the thing given. Giving is a transfer of property. Now right is a matter of law, and law is a matter of thought and meaning. (1.345)

We cannot give an adequate account of the relation of giving by describing it in terms of physical (or even mental) juxtaposition – a series of dyadic relations. What is distinctive about giving are the conventions, rules, or customs by virtue of which an act is giving and not just displacement. These conventions, rules, or customs are essential constituents of the type of action or conduct that is properly designated 'giving.' Consider the closely related example of A's making a contract with C. "To say that A signs the document D and C signs the document D, no matter what the contents of that document, does not make a contract. The contract lies in the intent. And what is the intent? It is that certain conditional rules shall govern the conduct of A and of C" (1.475). As Rorty has shown, Peirce's Thirdness anticipates Wittgenstein's discussion of rules and the application of rules that has played such a prominent role in analytic philosophy (Rorty 1961a). The most notable example of Thirdness is a sign. In one of his several definitions of "sign" he tells us that a sign is "anything which is so determined by something else, called its Object, and so determines an effect upon a person, which effect I call its Interpretant, that the latter is thereby mediately determined by the former" (Peirce 1998, p. 493). Or again: "I will say that a sign is anything, of whatsoever mode of being, which mediates between an object and an interpretant; since it is both determined by the object *relatively to the interpretant*, and determines the interpretant *in reference to the object*, in such wise as to cause the interpretant to be determined by the object through the mediation of this 'sign'" (Peirce 1998, p. 410).[8] These are not the clearest statements, but what is crucial is that Peirce objected to any account of signs that restricts the analysis to the sign and the signified (a dyadic account). An adequate theory of signs must take account of the *interpretant*.[9] (Peirce's insistence on the triadic character of signs became the basis for Charles Morris's introduction of the technical term 'pragmatics,' which he distinguished from semantics and syntax. Syntax is restricted to the formal relations of signs; semantics deals with the relations of signs and the objects that signify, but pragmatics makes essential reference to the use and interpretation of signs.)

Let us stand back and see what Peirce is showing us with the phenomenological application of his categorial scheme. Early modern empiricists assigned prominence to experience because the appeal to experience was taken to be vital for testing what we claim to know. Experience constrains and checks our fancies, prejudices, and speculations. When empiricist and phenomenalist philosophers became more concerned with the character of "sensations," "impressions," "sense data," etc., the brute constraining force of experience tended to get obscured and neglected. But the insight that originally led philosophers to valorize experience – its brute compulsiveness – is what Peirce underscores with Secondness. Acknowledgment of this bruteness – the way in which experience "says NO!" – is required to make sense of the self-corrective character of inquiry and experimentation. Experiments must always finally be checked by experience. Peirce would have been repelled and horrified by Rorty's claim that the *only* constraints upon us are "conversational constraints." To speak in this manner is to ignore the facticity, the surprise, shock, and brute constraint of our experiential encounters.

One of the great dangers of the so-called "linguistic turn" is the way it keeps sliding into linguistic idealism, where there is nothing that constrains our language. When McDowell begins his *Mind and World* by describing the "interminable oscillation" between the appeal to the Given and a "frictionless coherentism," he expresses the anxiety that there is nothing that really constrains or ties down our network of beliefs. When Habermas engages in a self-critique of his epistemic theory of truth, and is worried that even an "ideal justification" may fail to do justice to "realistic intuitions," he is giving expression to the same philosophical anxiety (see chapter 8). When Popper criticizes the logical positivist appeal to verification and argues that falsification is essential for critical inquiry, he is reiterating Peirce's point (see "Falsifiability," in Popper 1959, pp. 57–73). Or again, when Gadamer shows how tragedy enriches our understanding of experience, he calls attention to the painful brute Secondness of experience. "[E]xperience is initially always experience of negation: something is not what we supposed it to be" (Gadamer 1989, p. 354).

Consider again McDowell's description of the oscillation between the temptation to appeal to some version of the Given and the temptation to adopt some version of coherentism that loses contact with reality. I have already argued that most of the arguments that Sellars and others have presented to expose the Myth of the Given are anticipated in Peirce's 1868–9 Cognition papers. So how does Peirce escape the "interminable oscillation" that McDowell takes to be endemic to modern philosophy? Peirce – like Wittgenstein, Sellars, McDowell, Brandom, Putnam, Habermas, Rorty, and Davidson – maintains that there is something irreducible about anything that we take to be epistemic.[10] In Peirce's scheme anything that is properly classified as epistemic exemplifies Thirdness. The epistemic *authority* of any cognitive claim is always – in principle – open to challenge, modification, revision, and even abandonment. One of the deepest and most pervasive confusions that gives rise to the Myth of the Given is the confusion of *brute constraint* and *epistemic authority*. This is the confusion of Secondness and Thirdness. There is an enormous temptation to confuse the fact that we are constrained (Secondness) with the claim that what constrains us has epistemic authority (Thirdness). This temptation gives rise to one of the most tenacious forms of the Myth of the Given – a Given that is supposed to serve as the epistemically authoritative foundation for empirical knowledge. Peirce even helps us to understand why it is so *tempting* to make this misleading identification. Secondness and Thirdness are distinguishable, but inseparable, elements or aspects of every phenomenon. Experience itself is *not* pure Secondness; it manifests elements of Firstness and Thirdness. We *prescind* the aspects of Firstness (quality), Secondness (brute compulsion), and Thirdness (the inferential or epistemic character) from experience.

Consequently, as soon as we raise the question, "*What* constrains us?" we are dealing with Thirdness. But there is nothing mysterious here. If we reflect again on Peirce's examples of Secondness, we say that we experience shock, surprise, resistance, constraint. But as soon as we ask *what* precisely the character of this experience is and seek to *describe* what constrains us, we are dealing with an epistemic issue (Thirdness). There may be multiple descriptions that are, of course, fallible. The distinction that Peirce makes between the compulsion of Secondness and the epistemic authority of Thirdness is closely related to the distinction that Wittgenstein makes between causal and logical determination – a distinction taken up by many philosophers influenced by Wittgenstein. But Secondness and Thirdness do not line up with the familiar distinction between *causes* and *reasons*. Thirdness includes far more than reasons. Habits, conduct, and signs are all examples of Thirdness. Although many linguistic analytic philosophers appeal to the distinction between reasons and causes, they rarely provide a clear explication of what they mean by *causes*. Some conceptions of causality involve the type of constraint that Peirce singles out as Secondness, but there are many accounts of causality (for example, Humean regularity theories) that don't involve constraint. Peirce himself argues that causality involves an appeal to laws. Consequently, causality involves Thirdness.

Peirce not only avoids the Myth of the Given and the aporias of linguistic idealism, he gives a nonfoundational account of experience that does justice to its brute compulsiveness and its epistemic openness and fallibility. His phenomenological account helps to undercut much of the sterile debate about realism and antirealism in contemporary philosophy. I don't think we need anything more than Secondness to do justice to what philosophers call their "realistic intuitions."[11] We do not need to reify a realm of facts that exist independently of any language, thought, or inquiry. Peirce does justice to the fallibility and openness of all justificatory practices and inquiry without losing touch with a reality "that is independent of vagaries of me and you" (Peirce 1992, p. 52). Contrary to the prevailing prejudice that the linguistic turn displaces old-fashioned talk about experience, Peirce's conception of experience helps us to escape from some of the dead-ends of the linguistic turn.[12]

James: The Varieties of Experience

Scholars of pragmatism debate the extent to which William James really understood Peirce. James publicly acknowledged his intellectual debt to Peirce. But when James tells us what he learned from Peirce, it is sometimes difficult to recognize the relation between "James's Peirce" and what Peirce actually says. Reading their correspondence during their lifelong friendship is painfully moving. Despite Peirce's sharp barbs and quixotic behavior, James always remained his loyal friend and supporter. (He created a fund to support Peirce at a time when he was barely earning any income.) And it is touching – almost pathetic – to witness how the isolated and lonely Peirce sought over and over again to "educate" his immensely popular and success-ful friend. Peirce thought that James made grave mistakes, and he patiently tried to correct them.[13] James never quite grasps the point of Peirce's categorical scheme; he simply doesn't "get it." But James is masterful in describing what Peirce calls Firstness – the qualitative immediacy of experience. If ever there was a philosopher who didn't just talk about getting back to the "things themselves," but showed us how to do it, it was William James. (James's phenomenological descriptions earned the respect of Husserl and endeared him to many later phenomenologists.) There is also plenty of evidence that James was sensitive to the brute compulsiveness that Peirce took to be characteristic of Secondness. But James was tone deaf to what Peirce meant by Thirdness; and there is little evidence that he ever grasped the point of Peirce's semiotics.

James sought to describe the variety of human experiences in all their thickness and fluid living quality. James complements Peirce, although there are also some sharp conflicts.[14] I will limit myself to four aspects of James's reflections on experience: (1) his critique of traditional empiricist accounts of experience; (2) his radical empiri-cist understanding of 'pure experience'; (3) his pluralistic sense of the varieties of experience (including religious experience); and (4) his subtle interplay of language and experience.

(1) In his *Principles of Psychology*, James already criticized what he took to be the artificial and deeply misleading traditional empiricist accounts of experience. Experience does not consist of *discrete* atomic units that simply follow or are associated with each other. This is an intellectualist abstraction of philosophers, not an account of concrete experience as it is lived. James emphasizes the dynamic, flowing quality of the "stream of experience" – what he sometimes called the "muchness" and pluralistic variety of experience. Contrary to Hume and those influenced by him, James argued that we experience "relations," "continuity," and "connections" *directly*. We experience *activity* – its tensions, resistances, and tendencies. We feel "the tendency, the obstacle, the will, the strain, the triumph, or the passive

giving up, just as [we feel] the time, the space, the swiftness or intensity, the movement, the weight and color, the pain and pleasure, the complexity, or whatever remaining characters the situation may involve" (James 1997, p. 282). He does not denigrate or underestimate the importance of our conceptual activity, but concepts are never quite adequate to capture the concreteness of experience. To say this is not to claim that there is something about experience that is in principle knowable, but that we cannot know. Rather, it is to affirm that there is more to experience than *knowing*. James criticizes the epistemological prejudice, which assumes that the only or primary role that experience plays in our lives is to provide us with knowledge. Paraphrasing Hamlet, James might well have said to his fellow philosophers: "There are more things in experience than are dreamt of in your philosophy."

(2) James characterizes his version of empiricism as "radical empiricism" and speaks of "pure experience."[15] As so frequently happens with James, he gives many different (not always consistent) descriptions of what he means by "radical empiricism."[16] Let us pursue a line of thought developed in his famous "Does 'Consciousness' Exist?" There James declares:

> To deny plumply that 'consciousness' exists seems so absurd on the face of it – for undeniably 'thoughts' do exist – that I fear some readers will follow me no farther. Let me then immediately explain that I mean only to deny the word stands for an entity, but to insist most emphatically that it does stand for a function. There is, I mean, no aboriginal stuff or quality of being, contrasted with that of which material objects are made, out of which our thoughts of them are made; but there is a function in experience which thoughts perform, and for the performance of which this quality of being is invoked. (James 1997, pp. 169–70)

James introduces his notion of "pure experience" and succinctly states his thesis:

> My thesis is that we start with the supposition that there is only one primal stuff or material of the world, a stuff of which everything is composed, and if we call that stuff 'pure experience,' the knowing can

easily be explained as a particular relation towards one another into which portions of pure experience may enter. (James 1997, p. 170)

What precisely does James mean by this striking claim? And what is his philosophical motivation for making this seemingly paradoxical assertion? Basically, James is rejecting the standard epistemological and ontological dichotomies: thoughts and things, consciousness and content, the mental and the physical. He is not denying that we make such distinctions, but they are functional and internal to "pure experience." Against the idea of some sort of basic dualism, James writes:

> *Experience, I believe, has no such inner duplicity; and the separation of it into consciousness and content comes, not by way of subtraction, but by way of addition* – the addition, to a given concrete piece of it, of other sets of experiences, in connection with which severally its use or function may be of two different kinds. (James 1997, p. 172)

Suppose we consider the example of the experience of a room with a desk and a book that I am reading. I may treat this in a commonsense manner where I think of it as a "collection of physical things cut out from the environing world of other physical things with which these physical things have actual and potential relations" (James 1997, p. 173). But I can also treat "those self-same things" as part of my subjective mental life – as part of my own biography. In effect, one and the same experience can function in two different narratives. So the same bit of experience may be part of the "reader's personal biography" or part of the "history of which the room is part."

> The physical and mental operations form curiously incompatible groups. As a room, the experience has occupied that spot and had that environment for thirty years. As your field of consciousness it may never have existed until now. As a room, attention will go on to discover endless new details in it. ... As your mental state merely, few new ones will emerge under attention's eye. As a room, it will take an earthquake, or a gang of men, and in any case a certain amount of time to destroy it. As your subjective state, the closing of your eyes, or any instantaneous play of your fancy will suffice. (James 1997, p. 174)

James expands his proposal in order to show that it is applicable to our concepts. Despite the initial attractiveness of James's thesis about the double function of pure experience, there are many serious problems that he doesn't squarely confront. When James asserts that "there is only one primal stuff or material of the world, a stuff of which everything is composed," he invites all sorts of misunderstandings because this phrasing suggests that there is a monistic primal stuff – a claim that contradicts his pluralism. Bertrand Russell thought that the term 'pure experience' pointed "to a lingering influence of idealism." " 'Experience,' " Russell claimed, "like 'consciousness,' must be a product, not part of the primary stuff of the world" (Russell 1949, p. 24). Although James asserts that one and the same bit of experience can be taken as physical and mental, objective and subjective, he doesn't really explain why or how this comes about. He vividly indicates the characteristics that we normally associate with the physical features of a room and with our subjective awareness of a room – but this is not an *explanation* of the genesis of the two different narratives to which one and the same piece of experience belongs.

There are many questions that can be raised about James's conception of 'pure experience'; nevertheless, the problem he is struggling with is a difficult one – one that continues to preoccupy philosophers (even after the linguistic turn). James argues for an alternative to representational theories of mind – theories that presuppose that the mind has impressions or ideas that *represent* objects that are "outside of the mind." These representative theories can take a variety of forms – Cartesian, Lockean, Humean, Kantian, neo-Kantian – but they all presuppose a dualism (ontological or epistemological) between the mental representation and what is represented. "Representative theories ... violate the reader's sense of life, which knows no intervening mental image but seems to see the room and book immediately just as they are" (James 1997, p. 173). Normally, we take the room that we perceive to be one and the same as the room that actually (physically) exists.[17]

There is still another perspective for understanding "pure experience." Whitehead was more perceptive than he realized when he claimed that "Does 'Consciousness' Exist?" marks the end of an era that began with Descartes. It also marks the beginning of a new era – *the decentering of the subject* – a theme that has been in the foreground of linguistic poststructuralist thought in writers like Foucault, Derrida, and Lyotard.[18] James's dismantling of the subject – the autonomous ego – anticipates the post-linguistic critiques of the philosophy of consciousness and subjectivity.

(3) Philosophers frequently focus on the advantages of making the linguistic turn, but they rarely take account of the losses. Rorty, for example, takes James and Dewey to be among his heroes, but as he tells the story of contemporary philosophy, he sees Quine, Sellars, and Davidson as advancing pragmatic themes precisely because of the philosophical finesse they have achieved by making the linguistic turn. The drawback is the shrinkage of what we consider to be a legitimate topic for philosophical investigation. Nowhere is this more evident than in the way in which analytically trained philosophers have neglected any serious discussion of religious experience.[19] Today, when the topic of religion has become so alive and pressing throughout the world, it is striking how little philosophers have to say about it. This was certainly not true for James. Throughout his career, James's most central concern was religious experience – and it colors almost everything he wrote about pragmatism, radical experience, and free will. When James introduced the "principle of pragmatism" in 1898, he first applied it to confronting the question: "Is matter the producer of all things? Or is there a God too?" (James 1997, p. 350). Even before he introduced pragmatism, his early collection of philosophical articles contained his controversial essay, "The Will to Believe" (which he subsequently declared should have been more appropriately entitled "The Right to Believe"). But it was only with his Gifford Lectures (1901–2), subsequently published as *The Varieties of Religious Experience*, that James turned his full attention to exploring religious experience with enormous sensitivity and breadth.

To appreciate how James approaches religious experience, it is helpful to sketch his existential situation. James had many loyalties. We should never forget that he was a scientist. He attended medical school and studied medicine in Germany. He spent three years as an assistant to Louis Agassiz on a biological expedition along the Amazon River. His first position at Harvard was as instructor in anatomy and physiology. Even in his *Principles of Psychology*, he typically traces psychological functions back to their biological and neurobiological origins. He was a consistent defender of the Darwinian theory of evolution. He was a committed fallibilist; he hated all forms of dogmatism and fanaticism. James – perhaps, in part, due to his father's influence – always felt that religious experience enhanced human life. For all his commitment to the rigorous demands of scientific inquiry, he had an almost visceral reaction to doctrines of reductive materialism, determinism, and scientism. For James there is *no* incompatibility between taking the canons of scientific inquiry seriously and responding in depth to religious and spiritual concerns.[20] To be sure, he never had much interest in the communal or institutional aspects of religion. He was indifferent to theology; it left him cold. But he was also suspicious of philosophical "intellectualism" that failed to capture the vividness and variety of religious experiences. He did not approach the topic of religious experience dispassionately; it had deep personal significance for him – and he never denied this. Throughout his life he suffered from bouts of melancholic depression and was tempted to commit suicide. He felt that it was his personal religious experience that got him through these dark periods. James wanted to achieve two goals in his *Varieties*:

> *first*, to defend (against all the prejudices of my class) "experience" against "philosophy" as being the real backbone of the world's religious life – I mean prayer, guidance, and all that sort of thing immediately and privately felt, as against high and noble general laws of our destiny and the world's meaning; and *second*, to make the hearer or reader believe, what I myself invincibly do believe, that although all the manifestations of religion may have been absurd (I mean the creeds and theories) yet the life of it as a whole is mankind's most important function. (James 1920, vol. 2, p. 127)[21]

Consequently, James identified with *"the feelings, acts, and experiences of individual men in their solitude, so far as they apprehend themselves to stand in relation to whatever they may consider the divine"* (James 1920, pp. 31–2). The *Varieties* is rich in its detailed descriptions of the accounts of mystics, saints, born-again converts, and other "religious geniuses," as James called them. James was drawn to the more extreme forms of religious feeling and expression because he felt that such limit cases helped to clarify more normal expressions of religious feeling. He was fascinated with what the subliminal, subconscious self contributes to religious experience. "James," as Martin Jay comments "felt most warmly toward the religions that he saw as experimental, non-dogmatic, open-minded, and spiritually alive" (Jay 2005, p. 107, n. 100). Yet at the same time, James explored some of the darker and more intense religious experiences of the "sick soul" (which many have suggested is actually a description of his own intense suffering). The *Varieties* slights the epistemological and metaphysical questions that frequently preoccupy philosophers of religion. But there is a great lesson to be learned from James, which extends far beyond his description of religious experiences. Few philosophers before or after William James have been his equal in their ability to find language to describe the precise shading of the varieties of the full range of human experiences.

(4) Readers of James – especially philosophers – frequently have two extreme reactions to him. They detest him or love him. His style is charming, but charm is not normally a virtue that philosophers prize highly. Trying to pin down any of his key terms such as 'experience' or even 'pragmatism' is frustrating. At his best he reads like a virtuoso of *belles-lettres* and at his worst he is just fuzzy, vague, and superficial – or so his unsympathetic critics complain. He can't be taken seriously as a philosopher. Many analytically trained philosophers who cherish clarity, precision, and rigorous argumentation take a dim view of James (although one of the most tough-minded, analytically trained philosophers, Hilary Putnam, has consistently argued that many of James's *arguments* are sophisticated and subtle). For those who love him (philosophers and nonphilosophers), James's style, wit, insouciance, and deflationary prose are extremely attractive. James brilliantly deflates grandiose philosophical pretensions, for he has the knack of vividly bringing us back to everyday experiences. James would have been unimpressed by the reasons that Gustav Bergmann gives for why philosophers should make the linguistic turn. He would have thought that it was downright perverse to advocate that philosophers *limit* themselves "to talk about the world by means of talking about a suitable language." If James were alive today, he might have reminded Bergmann that Wittgenstein taught us that there are many varieties of description, oriented by different human purposes and interests. James did not develop a systematic "philosophy of language," but he *showed* us (to use another Wittgensteinian expression) what language could do in

the hands of a skillful stylist to elicit and describe the nuances of human experience.

Dewey: The Darwinian Naturalization of Hegel

Earlier I cited Rorty's complaint that Dewey never developed a coherent account of experience that combines Hegel's historicism with Darwinian naturalism. To the contrary, I believe that Rorty is mistaken. That is precisely what Dewey *succeeded* in doing – or so I want to argue. Dewey's occasional vague talk about the meaning of experience should not keep us from appreciating his distinctive contribution. In my Prologue, I indicated that a source for the rich diversity of the classical pragmatists was their ability to draw upon different philosophical traditions. Dewey agreed with Hegel's critique of the fragmented quality of modernity and the disintegrative ethical and political consequences of rampant individualism. This early appeal of Hegelianism is reflected in Dewey's frequent use of organic metaphors and his reliance on the theory of the "social organism." Dewey recognized that Hegel had left a permanent deposit on his thinking. In his 1930 autobiographical essay, he wrote:

> I drifted away from Hegelianism in the next fifteen years; the word "drifting" expresses the slow and, for a long time, imperceptible character of the movement, though it does not convey the impression that there was an adequate cause for the change. Nevertheless I should never think of ignoring, much less denying, what an astute critic occasionally refers to as a novel discovery – that acquaintance with Hegel has left a permanent deposit in my thinking. The form, the schematism, of his system now seems to me artificial to the last degree. But in the content of his ideas there is often an extraordinary depth; in many of his analyses, taken out of their mechanical dialectical setting, an extraordinary acuteness. Were it possible for me to be a devotee to any system, I still should believe that there is greater richness and greater variety of insight in Hegel than in any other single systematic philosopher – though when I say this I exclude Plato, who still provides my favorite philosophic reading. (Dewey 1981, p. 8)

Nowhere is this "permanent deposit" more evident than in Dewey's appropriation and transformation of the Hegelian concept of experience (*Erfahrung*). Dewey shows how Hegel's insights into the rhythms of experience – its internal tensions and conflicts that give rise to a dynamic movement toward integration (*Aufhebung*) – take on more concrete experimental meaning when reformulated in the biological language of Darwin.[22] The early fruits of this naturalized Hegelianism are evident in Dewey's classic article "The Reflex Arc Concept in Psychology" (1896). Dewey criticizes the notion (popular at the time) of a reflex arc that presupposes "rigid distinctions between sensations, thoughts and acts." "The sensory stimulus is one thing, the central activity, standing for the idea, is another thing, and the motor discharge, standing for the act proper, is a third. As a result, the reflex arc is not a comprehensive, or organic, unity, but a patchwork of disjointed parts, mechanical conjunctions of unallied processes" (Dewey 1981, p. 137). We should replace this mechanical conception of the reflex arc with the idea of a dynamic *coordination* in which distinctions of sensory stimulus and motor response are changing functional phases within a unified circuit.

> The circle is a co-ordination, some of whose members have come into conflict with each other. It is the temporary disintegration and need of reconstitution which occasions, which affords the genesis of, the conscious distinction into sensory stimulus on one side and motor response on the other. The stimulus is that phase of the forming co-ordination which represents the conditions which have to be met in bringing it to a successful issue; the response is that phase of one and the same forming co-ordination which gives the key to meeting these conditions, which serves as instrument in effecting the successful co-ordination. They are therefore strictly correlative and contemporaneous. (Dewey 1981, p. 147)

This early article contains the germ of Dewey's conception of experience, which he elaborated and refined throughout his life.[23] Experience has both spatial and temporal reach; it is neither purely "subjective" nor "objective," neither "mental" nor "physical." The language that Dewey uses to characterize this coordination is incorporated in the instrumental logic of inquiry that he was soon to develop: "conflict," "problem," "reconstitution."

Like Peirce and James, Dewey is critical of traditional empiricist conceptions of experience (and for many of the same reasons).[24] He also felt – as James had emphasized – that the obsession with epistemology in modern philosophy distorted our approach to experience. Dewey wanted to recover the viability of our ordinary ways of speaking about experience: for example, when we speak about an "experienced craftsman" or the "memorable experiences" of hearing a great performance of Beethoven's last sonatas or having a fantastic meal at a Michelin three-star restaurant.

Inquiry typically arises from the conflicts and tensions within those experiences that are not primarily cognitive or reflective.[25] These experiences "may contain knowledge resulting from prior inquiries ... but not so that they dominate the situation and give it its peculiar flavor."

> Positively, anyone recognizes the difference between an experience of quenching thirst where the perception of water is a mere incident, and an experience of water where knowledge of what water is, is the controlling interest; or between the enjoyment of social converse among friends and a study deliberately made of the character of one of the participants; between aesthetic appreciation of a picture and an examination of it by a connoisseur to establish the artist, or by a dealer who has a commercial interest in determining its probable selling value. The distinction between the two types of experience is evident to anyone who will take the trouble to recall what he does most of the time when not engaged in meditation or inquiry. (Dewey 2007, p. 4)

To use a Heideggerian expression, our "being-in-the-world" consists of encounters and experiences that are not primarily "knowledge affairs."

In the above passage, Dewey speaks of "*an* experience," so the question arises, what is it that individuates *an* experience, what sets it apart from other experiences? "Experience occurs continuously, because the interaction of [a] live creature and environing conditions is involved in the very process of living. ... Oftentimes, however, the experience had is inchoate. Things are experienced but not in such a way that they are composed into *an* experience. There is distraction and dispersion" (Dewey 1981, p. 555). There may be a great variety of factors involved in *an* experience spanning stretches of space and time, but *an* experience is "saturated with a pervasive quality. Being ill with the grippe is an experience which includes an immense diversity of factors, but none the less is the one qualitatively unique experience which it is" (Dewey 2007, p. 6). Pervasive quality is close to Peirce's Firstness. Like Peirce, Dewey emphasizes that these qualities are not "merely subjective"; pervasive quality is not to be "regarded as a subjective state injected into an object which does not possess it" (ibid.). When Dewey first introduces the idea of a pervasive quality that unifies *an* experience, he doesn't refer to Peirce. But when Peirce's *Collected Papers* were published in the 1930s, Dewey acknowledged the strong convergence of Peirce's phenomenological description of Firstness with his notion of pervasive quality.[26] Dewey illustrates what he means by indicating how inquiry emerges out of and against the background of an "indeterminate situation." It is the situation itself that is "disturbed, troubled, ambiguous, confused, full of conflicting tendencies, obscure, etc."

> It is the *situation* that has these traits. *We* are doubtful because the situation is inherently doubtful. Personal states of doubt that are not evoked by and are not relative to some existential situation are pathological. ... Consequently, situations that are disturbed or troubled, confused or obscure, cannot be straightened out, cleared up and put in order, by manipulation of our personal states of mind. ... The habit of disposing of the doubtful as if it belonged only to *us* rather than to the existential situation in which we are caught and implicated is an inheritance from subjectivistic psychology. The biological antecedent conditions of an unsettled situation are involved in that state of imbalance in organic-environmental interactions. ... Restoration or integration can be effected ... only by operations which actually modify existing conditions, not merely "mental" processes. (Dewey 1981, pp. 227–8)

Dewey approaches inquiry and knowing from the perspective of those experiences or indeterminate situations that become problematic for us. And what individuates a situation or an experience is its pervasive quality.[27]

When Dewey speaks of *"an* experience," he highlights another important feature of experience. We can see the traces of a naturalized Hegel when Dewey writes:

> For life is no uniform uninterrupted march or flow. It is a thing of histories, each with its own plot, its own inception and movement toward its close, each having its own particular rhythmic movement; each with its own unrepeated quality pervading it throughout. (Dewey 1981, p. 555)

In this rhythmic temporal development, experiences achieve fulfillment. Dewey calls this the consummatory or the *aesthetic* phase of experience. Interpreters of Dewey frequently neglect the importance of this consummatory phase of experience.[28] But this consummatory aesthetic dimension can qualify any experience. "The enemies of the esthetic are neither the practical nor the intellectual. They are the humdrum: slackness of loose ends: submission, tightness on the one side and dissipation, incoherence and aimless indulgence on the other, are deviations in opposite directions" (ibid.). Solving a complex intellectual problem, or struggling with a complex moral or political dilemma, or creating a work of art, can all have their distinctive consummatory or aesthetic quality. Dewey's approach to the emotional and aesthetic sense of fulfillment also has the utmost significance for his vision of creative democracy. Like the early Marx (and Hegel), Dewey was distressed by the fragmentation and alienation characteristic of so much of modern life. Dewey's vision of the good society is aesthetic insofar as he calls for the type of education and social reform that can enrich experience – fund it with consummatory meaning. Speaking of *Art as Experience*, Robert Westbrook says that the book

> was not incidental to the radical politics that absorbed Dewey in the 1930's. Indeed, it was one of the most powerful statements of that politics, for it clearly indicated that his was not a radicalism directed solely to the material well-being of the American people but directed as well to the provision of consummatory experience that could be found only outside the circulation of commodities. (Westbrook 1991, pp. 401–2)[29]

I can now justify my claim that Rorty is mistaken when he suggests that Dewey never developed a coherent conception of experience – one that combines Darwinian naturalism and Hegelian historicism. There is a coherent theory of experience that is already evident in "The Reflex Arc Concept," one that Dewey refined throughout his career. Inspired originally by Hegel, Dewey thoroughly naturalized his understanding of experience in light of Darwin's theory of evolution. Dewey also has an acute sense of the changing historical role of experience. Dewey illustrates how philosophy is conditioned by its cultural context in "An Empirical Survey of Empiricisms." Dewey distinguishes "three historic conceptions of experience": the first, formulated in classic antiquity; the second, characteristic of eighteenth- and nineteenth-century empiricisms; and the third, which is still in the process of developing (and with which Dewey identifies).

The Greek conception of experience (*empeiria*) "denotes the accumulation of the past, not merely the individual's own past but the social past, transmitted through language and even more through apprenticeship in the various crafts, so far as this information was condensed in matter-of-fact generalizations about how to do certain things like building a house, making a statue, leading an army, or knowing what to expect under given circumstances" (Dewey 1960, pp. 71–2). Plato and Aristotle point out three great limitations of experience: empirical knowledge is contrasted with genuine scientific knowledge (*epistēmē*); experience is dependent on practice, in contrast with the truly free character of rational thought; and experience is limited because it is closely connected with the body. This Greek conception of experience is "an honest empirical report." "In short, the account given of experience was a correct statement of the conditions of [their] contemporary culture" (Dewey 1960, p. 78). The Greek philosophers were mistaken only insofar as they took this historical notion of experience to be the permanent account of experience. "The mistake involved in the philosophy of the period was in its assumption that the implications of a particular state of culture were eternal – a mistake that philosophers as well as others readily fall into" (ibid.).

> If the experience of the time had been the measure of all possible, all future, experience I do not see how this conception of experience could be attacked. But the significant point to be borne in mind (one philosophers at the present period have little excuse for ignoring) is that subsequent developments show that experience is capable of incorporating rational control within itself. (Ibid.)

Dewey's account of the Greek conception of experience is sensitive to the cultural context in which it was developed.[30] So, too, Dewey emphasizes the historical significance of Locke's conception of experience and its subsequent development in British empiricism through the nineteenth century. Like Peirce, Dewey notes that "what characterizes sensation and observation and hence experience, is, in Locke's thought, their coerciveness. ... Compulsion is the safeguard against the vagaries of fancy and accidents of conventional belief" (Dewey 1960, p. 80).

> On the positive side, empiricism was thus an ideal, whether realized or not, associated with the eighteenth-century concept of progress and

the opening up of vistas of the infinite perfectibility of humanity, when once the corruption that comes from bad institutions, political and ecclesiastical, had been done away with and education and rationality given a chance. (Dewey 1960, p. 83)

This appeal to experience originally served a *critical* function against prejudices. But it became evident that it failed to account for the active, experimental character of inquiry.

For all experiment involves regulated activity, directed by ideas, by thought. ... Therefore it would seem that those ideas which function as theories and hypotheses in scientific experimentation and organization are not copies of sensations nor suggested by past experience, by past observation, but that they have a free, imaginative quality that no direct sensation or observation can have. (Dewey 1960, pp. 85–6)

Dewey concedes that the third concept of experience is still very much in the process of being articulated. But he underscores two of its key features. The first is the shift from antecedents to the consequences of ideas, hypotheses, and theories.

[T]he whole point of James's philosophy, which comes out better in some chapters of his *Psychology*, I think, especially in the last chapter of the second volume, than in his lectures on *Pragmatism*, is that the value of ideas is independent of their origin, that it is a matter of their outcome as they are used in directing new observation and experiment. (Dewey 1960, p. 86)

The second is "the breakdown of the old introvert psychology and the development of a psychology having an objective basis, essentially a biological basis" (ibid.).[31] Dewey self-consciously integrates a historical account of changing philosophical conceptions of experience with the lessons he has learned from Darwinian naturalism.

Experience and the Linguistic Turn Again

Before concluding, I want to return to the question of *the* linguistic turn. When did this turn originate? This is a badly formulated question, because everything depends on what we intend by the expression "linguistic turn." Bergmann suggested that it began with Wittgenstein's *Tractatus*. I suspect that many analytic philosophers would sharply disagree and give much more credit to the philosopher who inspired the early Wittgenstein, Frege. But if one thinks that the most important aspect of the linguistic turn is its hermeneutical dimension, then we would tell a different story that would give a prominent place to the contributions of Hamann, Humbolt and Herder, Dilthey and Gadamer.[32] Still others, influenced by French "theory," would date the linguistic turn from the poststructuralist critique of structuralism.

Habermas offers still another perspective on the "linguistic turn" when he distinguishes between *representation* and *communication*. He asserts that "even after the linguistic turn, the analytic mainstream held fast to the primacy of assertoric propositions and their representative function" (Habermas 2003, p. 3). Although Habermas thinks that the representational and communicative functions of language are equiprimordial and mutually presuppose each other, his major focus has been the communicative function of language.[33] Habermas develops a subtle and complex communicative theory of action and rationality and offers an illuminating historical account of the paradigm shift that took place at the end of the nineteenth century from the philosophy of consciousness or subjectivity (that dominated philosophy since the time of Descartes) to a post-Hegelian intersubjective (social), dialogical paradigm of language and communication. As Habermas tells this story, a key figure in bringing about this paradigm shift was George Herbert Mead. This paradigm shift was anticipated in Peirce's critique of a philosophy of subjectivity and in his intersubjective theory of signs. But it was Mead who sought to work out in detail an account of the genesis of language as a *social* phenomenon – a theory that brings out the continuity between non-human and human communication and also seeks to explain human symbolic communication. Mead is in basic agreement with Dewey's account of experience. "The Reflex Arc Concept" was one of the sources of his own social psychology. Although Mead's theory of the social communicative function of language leaves many difficult questions unresolved, Habermas and others have explored and further developed Mead's basic insights. The following themes have been taken up and developed in original ways by philosophers working after the linguistic turn: the "conversations of gestures"; "the dialogical character of language"; "the generalized other"; "role taking"; the

interplay of the "I and me"; "the social character of the self"; how
human "subjectivity" emerges from symbolically mediated interaction; and how reciprocal linguistic perspective-taking is the basis for
both ethics and the theory of radical democracy.[34]

By exploring the reflections on experience by the classical pragmatists, I hope to have undercut the sterile contrast that is sometimes
drawn between experience and language. It is a slander to suggest
that the pragmatic thinkers, who did so much to undermine all forms
of foundationalism, were guilty of appealing to experience as some
sort of foundation. I have urged that the dichotomy that is sometimes
drawn between experience and language is just the sort of dichotomy
that ought to be challenged from a pragmatic perspective. A "linguistic pragmatism" that doesn't incorporate serious reflection about
the role of experience in human life is impoverished in at least two
serious ways. For it slides into linguistic idealism, which tends to lose
contact with the everyday life world of human beings and fails to do
justice to the ways in which experience (Secondness) constrains us.
But even more seriously, linguistic pragmatism severely limits the
range of human experience (historical, religious, moral, political, and
aesthetic experience) that should be central to philosophical reflection. Philosophers working after "the linguistic turn" (no matter how
it is defined) still have a great deal to learn about experience and
language from Peirce, James, Dewey, and Mead.

7

Hilary Putnam: The Entanglement of Fact and Value

If one wanted to write a history of the most important and exciting philosophical debates of the past half-century, there would be no better place to begin than with the writings of Hilary Putnam. His philosophical range is enormous and deep. In the philosophy of science, logic, mathematics, language, mind, perception, epistemology, and metaphysics, Putnam's challenging and controversial claims have been at the very center of discussion. He has critically engaged virtually every major contemporary Anglo-American and Continental philosopher. He frequently brings to his philosophical encounters a subtle knowledge of the history of philosophy that reaches back to classical Greek philosophy. The variety of theses that he has defended, revised, and sometimes abandoned can strike one as bewildering. But a careful reading of his works reveals an underlying coherence to the philosophical vision that he has been articulating – one that is genuinely dialectical in the sense that we can see why he has advocated certain theses as well as his reasons for revising, correcting, and even abandoning them. We can also detect what he seeks to preserve and integrate in his comprehensive vision. "Philosophers," he tells us, "have a double task: to integrate our various views of the world and ourselves ... and to help us find a meaningful orientation in life. Finding a meaningful orientation is not, I think, a matter of finding a set of doctrines to live by, although it certainly includes having views; it is much more a matter of developing a *sensibility*" (Putnam 1997, p. 52).[1]

In this chapter, I shall probe a theme that has become increasingly dominant for Putnam, especially during the past few decades when he has reflectively sought to take pragmatism seriously. Putnam finds in American pragmatism "a certain group of theses which can and indeed were argued differently by different philosophers with different concerns, and which became the basis of the philosophies of Peirce, and above all James and Dewey" (Putnam 1994, p. 152).

> Cursorily summarized, those theses are (1) antiskepticism: pragmatists hold that doubt requires justification just as much as belief (recall Peirce's famous distinction between "real" and "philosophical" doubt); (2) *fallibilism*: pragmatists hold that there is never a metaphysical guarantee to be had that such-and-such a belief will never need revision (that one can be both fallibilistic *and* antiskeptical is perhaps *the* unique insight of American pragmatism); (3) the thesis that there is no fundamental dichotomy between "facts" and "values"; and (4) the thesis that, in a certain sense, practice is primary in philosophy. (Ibid.)

Putnam defends each of these theses in a distinctive manner. In the preface to *Realism with a Human Face*, he writes: "All of these ideas – that the fact/value dichotomy is untenable, and that the fact/convention dichotomy is also untenable, that truth and justification of ideas are closely connected, that the alternative to metaphysical realism is not any form of skepticism, that philosophy is an attempt to achieve the good – are ideas that have been long associated with the American pragmatic tradition" (Putnam 1990, p. xi).

The Context of Putnam's Thesis

I shall focus on the thesis that the fact/value dichotomy is untenable. Or, to put his point positively, that there is an entanglement of fact and value. We will see that this thesis has ramifications for a wide range of philosophical issues. To set the context for my discussion, I want to situate Putnam's thinking – both philosophically and existentially. One cannot underestimate the influence of his early mentors, Hans Reichenbach and Rudolf Carnap. Putnam was never a slavish disciple. He began his career criticizing specific claims that these two philosophers advanced, but he certainly took the challenges they presented with the utmost seriousness – especially their claims about the fact/value and the fact/convention dichotomies. In the opening chapter of *The Collapse of the Fact/Value Dichotomy*, he offers a succinct statement of how these dichotomies were understood by the logical positivists.

> The logical positivists famously introduced a tripartite classification of all putative judgments into those that are "synthetic" (and hence – according to the logical positivists – empirically verifiable or falsifiable), those that are "analytic" (and hence – according to the logical positivists, "true [or false] on the basis of the [logical] rules alone"). And those – and this, notoriously included all of our ethical, metaphysical, and aesthetic judgments – that are "cognitively meaningless." (Putnam 2002a, p. 10)

He also declares:

> But the confidence of the logical positivists that they could expel ethics from the domain of the rationally discussable was in part derived from the way in which the analytic–synthetic and the fact–value dualism reinforced one another in their hands. According to the positivists, in order to be knowledge, ethical "sentences" would have either to be analytic, which they manifestly are not, or else would have to be "factual." And their confidence that they could not be factual ... derived from their confidence that they knew exactly what a *fact* was. (Putnam 2002a, pp. 20–1)

Ever since Quine's critique of the analytic–synthetic dichotomy in 1951, this dichotomy has been discredited. Putnam introduces an important caveat; he distinguishes between a *distinction* and a *dichotomy*. Following John Dewey, Putnam insists that making distinctions (even if changing and open-ended) is important for specific philosophical purposes, but can be disastrous when functional distinctions are reified into rigid dichotomies (as the logical positivists reified the analytic–synthetic distinction). For specific purposes in particular contexts, we may want to draw a distinction between analytic and synthetic sentences, but not a fixed dichotomy. Furthermore, it is a mistake to think that *all* meaningful sentences divide neatly into these two categories. Even though the analytic–synthetic and the fact–convention dichotomies (at least as drawn by the logical positivists) have collapsed, the idea that there really is an unbridgeable gap between fact and value stubbornly persists. This is closely related to an older dichotomy, the allegedly categorical gap between *is* and *ought*.[2] According to Putnam – and I completely agree with him – the fact–value dichotomy has had a pervasive and pernicious influence on the social sciences, as well as on our everyday understanding of ethical and political judgments.[3] Few philosophers today who endorse the fact–value dichotomy endorse "emotivism" – the doctrine that the *primary* function of ethical sentences is to express or evince emotions. But many would assert that value judgments are noncognitive: they are not the sort of judgments that can be true or false. At best, such judgments are nothing more than the expression of individual (or group) preferences or attitudes. They are "merely subjective." Those who subscribe to the fact–value dichotomy may be open to a variety of ways of characterizing precisely what makes a fact a fact, but they still insist that factual claims must be sharply distinguished from value judgments. Facts are facts, and values are values; it is a "category mistake" to confuse the two – or so it is claimed. It is just this claim, however, that Putnam calls into question. We might even label this the "fourth dogma" of empiricism, except that it has also been held by many nonempiricists.

I mentioned that there is also an existential context for understanding why Putnam challenges the fact–value dichotomy. In his essay "The Place of Facts in the World of Values" (Putnam 1990), he gives a brief autobiographical account of his changing views. He tells us that his training as a philosopher of science came from the logical positivists. Although Putnam never advocated the emotive theory of ethical discourse, he did subscribe to a version of a sharp fact–value dichotomy. Concerning moral values, he thought "something was good in a specifically moral sense if it 'answers to the interests associated with the institution of morality'." This means that "the decision to try to be or do good is just a 'choice of a way of life', namely to subscribe or not to an 'institution'." But Putnam tells us that when he held this meta-ethical conviction "he found himself with a severe moral problem" and agonized over whether what he was doing "was *right – really* right" (Putnam 1990, pp. 144–5).

> And I did not just mean whether it was in accord with the Utilitarian maxim to do what will lead to the greatest happiness of the greatest number ... , but whether, if it was, then was that the *right* maxim for such a case? And I do not think I meant would some semantic analysis of the word "good," or some analysis of "the institution of morality,"

support what I was doing. But the *most* interesting thing is that it never occurred to me that there was any inconsistency between my meta-ethical view that it was all just a choice of a "way of life" and my agonized belief that what I was doing had to be either *right* or *wrong*. (Putnam 1990, p. 145)

Cognitive Values

What precisely does Putnam mean by the entanglement of fact and value, and how does he argue for this thesis? In a pragmatic spirit, he notes that there are different types of values – and that we must be philosophically sensitive to their differences. There is a class of values that Putnam calls "epistemological" or "cognitive." Some of his strongest arguments concerning the entanglement of fact and value deal with these epistemological values. He declares that "value and normativity permeate *all* of experience," and "normative judgments are essential to the practice of science itself" (Putnam 2002a, p. 30). "Judgments of 'coherence,' 'plausibility,' 'reasonableness,' 'simplicity,' and what Dirac famously called 'beauty' of a hypothesis are all normative judgments in Charles Peirce's sense, judgments of 'what ought to be' in the case of reasoning" (Putnam 2002a, p. 31).

It is difficult to imagine any philosopher of science – including the most orthodox positivists – denying that such criteria as simplicity, coherence, and plausibility are relevant to the assessment of scientific hypotheses and theories, so one may wonder what the force of Putnam's claim is. His point is that there is *no* way of making sense of these concepts unless we understand that they are values and involve normative judgments; they cannot be analyzed or reduced to what is "merely" factual.[4] He appeals to what he calls "indispensability arguments."[5] Values and norms are indispensable for an analysis and assessment of knowledge claims.

To suppose that "coherence" and "simple" are themselves just emotive words – words that express a "pro attitude" toward a theory, but which do not ascribe any definite properties to the theory – would be to regard *justification* as an entirely subjective matter. On the other hand, to suppose that "coherent" and "simple" name *neutral* properties – properties toward which people may have a "pro attitude" but there is no objective rightness in doing so – runs into difficulties at once. Like the paradigm value terms (such as "courageous," "kind," "honest," or "good"), "coherent" and "simple" are used as terms of praise. Indeed, they are *action guiding* terms: to describe a theory as "coherent, simple, explanatory" is, in the right setting, to say that acceptance of the theory is *justified*; and to say that acceptance of a statement is (completely) justified is to say that one ought to accept the statement or theory. (Putnam 1990, p. 138)

Putnam stresses that our views about the character of coherence and simplicity are themselves historically conditioned, just as our views on the nature of justice or goodness are. But this is not an argument for relativism. Rather, it indicates that "there is no neutral conception of rationality to which one can appeal when the nature of rationality is itself what is at issue" (Putnam 1990, p. 139). Putnam is right when he says that the classical pragmatists sought to support the claim that there is an entanglement of fact and value in *this sense*, that we cannot make sense of science and rationality without appeal to normative considerations. And he can also draw support from the development of this pragmatic theme in such thinkers as Sellars, McDowell, and Brandom, as well as from Apel and Habermas. All would agree with what Sellars says when he declares: "The essential point is that in characterizing an episode or state as that of knowing ... we are placing it in the logical space of reasons, of justifying and being able to justify what one says" (Sellars 1997, p. 169). This is just as true of the facts that we claim to know. Without the indispensable commitment to values and norms, there is no world, and there are no facts.

Ethical and Political Values

Suppose we grant Putnam's pragmatic claim about the entanglement of fact with epistemological values and norms. We still want to know its relevance for ethical and political values and norms.[6] Here we encounter another characteristic theme in Putnam's reflections on value – one that also resonates with the classical pragmatists and has recently been discussed by Iris Murdoch, John McDowell, and Bernard Williams. Putnam tells us that Murdoch perceptively notes that languages "have two very different sorts of ethical concepts: abstract ethical concepts (Williams calls them 'thin' ethical concepts), such as 'good' and 'right,' and more descriptive, less abstract concepts (Williams calls them 'thick' ethical concepts) such as, for example, *cruel, pert, inconsiderate, chaste"* (Putnam 1990, p. 166). The point is "that there is no way of saying what the 'descriptive component' of the meaning of a word like cruel or inconsiderate is without using a word of the same kind. ... The attempt by non-cognitivists to split such words into a 'descriptive meaning component' and 'a prescriptive meaning component' founders on the impossibility of saying what the 'descriptive meaning' of, say, *cruel* is without using the word *cruel* itself, or a synonym" (ibid.).

Putnam, Murdoch, Williams, and McDowell are correct in noting the extreme artificiality of trying to sort out the "descriptive" and "prescriptive" components of thick ethical concepts. If we are already committed *a priori* to the thesis that there *must* be a dichotomy between description and prescription, then we will feel compelled to sort out these different components in ethical language. Here again we see how Putnam exhibits a pragmatic temper. It is, of course, true that there are some concepts and sentences that we normally classify as descriptive and some that we take to be clearly prescriptive or evaluative. Drawing such a distinction in specific contexts may be helpful. But we are on the very brink of misunderstanding if we think that there are and *must* be separable components in *all* ethical concepts and judgments. But what does this establish about ethical values? Putnam argues against ethical relativism. But the observation about the thickness of some ethical concepts is certainly not sufficient to defeat ethical or cultural relativism. On the contrary, the appeal to thick ethical concepts has been used to support cultural and ethical relativism. Consider such a thick ethical concept as *pert* or *inconsiderate*. There are communities in which such concepts do not play any role. And what one group or community may consider inconsiderate may be categorized as honest, blunt behavior in a different community. There is even a sense in which such concepts can be understood as "objective." We sometimes disagree about whether some action really is or is not cruel – and will offer reasons to support our judgments. We may even rationally persuade a conversation partner that she is *mistaken* in her belief that an action was really cruel. There are objective criteria and standards in a given community (even if they are fuzzy) for correctly judging whether some action is cruel. No one in our society is going to judge (correctly) that helping a blind person to cross a dangerous intersection is cruel. Consequently, such judgments can be *true* or *false*. In short, claiming that thick ethical or political concepts exhibit the entanglement of fact and value does not in any way challenge cultural or ethical relativism.

Putnam is aware of the point that I have been making about the compatibility of this analysis of thick ethical concepts with relativism. He makes the same point in his critique of Bernard Williams. Williams endorses this distinction between thin and thick concepts, and he uses it to support a version of ethical relativism. And, according to Putnam, Williams's dichotomy between science and ethics is a "sophisticated" version of an older form of noncognitivism.

> [Bernard] Williams still defends a sharp "science/ethics" dichotomy; and he regards his science/ethics dichotomy as capturing something that was essentially right about the old "fact/value" dichotomy.
>
> Something else has accompanied this change in the way the dichotomy is defended. The old position, in several versions – emotivism, voluntarism, prescriptivism – was usually referred to as "non-cognitivism." ... Today, philosophers like Williams do not deny that ethical sentences can be true or false; what they deny is that they can be true or false *non-perspectivally*. Thus, the position has been (appropriately) renamed: while the proprietary versions of the new approved drug still have various differences one from the other, they all accept the same relativism. *Non-cognitivism has been rebaptized as relativism.* (Putnam 1990, p. 165)

There is nothing quite so damning for Putnam as the label "relativism" except the twin label "metaphysical realism." He is attracted to pragmatism because he believes that it shows the right way to avoid these extremes. Putnam's main strategy in "going after" Williams is to criticize his claim that science is based on a notion of the world as it really is; that science depends on a nonperspectival concept of "absoluteness." Putnam argues that the "dichotomy between what the world is like independent of any local perspective [the absolute conception of the world] and what is projected by us" is not just mistaken; it is *incoherent* (Putnam 1990, p. 170). This dichotomy is "utterly indefensible." Putnam brings a whole battery of arguments to show this.[7]

Like John Dewey, one of his heroes, Putnam argues that philosophical dichotomies – whether metaphysical, ontological, or epistemological – are, at best, useful distinctions for limited purposes. His master strategy is to show that alleged hard-and-fast dichotomies (when closely scrutinized) turn out to be differences of degree. Contrary to what Williams claims, there is no absolute conception of the world; the idea of the world as it really is in itself, independent of any perspective, is illusory. The world does not have a structure that is independent of any of our conceptual schemes. This is a lesson that philosophers should have learned from Kant. All knowing is perspectival and involves conceptual choices. That is why knowledge always involves human interests. This is just as true of the formal sciences and the hard physical sciences as it is of ethics, history, and politics. Putnam writes: "Mathematics and physics, as well as ethics and history and politics, show our conceptual choices: the world is not going to impose a single language upon us, no matter what we choose to talk about" (Putnam 1990, p. 171).[8] Because he realizes that some of his central claims sound "relativistic," Putnam is at pains to stress his pragmatic realism – realism with a human face. There *are* facts of the matter, even though these facts are relative to the adoption of a conceptual scheme – and even though alternative conceptual schemes may be incompatible with each other.

Putnam's pragmatic strategy is to soften rigid dichotomies by showing that they turn out to be flexible differences related to human interests. This strategy is closely related to his attack on metaphysical realism, his relentless critique of relativism, his rejection of scientism, his rejection of the God's-eye point of view, his critique of absolutes, and his defense of pluralism. Putnam's claims about the entanglement of fact and value stand at the heart of his philosophical vision.

Moral Objectivity

But how does Putnam's argument that there is no intrinsic difference between science and ethics, and his claim that the range of rational argument is much broader than science, bear on the issue of moral objectivity? Let me begin by clarifying what Putnam means (and does not mean) by objectivity. Objectivity is not to be confused with metaphysical realism. There are philosophers who think that unless one endorses metaphysical realism, then there is no possibility of giving a proper account of objectivity. Presumably we achieve objectivity when our knowledge corresponds to a "real world" that is independent of us. This is the dogma that Putnam has been criticizing ever since he rejected metaphysical realism. His articulation of a "conceptual," "internal," and, more recently, "pragmatic realism" can be viewed as successive stages in showing how objectivity is compatible with different conceptual choices. Furthermore, objectivity is not to be confused or identified with algorithmic reasoning, wherein we assert that there is a univocal solution to a problem. There is a place for *phronēsis* and reasonable objective disagreement. This is a feature of objectivity that turns out to be highly relevant for ethical and political disputants, but it also has a place in the physical sciences. More generally, objectivity is compatible with pluralism (and pluralism is not to be confused with relativism). We see how deep his commitment to pluralism is, from his recent response to Habermas.

> The following claim is at the heart of my own pluralism:
>
> *One cannot be a consistent pluralist and accept that at least some people who have other ways of life, religious traditions, and sexual orientations, etc., is "light" and the others are all "darkness."* But this claim defines only a "minimal pluralism." A stronger form is defined by the claim, which I also accept, that at least some people who have other ways of life, religious traditions, sexual orientations, etc., than mine have insights that I do not have, or that I have not developed to anything like the same extent, precisely because they have those other ways of life, religious traditions, sexual orientations, etc.[9]

But even if we concede all of this, we may still feel some uneasiness with Putnam's claims about moral objectivity. After all, even if we claim that there is no difference in *kind* between scientific objectivity and moral objectivity, a good pragmatist is still going to ask for an account of the *apparent* differences between scientific and ethical reasoning. Putnam is frequently far more effective in criticizing dichotomies than he is in doing justice to important differences. Stated in another way, I do not think that even Putnam would deny that normally there is much more agreement in the formal and natural sciences about the criteria of objectivity (even when there are sharp disagreements) than we find when we turn to serious ethical and political disputes. And, even more important, in scientific matters there is frequently (but not always) some overlapping agreement about the type of criteria and evidence that are relevant for resolving current disputes. How, then, are we to account for these differences?

Objectivity, Moral Realism, and Democratic Openness

Putnam is not claiming that moral and political philosophers have disregarded a type of moral objectivity that *already exists*. It is not as if there are moral facts "out there" that we are ignoring. He is not advocating the existence of queer facts. His case for moral objectivity is not about how matters now stand. It is rather self-consciously a normative argument about what ought to be – or, more accurately, for a state of affairs that we ought to strive to achieve. We ought to strive to cultivate those practices in which there will be greater moral objectivity, in which there will an open democratic community where reasonable argument flourishes about what is right and wrong and what is morally true or false.

It may be objected that even if there is not a difference in kind, there is nevertheless a major difference between science and ethics. In science we do not have to argue about the standards of objectivity; they exist. But in morality or politics they do not exist; they must be instituted. But this objection misfires. It fails to acknowledge that even in the "hard" sciences there is ongoing discussion and debate about what constitutes objectivity and objective standards. What counted as an objective fact for Copernicus, Kepler, or Galileo is not what counts as an objective fact today. There are not only ongoing disputes about scientific hypotheses and theories but also disputes about standards and criteria of objectivity. Objectivity is not a metaphysical or epistemological given; it is an ongoing conflictual *achievement* – one that must be constantly rethought. "Our norms and standards of anything – including warranted assertibility [and including the norms and standards of objectivity] are capable of reform. There are better and worse norms and standards" (Putnam 1990, p. 21).

Some advocates of moral realism and moral objectivity do argue as if there really are moral facts "out there" in the world, independent of us. They argue as if moral objectivity and metaphysical realism are inextricably linked. But Putnam argues that this linkage is mistaken. Objectivity, whether in science or in ethics, has nothing to do with metaphysical realism or "queer facts." Metaphysical realism in any realm – epistemology, science, ethics, or politics – is mistaken. Putnam advocates a nonmetaphysical way of thinking about objectivity. He also argues for an "epistemological justification of democracy." "The claim, then is this: Democracy is not just a form of social life among other workable forms of social life; it is the precondition for the full application of intelligence to the solution of problems" (Putnam 1991, p. 217). Putnam agrees with Dewey.

> Nevertheless, Dewey believes (as we all do, when we are not playing the skeptic) that there are better and worse resolutions to human predica-ments – to what he calls "problematical situations." He believes that of all the methods for finding better resolutions, the "scientific method" has proved itself superior to Peirce's methods of "tenacity," "authority," and "what is agreeable to reason." For Dewey, the scientific method is simply the method of experimental inquiry combined with free and full discussion – which means, in the case of social problems, the maximum use of the capacities of citizens for proposing courses of action, for testing them, and for evaluating the results. And, in my view, that is all that Dewey really needs to assume. (Putnam 1991, p. 227)[10]

In a similar vein, Putnam argues that we ought to give up the meta-physical picture of objectivity and "accept the position we are fated to occupy in any case, the position of beings who cannot have a view of the world that does not reflect our interests and values, but who are, for all that, committed to regarding some views of the world – and, for that matter, some interests and values – as better than others" (Putnam 1990, p. 178).

> This may mean giving up a certain metaphysical picture of objectivity, but it does not mean giving up the idea that there are what Dewey called "objective resolutions of problematical situations" – objective resolutions to problems which are situated in a place, at a time, as opposed to an "absolute" answer to "perspective-independent" ques-tions. And that is objectivity enough. (Ibid.)

I want to go over Putnam's claims a bit more carefully, because, from one perspective, his reasoning about objectivity in ethical and politi-cal disputes is circular. It is not a vicious circularity, however, but something that is analogous to the hermeneutical circle. Putnam is not claiming that – as things now stand – there is significant moral or political objectivity. He is arguing that we *ought* to cultivate and institute the social practices – practices that he associates with delib-erative democracy – that will enhance objectivity and reasonable argumentation in confronting complex moral situations. This is the way in which an ethical community *ought* to organize itself. To the extent that we achieve the concrete realization of such a democratic community, to that extent moral objectivity becomes a real fact of the matter. "[A]n ethical community – a community which wants to know what is right and good – should organize itself in accordance with democratic standards and ideals, not only because they are good in themselves (and they are), but because they are the prerequisites for the application of intelligence to inquiry" (Putnam 1994, p. 175). He goes on to tell us:

> It may look as if Dewey is "pulling himself up by his own bootstraps." For even if we assume that inquiry into values should be democratized, that the participants should, *qua* seekers after the right and the good, respect free speech and the other norms of discourse ethics, not instrumentalize one another, and so on, what *criteria* should they use to tell that their inquiry has succeeded? (Ibid.)

But it looks as if Putnam is also "pulling himself up by his own bootstraps." He argues that we ought to strive for a democratic open society in which there will be a broader and deeper moral objectivity. Making such a democratic community a living reality means making the type of objectivity that he favors a concrete reality. This is a type of "bootstrapping" because it is intended to bring about a moral objectivity that does not yet exist (and may never fully exist). But this bootstrapping is not necessarily objectionable. Putnam might have been more forthright if he made it clear that he is not describing the current state of affairs but rather what he claims is a desirable future world.

Another objection might be raised against Putnam. Isn't he really seeking to impose or construct standards of moral objectivity rather than discover them? If this is his aim, then wouldn't his goal be achieved more effectively by authoritarian regimes that enforce standards of right and wrong and the "objectively correct" view? But this objection also misfires, because it falsely assumes that Putnam fails to distinguish the type of moral realism and moral objectivity that he wants to defend from the view that he rejects.

> But not every defense of moral objectivity is a good thing. We live in an "open society," a society in which freedom to think for oneself about values, goals, and mores is one that most of us have come to cherish. Arguments for "moral realism" can, and sometimes unfortunately do, sound like arguments against the open society; and while I do wish to undermine moral skepticism, I have no intention of defending either

authoritarianism or moral apriorism. It is precisely for this reason that in recent years I have found myself turning to the writings of the American pragmatists. (Putnam 1994, p. 152)

In Putnam's declaration of his affinity with the American pragmatists, we see the basis for a difference that makes a difference. He advocates that the moral objectivity we should strive to achieve is through open discussion, debate, and reciprocal give-and-take. He is sympathetic to the spirit of Habermas's discourse ethics. The democratic practices that Putnam favors are not simply "subjective" preferences. He argues that these practices provide the conditions for the norms and standards for achieving moral objectivity.

In his essay "Pragmatism and Moral Objectivity," originally delivered at a conference dedicated to the issues of justice and equality in developing countries, Putnam concedes that his paper is more "abstract" than most of the others. He defends this abstractness when he declares: "If it ended up being more 'abstract' than most of the others, that is not because the author got 'carried away' by a particular line of abstract thought. Rather, it is because it was my conviction ... that positions on the 'abstract' question of moral objectivity have real world effects." And he adds: "To show that the justifications which are offered for ethical skepticism at a philosophical level will not stand up to examination, that the foundations of the idea that there is no rationality beyond purely instrumental rationality are in trouble, *may* help to combat that instrumentalization and that manipulation" (Putnam 1994, p. 151). This is a modest but important claim about "abstract" philosophical discussions and "real world effects." I am sympathetic to Putnam's arguments against ethical skepticism, his defense of an enlarged conception of rationality and a liberal sense of moral objectivity. I do think he is effective in showing the entanglement of fact and value. He has elucidated a way of thinking about moral objectivity that escapes the snares of moral metaphysical realism. He is also effective in challenging a rigid dichotomy between science and ethics, and in exposing the appeals to "absoluteness." But I also think that his general line of argument is "abstract." It is as if he is clearing the space for a deliberative democratic way of dealing with value judgments and decisions. But a good pragmatist will also want to know how this really works when we get down to the nitty-gritty, how we are to decide what is right and wrong, and how we are to figure out which value judgments are true and false in specific situations. It is not good enough to be told that this will always depend on context and the background assumptions of the participants in a dispute. This is true but unhelpful. The really hard moral and political issues concern just how we are to figure out what is to be done and how we are to judge competing claims. On the abstract level, Putnam has made a good case for nonmetaphysical ways of thinking about moral objectivity. But he has not shown us how we are to determine which of our value judgments are objectively true and false. He hasn't shown us how we are to resolve the type of conflicts that constantly arise in a democratic society – especially when reasonable citizens sharply disagree over fundamental issues. I am not asking for clear and determinate criteria or demanding more exactness of ethical and political objectivity than the subject matter warrants. Aristotle taught us this lesson long ago. But an abstract argument for moral objectivity must at least be complemented by some guidance about how we decide what is right and wrong, true and false, when confronted with seriously competing claims. This is especially pressing in a world in which extremist positions are becoming dangerously fashionable and in which there is a violent clash of "absolutes" – where there seems to be very little agreement even in democratic societies about what really counts as an "objective" solution to an ethical or political problem. If we are to be fully persuaded by Putnam, then these are the sorts of questions that must be answered. Putnam leaves himself open to the objection that his version of "moral realism" is a misleading way of projecting an ideal democratic polity. What Putnam has shown is illuminating and helpful, but it is still only a very abstract sketch – one that on pragmatic grounds demands filling in with concrete details. Without working out these concrete details, a certain skepticism about moral objectivity and moral realism is still warranted.

8

Jürgen Habermas's Kantian Pragmatism

Several years ago when Habermas was asked "What do you see as the most lasting contribution of pragmatism to the tradition of Western philosophy and social thought?" he replied:

> Alongside Marx and Kierkegaard ... pragmatism emerges as the only approach that embraces modernity in its most radical forms, and acknowledges its contingencies, without sacrificing the very purpose of Western philosophy – namely, to try out explanations of who we are and who we would like to be, as individuals, as members of communities, and as persons *überhaupt* – that is, as man. (Habermas 2002, p. 229)

This response echoes an interpretation of post-Hegelian philosophy that Habermas (together with Karl-Otto Apel) worked out in great detail. Hegel is the philosopher *par excellence* who deeply grasps the aporias of modernity – aporias concerning the many forms of rupture and fragmentation as well as their potential for healing and reconciliation. Marxism, Kierkegaardian existentialism, and pragmatism represent the three major attempts to rethink and resolve these aporias. The above passage also tells us something about Habermas's philosophical trajectory – where he has come increasingly to think of his comprehensive philosophical investigations as developing what he calls a "Kantian pragmatism." My aim in this chapter is to sketch the outlines of this Kantian pragmatism and raise some critical questions about it. (We will see just how important it is to explicate both terms: 'Kantian' and 'pragmatism.')

Kant Detranscendentalized

But first I would like to say a word about the influence of American pragmatism on Habermas. Habermas is one of the very few European philosophers who have taken classical American pragmatism seriously. He appropriates, reconstructs, and integrates pragmatic themes into his own thinking. "Influence" is perhaps too flat a word, because it suggests that Habermas read the pragmatic thinkers carefully and learned from them. This is certainly true. But what is more philosophically interesting is that Habermas – following his own distinctive dialectical journey – has come to realize how many of his central ideas were anticipated by the classical American pragmatists. This is, of course, compatible with the ways in which he has also been critical of the pragmatists (see Habermas 2002). Habermas has also critically engaged those contemporary American philosophers who (in different ways) strongly identify with the pragmatic tradition: Richard Rorty, Hilary Putnam, and Robert Brandom. In these exchanges he has refined and defended his Kantian pragmatism.

We must remember how deeply Peirce, the founder of pragmatism, was shaped by his encounter with Kant.[1] Peirce began his philosophical investigations with an attempt to rethink the Kantian categories – or to use Habermas's expression – to "detranscendentalize" Kant. Habermas tells us: "In epistemology – and the theory of truth – Peirce had the strongest influence, from my Frankfurt inaugural lecture on *Knowledge and Human Interests* (1971) onwards up to *Wahrheit und Rechtfertigung* (1999)." Habermas (and Karl-Otto Apel) "perceived Peirce's pragmatist approach as a promise to save Kantian insights in a detranscendentalized yet analytical vein" (Habermas 2002, p. 227). What does Habermas mean by a "detranscendentalized" Kant? I begin with an initial characterization, which I will refine as I proceed. Habermas has always felt that there is something profoundly right about the core idea of the Kant's transcendental project.

> Transcendental philosophy, as the famous phrase has it, "deals not so much with objects as rather with our way of cognizing objects in general insofar as that way of cognizing is to be possible a priori." It takes itself to be reconstructing the universal and necessary conditions under which something can be an object of experience and cognition. The significance of this transcendental problematic can be generalized by divorcing it from the basic mentalistic concept of self-reflection as

well as from a foundationalist understanding of the conceptual pair
a priori – a posteriori. After the pragmatist deflation of Kantian con-
ceptuality, "transcendental analysis" refers to the search for presumably universal but only *de facto* unavoidable conditions that must be
fulfilled in order for fundamental practices or achievements to emerge.
(Habermas 2003, pp. 10–11)

One may think initially that this "pragmatist deflation" is so radical
that there is very little of the "historical" Kant left. Habermas
doesn't deny this; transcendental philosophy no longer deals with
"consciousness *überhaupt*." It now becomes the investigation that aims
"to discover deep-seated structures of the background of the lifeworld. These structures are embodied in the practices and activities
of subjects capable of speech and action" (Habermas 2003, p. 11).
The linguistic turn in philosophy requires that we give up talk about
"consciousness," "self-consciousness," and "apperception" as exclusively *mental* activities. There is no way of analyzing concepts and
judgments without reference to language. And we cannot understand
language and speech acts except in the context of social and communal practices. "Detranscendentalization leads, on the one hand,
to the embedding of knowing subjects into the socializing context of
a lifeworld and, on the other hand, to the entwinement of cognition
with speech and action" (Habermas 2003, pp. 88–9). A great deal is
packed into this brief statement. When Habermas speaks of "embedding of knowing subjects into the socializing context of a lifeworld,"
he is alluding to his (and the Peircian) sustained critique of "the
philosophy of consciousness" that has dominated so much of modern
philosophy. He is underscoring the paradigm shift from a philosophy of subjectivity or consciousness to an intersubjective or social
understanding of human beings that stands at the very heart of his
communicative theory of action and rationality. When he speaks of
the "entwinement" of cognition with speech and action, he is alluding to the linguistic turn that is characteristic of twentieth-century
philosophy – especially the appreciation of the pragmatic dimension
of speech acts, which can also be traced back to Peirce's semiotics and
Mead's communicative analysis of speech acts.

Many of the classic Kantian distinctions – noumena/phenomena,
appearance/thing-in-itself, understanding/sensibility – are no longer
acceptable as they were originally developed by Kant. Habermas
rejects Kant's transcendental idealism (as well as Hegel's absolute

idealism) in favor of a post-Kantian and post-Hegelian epistemological realism. Nevertheless, even after the linguistic and pragmatic turns in philosophy, there is a proper role for a chastened transcendental philosophy: that is, the attempt to reconstruct the universal conditions that form the deep structures of everyday speech and action. This is the investigation that Habermas carries out in his theory of communicative action, a project that abandons any claims to finality, completeness, or epistemic certainty. Habermas is a thoroughgoing fallibilist – another basic conviction that he shares with Peirce and the classical American pragmatists. Furthermore, Habermas, as we shall see, follows Kant in maintaining a sharp distinction between theoretical and practical philosophy. In this respect, he differs from the classical American pragmatists (with the possible exception of Peirce). In sorting out the ways in which Habermas follows and departs from Kant, one should also mention his interest in naturalism. Habermas has always opposed a reductive form of naturalism: the type of naturalism closely allied to reductive materialism and scientific realism, which identifies nature with the entities ultimately countenanced by an "ideal" physical science. But in *Truth and Justification* he sketches a "weak naturalism." The question he wants to answer is: "How can the normativity that is unavoidable from the perspective of the participants in this lifeworld be reconciled with the contingency of sociocultural forms of life that have evolved naturally?" (Habermas 2003, p. 2). Weak naturalism, as Habermas understands it, is "based on a single metatheoretical assumption: that 'our' learning processes, that are possible within the framework of sociocultural forms of life, are in a sense simply the continuation of 'evolutionary learning processes' that in turn gave rise to our forms of life. ... [W]eak naturalism contents itself with the basic background assumption that the biological endowment and the cultural way of life of *Homo sapiens* have a 'natural' origin and can in principle be explained in terms of evolutionary theory" (Habermas 2003, pp. 27–8). In short, Habermas wants to combine a version of a detranscendentalized Kant with Darwin.[2]

When Habermas developed his theory of communicative action and rationality originally, he set aside theoretical issues of epistemology that preoccupied him in *Knowledge and Human Interests*. The linguistic turn did not acquire its significance for him in dealing with traditional epistemological and semantic issues such as our knowledge of objects and facts or the form of assertoric propositions. "Rather, the pragmatic approach to language [*Sprachpragmatik*] helped me to develop a theory of communicative action and of rationality. It was the foundation for a critical theory of society and paved the way for a discourse-theoretic conception of morality, law, and democracy" (Habermas 2003, p. 1). The theory of communicative action situates rationality in the everyday practices of the lifeworld and shows that the critical power of reason is rooted in ordinary language. "The expression 'communicative action' designates social interactions where language use aimed at reaching mutual understanding plays the role of action coordination. Through linguistic communication, idealizing presuppositions enter into action oriented toward reaching mutual understanding" (Habermas 2003, p. 110). But Habermas stresses that his communicative theory of action and his formal pragmatics presupposes an understanding of truth and objectivity.

> Of course, the formal pragmatics that I have developed since the early 1970s cannot do without the fundamental concepts of truth and objectivity, reality and reference, validity and rationality. The theory relies on a normatively charged concept of communication [*Verständigung*], operates with validity claims that can be redeemed discursively and with formal-pragmatic presuppositions about the world, and links understanding speech acts to the conditions of their rational acceptability. However, I have not dealt with these themes from the perspective of theoretical philosophy. (Habermas 2003, p. 1)

Truth and Normative Rightness

To see why it is so important to deal with these themes from "the perspective of theoretical philosophy," we need to recall some of the key claims that Habermas makes in *The Theory of Communicative Action*. The heart of the theory concerns what Habermas calls "validity claims." Communicative interaction is primarily a matter of raising validity claims. There are three basic types of validity claim that are raised by speakers in their speech acts: a claim to the truth of what is said or presupposed, a claim to normative rightness, and a claim to truthfulness. All three claims are raised simultaneously, although typically only one of them is thematized or made explicit, while the others may remain implicit. Habermas is, of course, aware that in actual empirical communication, any or all of these validity claims may be violated. We may deliberately lie and misrepresent something as true that we know is false with the intent of deceiving a hearer about what is normatively right. One of the most misunderstood features of Habermas's theory is the way in which these "idealizing" counterfactual presuppositions of communicative action may be violated in any empirical speech act. These idealizations are not intended to delineate an "ideal" communication or an "ideal" community. On the contrary, they are intended to specify what is *counterfactually* presupposed in *every* communicative interaction. For example, we could not lie or deceive without presupposing that there are implicit standards for what counts as truth and truthfulness.[3] I shall concentrate on the validity claims to truth and normative rightness – for this is where we will see the full force of his Kantian pragmatism. Each of the validity claims is distinctive, but they are also interdependent. When, in a specific communicative exchange, a question is raised about the truth of one's claim or its normative rightness, then there is a call for argumentation (discourse) – the give-and-take of reasons. Consequently, disputes about truth and normative rightness are essentially cognitive. This sets Habermas apart from all those philosophers who claim that disputes about normative rightness are noncognitive. One of the key presuppositions of communicative action is that there is a common objective world about which we can make true and false assertions. If I claim that something is true and you challenge me, then at the very least we are both presupposing that there is a common objective world to which we can refer. Of course, this does not mean that in fact we will agree or be able to resolve our dispute. When Habermas initially sought to explain the validity claim of truth, there were some crucial ambiguities in his presentation. Unless Habermas can give an adequate account of the validity claim of truth, the very foundations of the theory of communicative action and rationality are seriously threatened.

The Epistemic Conception of Truth

Habermas originally approached the question of truth from an epistemic perspective. He calls this a "procedural" or "discursive" understanding of truth. The primary issue here is not how to characterize truth, but rather how to analyze what it means to *know* that a given

claim is true. He originally sought to answer this question by appealing to the "ideal" conditions of justification. But many critics have
argued that such an epistemic conception of truth is seriously flawed.
Habermas now concedes that his critics are right.

> For my part, I initially determined the meaning of truth procedurally,
> that is, as confirmation under the normatively rigorous conditions of
> the practice of argumentation. This practice is based on the idealiz-
> ing presuppositions (a) of public debate and complete inclusion of all
> those affected; (b) of equal distribution of the right to communicate;
> (c) of a nonviolent context in which only the unforced force of the
> better argument holds sway; and (d) of the sincerity of how all those
> affected express themselves. The discursive concept of truth was on
> the one hand supposed to take account of the fact that a statement's
> truth – absent the possibility of direct access to uninterpreted truth
> conditions – cannot be assessed in terms of "decisive evidence," but
> only in terms of justificatory, albeit never definitively "compelling,"
> reasons. On the other hand, the idealization of certain features of the
> form and process of the practice of argumentation was to characterize
> a procedure that would do justice to the context-transcendence of the
> truth claim raised by a speaker in a statement by rationally taking
> into account all relevant voices, topics, and contributions. (Habermas
> 2003, pp. 36–7)[4]

This procedural conception of truth comes close to identifying truth
with "ideal" justification.[5] Habermas now realizes that this is inad-
equate. In his introduction to *Truth and Justification*, he writes:

> I have given up an epistemic conception of truth and sought to distin-
> guish more clearly between the truth of a proposition and its rational
> assertibility (even under approximately ideal conditions). In retro-
> spect, I see that the discursive conception of truth is due to an overgen-
> eralization of the special case of the validity of moral judgments and
> norms. A constructivist conception of the moral "ought" does require
> an epistemic understanding of normative rightness. But if we want
> to do justice to realist intuitions, the concept of propositional truth
> must not be assimilated to this sense of rational acceptability under
> approximately ideal conditions. (Habermas 2003, p. 8)

Habermas certainly does not want to deny that there is an "unavoidable epistemological connection between truth and justification," but
this does not amount to "a conceptual connection between truth
and assertibility under ideal conditions" (Habermas 2003, pp. 37–8).
"Truth," he tells us, is a "property of propositions that they 'cannot

lose'" (Habermas 2003, p. 38). The proper characterization of truth is closely related to an understanding of objectivity and reference. Habermas now emphasizes that an epistemic understanding of truth is not *sufficient*, because no matter how strong our justification is – even if it were "ideal" – it may turn out that what is ideally justified is nevertheless false. Furthermore, serious problems arise when it comes to specifying what "ideal justification" really means. The epistemic account of truth does violence to our "realist intuitions." It violates our sense that there is a world that is independent of our justificatory practices and that our claims to truth ultimately presuppose an independent objective world. Habermas's realist intuitions are extremely strong. Although he emphasizes that philosophy is now post-metaphysical, he doesn't hesitate to use ontological language.

> What we want to express with true sentences is that a certain state of affairs "obtains" or is "given." And these facts in turn refer to "the world" as the totality of things about which we may state facts. This ontological way of speaking establishes a connection between truth and reference, that is, between the truth of statements and the "objectivity" of that about which something is stated. The concept of the "objective world" encompasses everything that subjects capable of speech and action do not "make themselves" irrespective of their interventions and inventions. (Habermas 2003, p. 254)[6]

This is strong stuff. Except for the claim that the world is "the totality of things about which we may state facts" rather than the world as the totality of facts, it sounds like the Wittgenstein of the *Tractatus*.

One of the fundamental questions that Habermas seeks to answer in *Truth and Justification* is: "How can we reconcile the assumption that there is a world existing independently of our descriptions of it and that is the same for all observers with the linguistic insight that we have no direct, linguistically unmediated access to 'brute' reality?" (Habermas 2003, p. 2). As I hope to show, the viability of Habermas's Kantian pragmatism depends on giving a satisfactory answer to this question.

Neither Contextualism nor Idealism

Let me first state what are Habermas's chief worries and what it is that he wants to avoid. This may seem like a circuitous route, but it will take us to the heart of the matter. Briefly stated, Habermas wants to avoid what he takes to be two unsatisfactory extremes: the extreme of Rorty's pragmatic contextualism and the extreme of Brandom's pragmatic neo-Hegelianism. Once one makes the linguistic turn, then one is committed to holding that an adequate explication of the procedures of argumentative justification must be related to language – or what Rorty calls "vocabularies." And if there is no "linguistically unmediated access to 'brute reality'" (as Hegel, Peirce, Wittgenstein, Sellars, and many others have argued), then how can we know that there is a world existing independently of our descriptions of it? Rorty's answer is straightforward: we can't! And because there is a plurality of vocabularies, and no apriori limits on inventing new vocabularies, all we can do is play off our vocabularies – our descriptions and redescriptions – against each other. The world is well lost! There is simply no "it," no world that stands independently of our descriptions. If we appeal to "realist intuitions" (as Habermas does), Rorty's advice is to abandon these intuitions and develop new ones. Rorty is quite explicit in mocking the philosophical appeal to intuitions, especially realist intuitions.

> What really needs debate between the pragmatist and the intuitive realist is not whether we have intuitions to the effect that "truth is more than assertibility". ... Of course we have such intuitions. How could we escape having them? We have been educated within an intellectual tradition built around such claims. ... But it begs the question between pragmatist and realist to say that we must find a philosophical view which "captures" such intuitions. The pragmatist is urging that we do our best to stop having such intuitions, that we develop a new intellectual tradition. (Rorty 1982, pp. xxix–xxx)

From Rorty's perspective, defenders of "realist intuitions" require philosophical therapy – a therapy that aims to relieve them of their anxieties and to abandon their "realist intuitions." These "intuitions" don't do any pragmatic work; they don't help us to cope. Consequently, Rorty deflates the philosophical idea of truth and replaces it with the appeal to social (that is, sociological) justification: he urges us to replace objectivity with solidarity. All we need is a "cautionary sense of true," which merely tells us that no matter how successfully we have justified a claim, it may turn out that we discover that the justification is no longer satisfactory; it no longer persuades. But if this happens, it is because we have come up with new forms of social justification: that is, procedures of justification that are more acceptable to our peers and the audience we are addressing – not because "realistic intuitions" have been vindicated. Rorty might claim that he is a more consistent "fallibilist" than Habermas, because he makes no pretence to speak about "ideal justification" or to anticipate what new forms of justification will be adopted in the future.

Habermas has raised a variety of objections against Rorty. He argues that this sort of contextualism cannot avoid relativism. Rorty doesn't think that we can give good reasons (indeed, he doesn't think he can give any context-transcending reasons) to justify one vocabulary over any other vocabulary. All we can do is try to persuade others to adopt the vocabulary we favor. Despite Rorty's claims to the contrary, this leads to a self-defeating relativism and involves a "performative contradiction." (Putnam has raised similar criticisms against Rorty. This is one reason why Habermas views Putnam as a fellow Kantian pragmatist who justifies a post-Kantian internal realism.) Habermas also argues that Rorty fails to make any sense of something that is implicit in our everyday linguistic practices: if I claim that something is true or just, I am not simply claiming that something is true or just for me or my group. I am making universal claims that "transcend" my context – "transcend" what I or my peers say or believe here and now. I may or may not be able to justify my claims, but I can't avoid making universal validity claims. So, even on pragmatic grounds, Rorty fails, because he can't make sense of the starting point for pragmatism – making sense of everyday practices.[7]

Habermas is far more sympathetic to Rorty's student, Robert Brandom, precisely because – unlike his teacher – Brandom struggles to give an account of truth and objectivity that tries to do justice to our "realist intuitions." Nevertheless, Habermas is skeptical of Brandom's neo-Hegelian turn.

> Brandom combines Wilfrid Sellars's inferential semantics step by step with a pragmatics of discourse in order to explain the objectivity of conceptual norms from the perspective of the intersubjectively shared "practice of giving and asking for reasons." In the end, Brandom is able to do justice to the intuitions underlying epistemological realism only at the price of a conceptual realism that obliterates the distinction between the intersubjectively shared lifeworld and the objective world. This assimilation of the objectivity of experience to intersubjectivity of communication is reminiscent of an infamous Hegelian move. (Habermas 2003, p. 8)[8]

So Rorty's pragmatism is too contextual, and Brandom's is too Hegelian. Neither fully appreciates the virtues of Kantian pragmatism. Habermas sees himself as closer to the Kantian pragmatism of Hilary Putnam. He draws upon Putnam's internal realism and his theory of direct reference to vindicate his own thesis that there is an objective world independent of us about which we can make true claims. "With regard to the objective world, the proposition's truth signifies a fact – the obtaining of a state of affairs." We will soon see that, according to Habermas, even Putnam is not a consistent Kantian pragmatist, because he fails – so Habermas claims – to make the important distinction between values and norms. Putnam fails to appreciate the important Kantian distinction between theoretical and practical philosophy and reason.[9]

The question now becomes, How does Habermas account for truth? How does he avoid identifying truth with ideal justification? How does he avoid the aporias of contextualism and neo-Hegelian idealism? Before answering these questions, we must deal with one further topic in order to appreciate fully the contours of Habermas's Kantian pragmatism.

Moral Rightness

The theory of communicative action and rationality is not yet an explicitly moral theory, even though normative rightness is one of the primary validity claims. Normative rightness is a much more general concept than moral rightness. Not all norms are moral norms. Nevertheless, the theory of communicative action and the formal pragmatic specification of the unavoidable conditions of communication serve as the basis for developing his discourse theory of moral discourse, law, and democracy. Barbara Fultner gives a succinct statement of the core of Habermas's cognitivist moral theory in the form of a discourse ethics.[10]

> The core of this theory is the so-called Principle of Universalization, according to which a moral norm is justified if all those affected would assent to it under conditions of an ideal speech situation. Moral norms, unlike ethical values, have a universal and unconditional validity. At the same time, moral rightness is an epistemic notion. That is, it

is defined in terms of what rational agents would agree on under (approximately) ideal conditions. (Fultner 2003, pp. viii–ix)

There are several features of the discourse theory of morality that call for comment. Although there is practical (moral) knowledge, it must not be confused or identified with theoretical knowledge about the objective world. "It seems that a cognitivist interpretation of the normative validity of binding norms, which takes account of the inescapable sense of the 'respect of the law' as a 'fact of reason,' is possible only if we conceive morality on analogy with cognition" (Habermas 2003, p. 239). And when a moral norm is contested, the only proper way to resolve the dispute is by discourse, by argumentation. In this argumentation we seek to justify moral norms. But what does justification mean here? It means that "all those affected would assent to it under conditions of an ideal speech situation." Once again, it is important to note that Habermas is not making a prediction about what will happen or suggesting that there will not always be moral disagreements; rather, he is specifying a demand and a condition for what counts as the justification of a moral norm. It begins to look as if much of what Habermas claimed with regard to the justification of truth claims is just as relevant to what he has to say about the justification of universal moral norms. Indeed, as we noted earlier, it was primarily Habermas's concern to develop an epistemic account of "normative rightness" that inspired his epistemic account of "truth." And it is this analogy between justifying normative validity claims and justifying truth claims about the objective world that initially led Habermas to claim that an epistemic account of truth was sufficient to explicate truth – the claim that he now rejects. This is why we need an account of truth that explains how truth involves *more* than justification – more than even "ideal" justification. Unless he can satisfy this need, he thinks that we will not be able to escape from the aporias of contextualism and linguistic idealism. Consequently, Habermas tries to give an account of truth that will explain our "ontological way of speaking [that] establishes a connection between truth and reference, that is, between the truth of statements and the 'objectivity' of that about which something is stated" (Habermas 2003, p. 254).

The substance of Habermas's "Kantian pragmatism" now emerges with greater clarity. Like Kant, Habermas claims that there is a sharp distinction between theoretical and practical philosophy and reason (although, of course, they are interdependent). The task of theoretical philosophy is to provide an adequate account of truth, and the task of practical philosophy, an adequate account of normative rightness and, especially, moral norms.

Moral norms are universal; these norms are binding on all human beings.[11] Ethics, as distinguished from morality, pertains to my personal life or the life of my group – whether this is an ethnic group, a religious group, or a national group. "Ethics" as Habermas uses this term is always oriented to the first-person singular or plural perspective. There is a plurality of ethical orientations, but there is only a single universal morality. In making and emphasizing the distinction between morality and ethics, Habermas is clearly identifying himself with the Kantian deontological conception of morality and justice that is applicable to all human beings. Theories of the good life – that is, theories about what is good for me or my group – are particularistic; they are not truly universal. Habermas gives the following illustration to indicate the difference between "a universalistic morality of justice and a particularistic ethics of the good life."

> We call the torture of human beings "cruel" not only here for us, but everywhere and for everyone. Yet we feel by no means justified to object against strange child-raising practices or marriage ceremonies, that is, against core components of the ethos of a foreign culture, as long as they do not contradict our moral standards. The latter are those central values that differ from other values in virtues of their universal claim to validity. (Habermas 2003, pp. 228–9)

Concerning the *analogy* between moral judgments and true descriptive statements, Habermas writes:

> Those moral judgments that merit universal recognition are "right," and that means that in a rational discourse under approximately ideal conditions they could be agreed to by anyone concerned. The analogy to the claim to truth consists in the demand for rational acceptability; the truth of descriptive statements can also come out and be confirmed only in rational discourses that are as comprehensive and persistent as possible. (Habermas 2003, p. 229)

But Habermas warns against blurring the distinction between these validity claims – between rightness and truth. To say that there is an *analogy* between moral judgments and true descriptive statements because both can be justified by argumentative discourse is not to *identify* them; there are crucial differences.

> The validity concept of moral rightness has lost the ontological con-
> notation of the justification-transcendent concept of truth. Whereas
> "rightness" is an epistemic concept and means nothing but worthi-
> ness of universal recognition, the meaning of the truth of statements
> cannot be reduced to epistemic conditions of confirmation, no matter
> how rigorous they might be: truth goes beyond idealized justification.
> This difference between "truth" and "moral rightness" mirrors the
> distinction between theoretical and practical reason. (Habermas 2003,
> pp. 229–30)

Despite Habermas's many criticisms of the "historical" Kant, we are now in a position to see just how Kantian he is – what he wants to appropriate from the Kantian legacy. First, there is the recon-struction of what he takes to be the viable core of the transcendental project – the formal-pragmatic statement of the unavoidable condi-tions of speech and action. Secondly, Habermas is Kantian in insisting on a sharp (categorical) distinction between the right and the good. Moral rightness is universal and can be justified only "in a type of discourse that (approximately) meets the ideal conditions that could be agreed to by anyone concerned." We might say that Habermas is a "communicative Kantian." Thirdly, he is Kantian in maintaining a strict distinction between theoretical and practical reason, and consequently between theoretical and practical philosophy. But here Habermas significantly departs from the classical pragmatists or, at least, from James and Dewey, who deny any sharp distinction between theoretical and practical philosophy. Most pragmatists – old and new – do not accept this Kantian distinction between theoretical and practical reason. And here Habermas also departs from Hilary Putnam, the contemporary Kantian pragmatist with whom he feels the greatest affinity, because Putnam questions the sharp distinction between values and norms.[12]

Action and Discourse

We are finally prepared to see how Habermas distinguishes rightness from truth. Here is a succinct statement of his guiding intuition:

> My guiding intuition can be characterized as follows. On the one hand,
> we discover the rightness of moral judgments in the same way as the
> truth of descriptions: through argumentation. We no more have direct
> access unfiltered by reasons to truth conditions than we do to the condi-
> tions under which moral norms merit universal recognition. In either
> case, the validity of statements can be established only through dis-
> cursive engagement using available reasons. On the other hand, moral
> validity claims do not refer to the world in the way that is characteristic
> of truth claims. "Truth" is a justification-transcendent concept that
> cannot be made to coincide even with the concept of ideal warranted
> assertibility. Rather it refers to the truth conditions that must, as it
> were, be met by reality itself. In contrast, the meaning of "rightness"
> consists *entirely* in ideal warranted acceptability. (Habermas 2003,
> pp. 247–8; emphasis added)

So the primary question now is, How does Habermas account for
truth? How does he complement an epistemic discursive concept of
truth with a non-epistemic account of truth that satisfies "realist
intuitions"? How does he account for the presupposition that there
is an objective world that is the same for everyone, and about which
we can make true assertions?

In order to give a more adequate theory of truth, Habermas returns
to the starting point for pragmatism – how truth claims function
within the lifeworld, that is, within the world of everyday actions and
practices.

> Pragmatism makes us aware that everyday practice rules out sus-
> pending claims to truth in principle. The network of routine prac-
> tices relies on more or less implicit beliefs that we take to be true
> against a broad background of intersubjectively shared or sufficiently
> overlapping beliefs. Everyday routines and habituated communication
> work on the basis of certainties that guide our actions. ... As soon as
> such certainties are dislodged from the framework of what we take
> for granted in the lifeworld and are no longer naively accepted, they
> become just so many questionable assumptions. In the transition from
> action to discourse, what is taken to be true is the first thing to shed
> its mode of practical certainty and to take on instead the form of a
> hypothetical statement whose validity remains undetermined until it
> passes or fails the test of argumentation. Looking beyond the level of
> argumentation, we can comprehend the pragmatic role of a Janus-
> faced truth that established the desired internal connection between
> performative certainty and warranted assertibility. (Habermas 2003,
> pp. 252–3)

Consider the following mundane example. If I take a subway to my office as I routinely do, I know how many blocks I have to walk to get to the subway, and that the train I take will stop at the same stations that it normally does. All of these are "more or less implicit beliefs" that I take for granted. They function as practical certainties and do not call for any further inquiry or argumentation. But suppose that, when I get to the subway station, I discover that, due to a breakdown, the train is not running. The situation has become problematic for me, and I may initially be somewhat uncertain about what to do. I may start a conversation with strangers about the best alternative way to get to my office. There may even be some dispute (an argument) about the best solution: for example, which is the best bus to take. And after listening to the pros and cons, I decide that it is best to take the Fifth Avenue bus. I walk to the bus stop and proceed with my journey.[13]

This example illustrates the way in which practical uncertainties arise in everyday life and how they may be resolved by discourse (my conversation with strangers about the best way to get to my office). It illustrates the movement from action to discourse and back again to action (taking the bus). But how do the appeal to action in the lifeworld and the move to argumentative justificatory discourse further our understanding of pragmatic truth?

In the lifeworld actors depend on behavioral certainties. They have to cope with a world presumed to be objective and, for this reason, operate with a distinction between believing and knowing. There is a practical necessity to rely intuitively on what is unconditionally held-to-be-true. This mode of unconditionally holding-to-be-true is reflected on the discursive level in the connotations of truth claims that point beyond the given context of justification and require the supposition of ideal justificatory conditions – with a resulting decentering of the justification community. For this reason, the process of justification can be guided by a notion of truth that transcends justification although it is always already operatively effective in the realm of action. The function of the validity of statements in everyday practices explains why the distinctive vindication of validity claims may at the same time be interpreted as the satisfaction of a pragmatic need for justification. The need for justification, which sets in train the transformation of shaken-up behavioral certainties into problematized validity claims, can be satisfied only by a translation of justified beliefs back into behavioral truths. (Habermas 2000b, p. 49)

Let me elucidate and simplify what Habermas is saying in this rather complicated passage. Habermas wants to explicate the relation of justification and truth. He realizes that an epistemic conception of truth – a conception that restricts itself to the discursive justification of truth claims – cannot by itself provide an adequate theory of truth, because, no matter how "ideal" our justification may be, it may nevertheless turn out to be false. So we have to complement this epistemic concept of truth with a non-epistemic concept – or, more accurately, we have to grasp the epistemic and non-epistemic aspects of the concept of truth. Taking his cue from the classical pragmatists, Habermas suggests that we return to the context of everyday practices and actions. In the "realm of action" we are always operating with behavioral certainties. We act as if we know what is true. But sometimes we encounter frustrations and resistances that compel us to question what we have taken as unproblematic. When this happens, we can react in many different ways; but one of our options is to engage in a discourse in which we problematize what we initially took for granted, and seek to resolve the problem by moving to a level of discourse in which we evaluate and justify our truth claims. We cannot account for truth by appealing solely to justificatory discourse; nor can we account for truth simply by appealing solely to the "behavioral certainties of everyday life." But if we grasp that truth is *Janus-faced* because it stands between action and discourse, then we can elucidate a notion of truth that transcends justification. By relating action to discourse in this manner, we can understand both why there is a "pragmatic need for justification" and how this need is satisfied by translating discursively established "beliefs back into behavioral truths."

On one interpretation, what Habermas says seems thoroughly noncontroversial, although one might object to his complicated form of expression. In our everyday lives we implicitly act on all sorts of beliefs that we take for granted – "practical certainties." Sometimes we are thwarted and face a practical uncertainty. This uncertainty may initiate a discourse in which participants offer reasons for the best solution about what is to be done. If the situation is resolved satisfactorily, I proceed on my way. If this is what it means to vindicate "realistic intuitions," then it is hard to see what all the fuss is about. Not even Rorty would deny that in our everyday lives we are frustrated and meet all sorts of obstacles, and sometimes we need to engage in inquiry and discussion to work out how to cope. (Rorty, of

course, would question whether it is helpful to describe this as commonsense "realism," or whether any of this requires us to speak about
a truth that transcends justification.)

Moral Constructivism and Epistemological Realism

Before probing further what Habermas means by his "Janus-faced"
concept of truth" and in what sense, if any, it helps us to "vindicate"
our "realist intuitions," I want to consider why it is so important
for him to come up with an adequate pragmatic theory of truth. In
advancing a pragmatic theory of truth, Habermas is not concerned
exclusively with vindicating our "realist intuitions." He wants sharply
to distinguish practical moral discourse, which is concerned with justifying universal moral norms, from theoretical discourse, which is
concerned with justifying truth claims. This distinction between these
two forms of discourse (and argumentation) is a fundamental doctrine of his Kantian pragmatism. In practical moral discourse, there
is nothing in the "objective world" to which we can appeal in order
to resolve our disagreements, whereas in theoretical discourse we do
appeal to the objective world (in a linguistically mediated manner)
to resolve disagreements.

> Moral validity claims lack reference to the objective world that is
> characteristic of claims to truth. This means they are robbed of a
> justification-transcendent point of reference. The reference to the
> world is replaced by an orientation toward extending the borders of
> the social community and its consensus about values. (Habermas 2003,
> pp. 256–7)

With moral norms, the only relevant consideration is the recognition
of the worthiness of norms by those affected by these norms.

> For the worthiness of norms to be recognized is based not on an
> objectively determined agreement of interests that are given, but on
> participants interpreting and evaluating interests from a first-person
> plural perspective. The participants can develop norms embodying
> shared interests only from a We-perspective. This perspective has to
> be constructed out of a reversible exchange of perspectives of all those
> affected. (Habermas 2003, p. 268)

So we must *not* identify or assimilate the type of "objectivity" we can achieve in moral discourse (intersubjective agreement by all those affected) with the strong realist objectivity indicated by an unanticipated reality – by a world that is independent of us. "The 'objectivity' of another mind is made of different stuff than the objectivity of an unanticipated reality" (Habermas 2003, p. 256). Theoretical reason is concerned with truth, and it deals with an objective world that is independent of us. Practical reason (in morals) is concerned with constructing and validating universal moral norms. Argumentation is essential for both forms of reason, but we corroborate moral beliefs "by consensually resolving interactions," and not by "successfully manipulating otherwise independently occurring processes" (ibid.). Habermas's Kantian pragmatism combines epistemological realism with moral constructivism.

Janus-Faced Truth?

Thus far, I have presented a sympathetic account of Habermas's Kantian pragmatism, explaining in what sense he is "Kantian" and "pragmatic." I want to raise some critical issues – primarily about his account of truth, his distinction between action and discourse, and his Kantian distinction between theoretical and practical reason.

We have seen that the core of his pragmatic conception of truth depends on the distinction between action and discourse (argumentation). This distinction is vital for his "Janus-faced" concept of truth. Habermas originally introduced this distinction and his pragmatic theory of truth in developing a critique of Rorty's contextualism. But here I agree with Rorty's response about this distinction.

> [W]hen Habermas makes a distinction between "two pragmatic roles ... played by the Janus-faced concept of truth in action-contexts and in rational discourses respectively," and when he goes on to say that "the concept of truth allows translation of shaken-up behavioral certainties into problematized propositions," I would rejoin that he is ignoring Peirce's point that beliefs are just habits of action. A rational discourse is just one more action-context in which a behavioral certainty evinces itself. There is no Janus-like role to be played, and no translation to be performed. (Rorty 2000a, p. 57)

Unlike Rorty, I do not want to deny that in some circumstances it is helpful to draw a distinction between action and discourse, but we should realize how misleading this distinction can be: how much "discourse" is embedded in action-contexts and how much action is embedded in discourse. Habermas's pragmatic theory of truth depends on drawing a clear distinction between action and discourse. But if we begin to question the rigidity of this distinction, we question the very idea of a Janus-faced concept of truth. When acting, I do take all sorts of things for granted without questioning them, but action is not dumb. It is – as Dewey says – funded with meaning and what I have learnt from the past. And as I act in the world, I am frequently adjusting my actions as I encounter unanticipated obstacles – as practical certainties turn into uncertainties. When I stop and reflect about how to resolve an uncertainty, I do not necessarily "move into" discourse. When I discover that the subway isn't running – being acquainted with New York's bus system – I, after some hesitation, decide to take the Fifth Avenue bus, without engaging in any discourse. But this feature of acting in the lifeworld is just as true for discourse. In any discourse, including sophisticated scientific discourse, I take all sorts of things for granted as "practical certainties," and I may well discover that what I have taken for granted is in fact problematic. Even in the "lifeworld," when my anticipations are frustrated, there are many different ways that I can adapt to the situation – and these adjustments are integral to acting in the world. Acting in the world is rarely simply routinized; it involves reflection and deliberation – and occasionally consulting with others about what is to be done. One of the primary aims of the classical pragmatists was to encourage the development of intelligent habits of action that would enable us better to cope with the world; to make our actions more intelligent and imaginative in responding to new situations. But Habermas makes it sound as if action is completely unreflective when he speaks of action and discourse as "two domains" and says: "Only once they make the transition from action to discourse do participants take a *reflective attitude* and dispute the now thematized truth of controversial propositions in the light of reasons for and against it" (Habermas 2003, p. 39; emphasis added). Furthermore, discourse frequently involves all sorts of actions, experiments, and interventions – as the classical pragmatists also emphasized. Experimentation and intervention are just as important and relevant to "discourse" as they are to "action." This is why I find Dewey's description of the

pattern of inquiry – where one begins with a "felt difficulty," moves
to specification of a problem, advances hypotheses, then tests these
hypotheses in order to resolve an "indeterminate situation" – more
illuminating than Habermas's analysis of the move from action to discourse and back to action. As Dewey stresses, this pattern of inquiry is
exemplified in ordinary everyday actions and sophisticated theoretical inquiry (as well as in what Habermas calls "ethical" and "moral"
inquiry).[14] But all of this can be described without any reference to
the "Janus-faced concept of truth."

Habermas recognizes the "embeddedness of discourses in the lifeworld," but nevertheless he claims:

> Convictions play a different role in action than in discourse and "prove
> their truth" in a different way in the former than in the latter. In every-
> day practices, a prereflexive "coping with the world" decides whether
> convictions "function" or are drawn into the maelstrom of problemati-
> zation, whereas in argumentation it depends solely on reasons whether
> controversial validity claims deserve rationally motivated recognition.
> (Habermas 2000b, p. 48)

Do "convictions play a different role in action and discourse"? I don't
think so. Whether it is action or discourse, I take all sorts of things for
granted – as practical certainties. Talk about a "prereflexive 'coping
with the world'" makes it sound as if in such coping there is no reflection and deliberation. But most of our acting in the lifeworld involves
some sort of reflection and deliberation – no matter how fleeting and
incidental it may be. To speak about the "maelstrom of problematization" exaggerates the difference between discourse and action.
"Problematization" is just as characteristic of everyday actions and
practices as it is of cultivated argumentation. So what we have here
is a difference of *degree*, ranging from routinized behavior that doesn't
involve reflection (but is typically funded by previous reflection) to
abstract forms of discursive argumentation. But this is a *continuum*
– not a movement from action to something that is categorically different, discourse. If we give up this (idealized) distinction between
action and discourse, this puts in question the relevance of speaking
of the "Janus-faced concept of truth." I am not denying that, in some
contexts, it is useful to introduce a distinction between action and discourse. But if we do so, it is *we* who make this distinction, and we do so
for specific reasons. Consequently, it is misleading to speak of "the

different roles played by the concept of truth in the two domains" (Habermas 2003, p. 39).

Habermas exaggerates the difference between action and discourse in order to make his "Janus-faced concept of truth" seem plausible. Consider the following passage:

> Although when we adopt a reflexive attitude we know that all knowledge is fallible, in everyday life we cannot survive with hypotheses alone, that is, in a persistently fallibilist way. The organized fallibilism of scientific inquiry can deal hypothetically with controversial validity claims indefinitely because it serves to bring about agreements that are uncoupled from action. This model is not suitable for the lifeworld. ... We would step on no bridge, use no car, undergo no operation, not even eat an exquisitely prepared meal if we did not hold assumptions employed in the production and execution of our actions to be true. At any rate, the performative need for behavioral certainty rules out a reservation in principle with regard to truth, even though we know, as soon as the naïve performance of actions is interrupted, that truth claims can be vindicated only discursively – that is, only within the relevant context of justification. Truth may be assimilated neither to behavioral certainty nor to justified assertibility. (Habermas 2000b, p. 44)

Of course, in everyday life we cannot survive on hypotheses alone; but neither is this the case in scientific inquiry. We could not conduct any inquiry – commonsense, scientific, ethical, or moral – unless we took all sorts of background knowledge and implicit convictions for granted – or, in Habermas's language, acted as if there were "behavioral certainties." (This is a lesson that Peirce taught us long ago.) It is misleading to say that the "organized fallibilism of scientific inquiry can deal hypothetically with controversial validity claims indefinitely because it serves to bring about agreements that are uncoupled from action." Scientific inquiry is rarely, if ever, uncoupled from action, because performing experiments and testing our hypotheses are actions integral to scientific inquiry. I would not step on a bridge unless I assumed it were relatively solid, but I would not conduct a scientific experiment unless I assumed that the instrument I am about to use is functioning properly. In both cases I may well discover that my "practical certainties" have been problematized.

But, even more troubling, it isn't clear what Habermas really explains with his non-epistemic conception of pragmatic truth.

Suppose, for the moment, we accept Habermas's characterization of practical certainties in the lifeworld – that we act as if many of our implicit beliefs are unquestionably true; that we bump up against a world that frustrates our expectations and compels us to question what we took to be certain; and that this questioning gives rise to a discourse in which we seek to evaluate and justify claims to resolve the problematic situation. In what sense does this contribute to an *explanation* that accounts for the philosophical understanding of realism and truth? Habermas says that, although justification (even if it were ideal) is not to be identified with truth, nevertheless there is an "internal connection between justification and truth," which explains "why we may, in light of the evidence available to us, raise an unconditional truth claim that aims beyond what is justified." But why not drop this talk of "unconditional truth" and simply say that no matter how rigorous and comprehensive our justifications, we may discover that they are not true? This is what Rorty calls the "cautionary" use of 'true.' It is hard to see what work the appeal to "unconditional truth" does. If we do discover that something we take to be thoroughly justified is false, it will be because we have reasons to question our justification, not because we presuppose that there is an "unconditional truth." For example, before the United States invaded Iraq in 2003, it seemed to be true that Saddam Hussein had some weapons – at least some chemical weapons – of mass destruction. After all, he had already used chemical weapons against the Kurds. But it turned out that this (justified) belief was false. We falsely believed that he still had these chemical weapons at the time of the Iraq invasion. Consequently, we now have good reasons to reject our earlier belief. We can *now* say that we have good reasons to say it was false, because no such weapons were discovered. And, of course, further investigation (the discovery of a hidden cache of such weapons) may, in the future, necessitate revising our current beliefs. We don't need to appeal to an "unconditional truth" or "justification-transcendent truth" to make sense of why we reject a former justification. Not only do we reject former "justifications," we sometimes also reject former criteria or standards of justification – as we learn from the history of science.[15]

We can put the difficulty in a slightly different way. Habermas tells us: "It is the goal of justifications to discover a truth that exceeds all justification" (Habermas 2003, pp. 33–4). But the phrase "exceeds all justification" is crucially ambiguous. It may simply mean that it is the goal of justification to discover a truth (full stop). But, of course, our justifications may fail to achieve this goal. This is why we need a cautionary use of 'true.' But Habermas thinks that something more is needed – "unconditional truth." He thinks that it is a deep and troubling question to ask: how is it that our justifications can tell us the truth about the "real world," especially since we know that no justification is sufficient to guarantee this truth? Although I have serious reservations about the way in which Rorty seeks to dismiss and/or trivialize the very idea of truth, I do think his critique of Habermas with regard to this issue on target.

> There is, to be sure, something unconditional about of truth. The unconditionality is expressed by the fact that once true, always true: we regard people who use the word in such expressions as 'true then, but not now' as using it incorrectly. Since "once justified, always justified" is obviously false, one can indeed express the contrast between truth and justification as a contrast between the unconditional and the conditional. But the unconditionality in question does not provide a reason for the fact that the cautionary use of 'true' is always apropos. ... The whole pragmatic force of the claim that truth is not conditional is to express willingness to change one's mind if circumstances alter, not to explain or justify this willingness. *We are not contritely fallible because we are in awe of the unconditionality of truth. Rather, to speak of truth as being unconditional is just one more way of expressing our sense of contrite fallibility.* (Rorty 2000a, p. 57; emphasis added)

Although we can speak of "unconditional truth" or "true" as a predicate that a proposition "cannot lose," it is difficult to see that appeal to such notions helps to explain anything. Habermas also declares that the "nonepistemic concept of truth, which manifests itself only operatively, that is, unthematically, in action, provides a justification-transcendent point of reference for discursively thematized truth claims" (ibid.). But in what sense do "behavioral certainties" – the facts we implicitly assume to be true – serve as a point of reference for a justification-transcendent concept of truth? Why not simply say that when something that we take to be practically certain in the lifeworld becomes problematic, we try to figure out what to do and say? And when Habermas goes on to say that "it is the goal of justifications to discover a truth that exceeds all justification" (ibid.), our perplexity is only increased. Does this mean anything more than that we expect (or hope) "the truth" that we have presumably discovered and sought to justify really is the truth – that our justification will withstand criticism and refutation?

Habermas is right when he claims that in the everyday lifeworld of actions, coping requires that we take all sorts of things for granted as practical certainties, and that reflection is provoked when these certainties become problematic. This was the starting point for the classical pragmatic conception of inquiry – when real doubt arises. (Not even Rorty would deny this. If something didn't resist and frustrate us, we could not even speak about coping.) But the basic question is whether the appeal to "unconditional truth" or "justification-transcendent truth" does any real work besides expressing "our willingness to change our minds if circumstances change." And if we are asked why we are willing to change our minds, why we are willing to reject justifications that we once accepted, we can answer: because we have learned over and over again that what we thought was thoroughly justified has turned out to be mistaken. It seems that – pragmatically speaking – Habermas's "realistic intuitions" come down to little more than what Peirce, in his categorical scheme, called Secondness – the non-epistemic sense of resistance, brute force, and compulsion, "the absolute constraint upon us to think otherwise than we have been thinking that constitutes experience" (1.336).[16]

Moral Constructivism Again

I have raised a number of questions about Habermas's pragmatic "Janus-faced" concept of truth, which is intended to clarify the validity claim of truth and help us to distinguish theoretical reason from practical reason. I now want to turn to the other pillar of his Kantian pragmatism – his understanding of normative rightness as a validity claim and his moral constructivism – in order to consider some of his key claims about practical (moral) reason. There are many issues that can (and) have been raised by critics. Do the Habermasian distinctions between norms and values, between rightness and goodness, between morality and ethics, really hold up? Many of Habermas's critics – including Rorty, Putnam, Brandom, McCarthy and I – have criticized Habermas on some or all of these issues.[17]

I will limit my discussion to Habermas's claim that truth and objectivity play a different role in theoretical and practical (moral) discourse, in order to challenge the thesis that is so fundamental for his version of Kantian pragmatism – that there is a fundamental distinction between theoretical and practical reason. I have already suggested that Habermas proposes his version of a pragmatic concept of truth not only to avoid Rorty's contextualism and Brandom's neo-Hegelianism, but also because of his concern to call attention to the analogy – yet fundamental difference – between truth and rightness. He thinks that we are tempted to confuse the two if we assume – as many analytic philosophers have – that the paradigm of a validity claim is the assertion of truth. "Realist intuitions" can be vindicated when it comes to matters of truth, but they have no place in relation to moral norms. Now why is this distinction so important for Habermas? Why does he have a "horror" of moral realism? He believes that moving in this direction, obliterating or softening the distinction between truth and rightness, would undermine his communicative theory of action (with its different types of validity claims) and his discourse theory of ethics. "The concept of 'normative rightness' can be reduced without remainder to rational justification under ideal conditions. It lacks the ontological connotation of reference to things about which we state facts" (Habermas 2003, p. 42).

Habermas concedes that there is a proper role for speaking about "moral truth" and "moral objectivity." But he insists that the meaning of "truth" and "objectivity" when we are speaking from a theoretical perspective is radically different from when we speak from a practical perspective. So now we must ask whether the role of the concepts of 'objectivity' and 'truth' are as different in theoretical discourse and practical (moral) discourse as Habermas claims.

Why Habermas Rejects Moral Realism

Before turning directly to these issues, I want to consider why the expression "moral realism" is loaded and misleading. (To the best of my knowledge, none of the classical pragmatists ever used this expression.) We might say that there is a picture here that holds one captive. And it certainly seems that this is the picture that Habermas has in mind when he categorically rejects moral realism and defends moral constructivism. Earlier I cited the passage where Habermas says: "What we want to express with true sentences is that a certain state of affairs 'obtains' or is 'given'. And these facts in turn refer to 'the world' as the totality of things about which we state facts." If we take this ontological way of speaking as presenting the paradigm of realism, then we can certainly understand why Habermas rejects moral realism. There don't seem to be any states of affairs that "obtain" in "the world" that *correspond* to our moral norms. When, for example, Habermas critiques Putnam's notion of "ought-implying facts," he declares that "to extend cognitive realism to values is to postulate facts that are 'queer' (in Mackie's sense) inasmuch as they run counter to our grammatical intuitions" (Habermas 2003, p. 224).[18]

But to appreciate fully why Habermas finds moral realism so objectionable and defends a version of Kantian constructivism, we need to grasp a deeper Habermasian theme: his understanding of how modernity has transformed the issue of moral autonomy and authority. Kant's great insight regarding moral norms is not only that they are universal, but that there is no higher moral authority than the appeal to our own practical rationality. The key to understanding moral autonomy is *self-legislation*. Any appeal to an authority other than our own practical reason is a form of heteronomy. Habermas accepts this claim, and he thinks of his own discourse theory as a continuation of this Kantian project. Moral constructivism shows that we, and we alone, have the responsibility for justifying universal moral norms. "If moral claims to validity nonetheless owe their binding force to something unconditional and analogous to truth, then the orientation toward ever increasing inclusiveness of other claims and persons must somehow compensate for the missing reference to the objective world" (Habermas 2003, p. 43). Because the expression "moral realism" is so loaded with misleading connotations and calls to mind a world of "queer" facts, I think it best to drop the expression altogether and concentrate on the role of truth and objectivity in moral argumentation.

Let us consider again the example that Habermas uses to illustrate the universality of moral norms, which he distinguishes from the particularity of ethical values:

> We call the torture of human beings "cruel" not only here for us, but everywhere and for everyone. Yet we feel by no means justified to object against strange child-raising practices or marriage ceremonies, that is, against core components of the ethos of a foreign culture, as long

as they do not contradict our moral standards. The latter are those central values that differ from other values in virtue of their universal claim to validity. (Habermas 2003, pp. 228–9)

I do not want to deny that there are some "central values that differ from other values in virtue of their universal claim to validity," where this is understood as being applicable to all human beings rather than to some specific group, people, or nation. The primary issue concerns how Habermas interprets this difference. He thinks that there is a sharp distinction between ethics and morals. The "domain" of ethics is that of values, and implicitly or explicitly they are limited to first-person singular or plural questions. And the "domain" of morals – or the moral point of view – concerns binding moral norms for which we claim universal validity.

> Ethical-existential questions – what is best for me overall? who am I and who do I want to be? – arise from the first-person perspective just as ethical-political questions about the collective identity and way of life do. Casting the issue in terms of ethics already means selecting the context of one's life history or of our collective life as the point of reference for this kind of hermeneutic self-reflection. This explains why practical wisdom is intuitive as well as context-dependent. ... And since such reflection guides what we do or don't do within the horizon of our own lifeworld, there is no universal validity claim connected with ethical wisdom. (Habermas 2003, p. 228)

I find this sharp distinction between ethics and morality unpersuasive. And this becomes evident if we turn to "real" ethical perspectives, especially those embedded in religious orientations. Ethical orientations embedded in religious world views have both particularistic and universal aspects (and sometimes it is difficult to draw a sharp line between these). As Jews, Christians, or Muslims, there are particular values that we share with our co-religionists, and we may also have binding obligations to them. But every one of the great religions also incorporates universal binding obligations to one's fellow human beings. And if I take my ethical responsibilities seriously as a member of a religious community, then I am committed to norms that apply to all human beings – whether or not the person is a member of my religious community. Habermas is right to point out that there are more particularistic and moral universal validity claims in every living ethical orientation, but it is misleading to speak of "ethical world views" as particularistic and "the moral point of view" as universalistic, and to contrast "a universalistic morality of justice" with "a particularist ethics of the good life" (ibid.).[19] Here one would like Habermas to be more pragmatic and recognize that our values and norms form a dynamic shifting continuum such that some are more particularistic and some more universalistic. Furthermore, we need to recognize just how open-ended "universalistic" moral claims are. It is not just that there are learning processes about what count as universal moral norms – a point that Habermas emphasizes. But in the course of history, unanticipated consequences and structural transformations require radical rethinking of the very meaning of morality, responsibility, and justice. Adorno argued that "after Auschwitz" we need a new categorical imperative, and Hans Jonas argued that, as a result of modern technology, we need a new imperative of responsibility. At its best, the universalistic characteristic of what Habermas calls the moral point of view is an *aspiration* that can take on radically different, and even incompatible, concrete meanings in novel historical circumstances. At its worst, it is merely formal and empty.[20]

Let us consider the role of truth and objectivity in practical discourse. Assume – as Habermas does – that the prohibition engaging in the practice of torture is a good candidate for a universal binding moral norm.[21] Consider some of the heated arguments that have been taking place recently in the United States about "waterboarding": whether it is a form of torture and whether or not it is a practice that can be morally justified – or at least be considered morally permissible – when used on suspected "terrorists." In these practical debates, issues arise about the practice of "waterboarding," its history and how it is used, and what are its effects on victims, what sorts of physical and psychological pain it inflicts, etc. Answering these questions in a responsible way requires making validity claims about what is true about objective practices. Now, of course, the type of facts that I will take to be relevant in arguing about the propriety of waterboarding will be quite different from the type of facts that are relevant in deciding the best way to get to my office; but I fail to see that Habermas has given us any reason to think that the meaning of 'true,' 'justify,' and 'objective' differs when we engage in these inquiries. There are factual issues concerning the practice and consequences of waterboarding.

Habermas sometimes suggests that the tasks of justifying and applying must be carefully distinguished. But this distinction, which is sometimes useful, can obscure the difficult practical issues that we have to face. It is not as if we have clear or fixed criteria for determining what constitutes torture, and can then decide whether they are applicable to the practice of waterboarding. The hard – and contestable – practical issue is to decide whether waterboarding should be judged as torture. We can't have a serious discussion about what moral norms ought to be binding unless we know what we mean by these norms and what are their consequences – the very meaning of such norms is always, in principle (and frequently, in fact), open to further determination and argumentation.[22] Habermas stresses the importance of "learning processes" in determining moral norms; but these learning processes frequently involve coming to a better understanding of the factual consequences of moral norms.

But still Habermas might object. There clearly is a difference between arguing about the truth of facts (even if these facts are relevant to practical disagreements) and arguing about universal moral norms. Again, the point is *not* to deny this difference, but rather to question how to interpret it. When we have to decide "moral," "ethical," or "merely pragmatic" issues, do we really engage in different *types* of practical deliberation? One wishes that Habermas had been less "Kantian" and more "pragmatic." Dewey, for example, characterized practical judgments as "judgments of a situation demanding action. There are, for example, propositions of the form: M.N. should do thus and so; it is better, wiser, more prudent, right, advisable, opportune, expedient, etc. to act thus and so. And this is the type of judgment I denote practical" (Dewey 1998, p. 234). This doesn't mean that judging what is right to do is the same as judging what is expedient. But insofar as they are both practical judgments, they form a continuum and differ only in degree. Furthermore, there is no dichotomy between theory and practice.

> The depersonalization of the things of everyday practice becomes the chief agency of their repersonalizing in new and more fruitful modes of practice. The paradox of theory and practice is that theory is with respect to all other modes of practice the most practical of all things, and the more impartial and impersonal it is, the more truly practical it is. And this is the sole paradox. (Dewey 1998, p. 268)

Although I have been critical of the way in which Habermas vindicates his "realistic intuitions," I certainly endorse his shift to the

pragmatic context of action in explaining what he means by 'truth.'
But I think he also needs to shift more radically to the context of
action and practice in his analysis of the justification of moral norms.
In the context of action we appeal to (tentative) norms to guide
our action. When we confront new problems, we have to clarify and
defend moral norms. We do not first discursively justify moral norms
and then apply them to new contexts. There is a more dynamic and
dialectical relation between confronting practical choices, clarifying
the precise meaning of the norms that guide us, and seeking to justify
them.

At times, especially when he describes his "epistemological
realism," Habermas sounds as if he is still wedded to what Dewey
called "the spectator theory of knowledge." This becomes evident in
the way in which he speaks about the "objective world." Typically,
he limits the expression "objective world" to what empirical descriptive judgments describe. "Empirical judgments say how things are
in the objective world whereas evaluative judgments enjoin us to
value or treat something in our lifeworld in the same way or other"
(Habermas 2003, p. 224). If this is taken to be the primary or privileged use of 'objective,' then, of course, we would have to conclude
that value and normative judgments do not describe the objective
world – or if we speak of them as "objective," we are using 'objective'
in a different sense. But we can challenge this limited or privileged
use of the expression 'objective.'[23] Whether we are speaking about
empirical judgments or normative judgments, we can speak of them
as 'objective' if they can properly be justified – insisting, of course,
that any specific justification may turn out to be unwarranted.

There is a tendency in Habermas, despite his disclaimers, to reify
fact talk, to think that facts are simply the way in which we (correctly)
describe the world. "What we want to express with true sentences is
that a certain state of affairs 'obtains' or is 'given'. And these facts
in turn refer to 'the world' as the totality of things about which we
may state facts" (Habermas 2003, p. 254). But Habermas might have
developed a more pragmatic understanding of facts viewed from the
perspective of agents (inquirers) solving problems if he had adopted
Dewey's "operational" perspective. Dewey writes:

> What is meant by calling facts operational? Upon the negative side
> what is meant is that they are not self-sufficient and complete in
> themselves. They are selected and described ... for a purpose, namely

statement of the problem involved in such a way that its material both indicates a meaning relevant to resolution of the difficulty and serves to test its worth and validity. ... They are not merely *results* of operations of observation which are executed with the aid of bodily organs and auxiliary instruments of art, but they are particular facts and kinds of facts that will link up with one another in the definite ways that are required to produce a definite end. (Dewey 1981, p. 234)

When facts are viewed in light of their pragmatic role in problem-solving, then they are just as relevant and essential for empirical description as they are for clarifying and justifying moral norms.

I have argued that when Habermas's "epistemological realism" is analyzed, it amounts to little more than the recognition of what Peirce called Secondness – that we encounter resistances in our "theoretical" and "practical" dealings with the world, resistances that limit our "theoretical" and "practical" justifications. "Truth" and "objectivity" are just as relevant to arguments about the empirical character of the world as they are to serious practical disputes about what ought to be morally binding. There are, of course, differences between different types of inquiry, but these differences have more to do with the context of inquiry than with the meanings of 'true' and 'objective.' Habermas's "Kantian pragmatism" is an *unstable* stopping stage. Habermas speaks about moving from Kant to Hegel and back again to Kant. Many of my criticisms of Habermas's Kantian dichotomies are in the spirit of Hegel. But the main point is not to move *back* again to Kant, but to move *forward* to a more dynamic, flexible pragmatism in the spirit of Dewey and Mead. Dewey and Mead clearly discerned – despite their many limitations – that although distinctions play a crucial role in philosophy, we must understand their functional changing roles in human experience, inquiry, and discourse.[24] They – and I fully agree with them – affirm the *continuity* between theoretical and practical reason.

9

Richard Rorty's Deep Humanism

I first met Dick Rorty in 1949 when I went to the "Hutchins College" at the University of Chicago – the institution described by A. J. Liebling as "the biggest collection of juvenile neurotics since the Children's Crusade." Rorty had already entered the University of Chicago in 1946 at the age of 15 and was beginning his M.A. in philosophy. After Chicago, he went on to Yale in 1952 for his doctoral studies, and he encouraged several of his Chicago friends (including me) to join him. From those early Chicago and Yale days, we became close personal friends – a friendship that lasted until his death in 2007. On the occasion of my seventieth birthday, Rorty wrote:

> Richard Bernstein and I are almost exact contemporaries, were educated in mostly the same places by mostly the same people, have been exalted by many of the same hopes, and have been talking to one another about how to fulfill those hopes for more than fifty years. We share not only many enthusiasms, but the vast majority of our convictions, both philosophical and political. (Rorty 2004, p. 3)[1]

No other contemporary philosopher has influenced me in such a creative manner. As I developed my own interpretation of pragmatism, I frequently felt I was addressing Rorty directly or indirectly – seeking to meet his penetrating challenges. Some of our philosophical disagreements were quite sharp, but they were always productive. Over the years I found myself defending Rorty as frequently as I criticized him, especially when I felt that attacks on him were grossly unfair.

I shall examine Rorty's deep humanism. It may seem strange and ironical to speak about Rorty's "deep humanism," because in *Contingency, Irony, and Solidarity*, he calls into question the very idea that there is anything "deep" and persistent about our selves. Yet, for all the complexity of his personality and his philosophical thinking, I believe that there has been a deep and persistent humanism that is characteristic of his life and his thinking. But to bring this forth, one needs some overall perspective on his life's work and development.

Rorty's Early Metaphysical Explorations

One of the misleading legends about Rorty is that he began his career as an analytic philosopher but turned against analytic philosophy. True, his early philosophical reputation was based on a number of outstanding articles that were at the cutting edge of analytic philosophy, especially those dealing with the mind–body problem and the misleading character of conceptual and transcendental arguments. But this ignores his ten years of philosophical study at Chicago and Yale. Although Rorty studied with a variety of philosophers at Chicago, including Richard McKeon, Rudolf Carnap, and Charles Hartshorne, he wrote his master's thesis on Alfred North Whitehead with Hartshorne. From McKeon and the general intellectual atmosphere at Chicago, Rorty developed a comprehensive and sophisticated knowledge of the history of philosophy. Rorty's characteristic wit and self-irony are already evident in a letter that he wrote to his mother, Winifred Raushenbush, in 1950 about a paper he wrote for Carnap:

> Finished a paper for Carnap – long, dull, of interest only to opponents of positivism. You can look at it if you like, but I can't see it interesting either you, Carnap, or anybody except the little clique of reactionary metaphysicians (the rank to which I aspire) who are trying to stop the positivist invasion. Title – "Logical Truth, Factual Truth, and the Synthetic A Priori." Someone suggested as a subtitle "How to Square the Vienna Circle." (Cited in Gross 2008, p. 123)

At Yale, Rorty worked with the boldest speculative metaphysician of the twentieth century, Paul Weiss. He wrote a dazzling 600-page dissertation entitled, "The Concept of Potentiality" (which he never published) under Weiss's supervision. He examined ancient (Aristotle), early modern (Descartes, Spinoza, and Leibniz), and contemporary (Carnap and Nelson Goodman) treatments of potentiality. Rorty's early metaphilosophical interests are already evident in his dissertation; he provides brilliant expositions and critiques of all three treatments of potentiality. But he tells us that "one of the motives in the choice of the topic of potentiality as the subject of this dissertation is the belief that it is in regard to this topic that the relation between the problems of logical empiricism and the problems of traditional metaphysics and epistemology may be most easily perceived" (Rorty 1956, p. xvi).

The importance of this early phase of Rorty's work for his subsequent philosophizing cannot be overestimated. Before he began to take analytic philosophy seriously, he already had a comprehensive and subtle understanding of the history of philosophy. He identified himself most closely with the grand metaphysical tradition (much later he called this "Platonism") and sought to show its contemporary relevance. His metaphilosophical interests are evident in some of his earliest published articles. In a stunning article, "Pragmatism, Categories, and Language" (1961), he claims that pragmatism is becoming relevant again and that the most up-to-date pragmatist is Charles S. Peirce. Much later, as we shall see, he dismissed the importance of Peirce, and claimed that the true progenitors of pragmatism were William James and John Dewey. But in 1961, he wrote:

> Peirce's thought envisaged, and repudiated in advance, the stages in the development of empiricism which logical positivism represented, and ... it came to rest in a group of insights and a philosophical mood much like those we find in the *Philosophical Investigations* and in the writings of philosophers influenced by the later Wittgenstein. (Rorty 1961a, pp. 197–8)

In his aloof metaphilosophical stance, he makes it clear that he is neither trying to show that "Peirce saw through a glass darkly what Wittgenstein saw face to face, nor the reverse. ... What I am trying to show is that the closer one brings pragmatism to the writings of the later Wittgenstein and of those influenced by him, the more light they shed on each other" (Rorty 1961a, pp. 198–9).

The Linguistic Turn

Rorty started reading analytic philosophy seriously when he was completing his dissertation. Wilfrid Sellars was the philosopher who initially had the greatest influence on him. I vividly recall discussing Sellars with Rorty in those early days. We both felt that Sellars represented the best of the analytic tradition, because he was leading the way in showing how the linguistic turn, with its subtle analytic techniques, could be used to clarify and further the discussion of many traditional philosophical issues.

During the 1960s Rorty published several papers that were important contributions to ongoing analytic debates. For example, in his "Mind–Body Identity, Privacy, and Categories" (1965), he developed an original approach to the mind–body identity theory, in which he defended the thesis that "it is sensible to assert that empirical inquiry will discover that sensations (not thoughts) are identical with certain brain-processes" (Rorty 1965, p. 24). Rorty was not predicting that this would happen – that descriptions of brain processes would displace descriptions of sensations – but only that it is sensible or conceptually meaningful to claim that it could happen. His interest in the mind–body identity theory was a case-study for dealing with a much larger issue. At the time, many proponents of conceptual analysis strongly believed that the genuine task of philosophy is to expose conceptual and linguistic confusions. They argued that to say that sensations can be identified with brain states is a conceptual confusion, an egregious category mistake (a howler!). But Rorty challenged the thesis that one can "draw a firm line between the 'conceptual' and the 'empirical', and thus ... differentiate between a statement embodying a conceptual confusion and one that expresses a surprising empirical result" (Rorty 1965, p. 25). The article was important for a number of reasons. Rorty showed a new way of thinking about the identity theory (sometimes labeled "eliminative materialism"); he also called into question one of the cherished dogmas of linguistic conceptual analysis – that we can sharply distinguish conceptual analysis from empirical inquiry. He challenged this "new" linguistic version of *a priori* transcendental argumentation. He concluded his article by warning linguistic philosophers that they should not "think that they can do better what metaphysicians did badly – namely, prove the irreducibility of entities" (Rorty 1965, p. 54). Reading this article from the perspective of Rorty's later development is revealing.

Although he doesn't mention "pragmatism," the thesis that "there is simply no such thing as a method of classifying linguistic expressions that has results guaranteed to remain intact despite the results of empirical inquiry" (Rorty 1965, p. 25) is the thesis that was advocated by the classical American pragmatists. Furthermore, he anticipates what he later called "vocabularies" and the ways in which new vocabularies can displace older ones.[2] His basic strategy is to show that there are no good philosophical reasons to believe that it is conceptually impossible that a language about brain states might some day displace our current language about sensations. And, finally, we can see here Rorty's fascination with metaphilosophy – his concern with understanding and criticizing the various strategies that philosophers use to make and justify their claims.[3]

In 1961, after three years at Wellesley, Rorty was invited by Gregory Vlastos to join the Princeton philosophy department as a one-year visitor. At the time, Princeton had one of the most outstanding graduate philosophy departments in the country. Vlastos, who had heard about Rorty's dissertation, initially asked him to help teach ancient philosophy. In his "Intellectual Autobiography," Rorty describes what happened:

> As soon as I got to Princeton in the fall of 1961 I realized that I did not know nearly enough Greek for Vlastos's purposes, and that I was probably not the man he wanted. So I assumed I would be back at Wellesley the following fall. But, again to my surprise, I was offered a three-year further appointment. (Rorty, "Intellectual Autobiography", cited in Gross 2008, p. 165)

Rorty remained at Princeton until 1982, when he left to become a professor of humanities at the University of Virginia.

In 1967, Rorty published his famous anthology, *The Linguistic Turn*, which was designed to show various ways in which linguistic philosophers had viewed philosophy and philosophical method over the previous 35 years. His introduction provides a metaphilosophical overview of the different strands of linguistic philosophy. In the concluding section of his introduction, he raises the question: "Is the linguistic turn doomed to suffer the same fate as previous 'revolutions in philosophy'?" (Rorty 1967, p. 33). He does not explicitly answer this question, but instead outlines "six possibilities for the future of philosophy, after the dissolution of traditional problems" (Rorty 1967,

p. 34). Although he does not take a definite stand on what will happen, he hints at the future direction of his own thinking. This becomes clear in the fourth possibility that he enumerates:

> It might be that we would end by answering the question "Has phi-losophy come to an end?" with a resounding "Yes," and that we would come to look upon a post-philosophical culture as just as possible, and just as desirable, as a post-religious culture. We might come to see philosophy as a cultural disease which has been cured, just as many contemporary writers (notably Freudians) see religion as a cultural disease of which men are gradually being cured. The wisecrack that philosophers had worked themselves out of a job would then seem as silly a sneer as a similar charge leveled against doctors who, through a breakthrough in preventive medicine, had made therapy obsolete. Our desire for a *Weltanschauung* would now be satisfied by the arts, the sciences, or both. (Ibid.)

Doubts about Analytic Philosophy

The 1970s was one of the most creative and turbulent decades of Rorty's intellectual life. His disenchantment with the pretensions of analytic philosophers increased dramatically. He was reading avidly the thinkers that most analytic philosophers dismissed as "not really" philosophers: Nietzsche, Heidegger, Sartre, Derrida, Foucault, Gadamer, and Habermas. In 1978, at the relatively early age of 47, he was elected vice-president (president-elect) of the Eastern Division of the American Philosophical Association before the publication of *Philosophy and the Mirror of Nature*. At the time, the Eastern Division was the fortress of analytic philosophy. (At the business meeting over which Rorty presided in 1979, there was a rebellion of the "plural-ist" philosophers, who elected John E. Smith as the new president.) When he was elected vice-president (president-elect) of the Eastern Division of the APA, Rorty's analytic credentials and reputation were based on his articles and the introduction to *The Linguistic Turn*.

But when *Philosophy and the Mirror of Nature* appeared in 1979, it caused a sensation. Many analytic philosophers were furious. They felt as if one of their own had betrayed them – like Judas. In a central chapter, "Privileged Representations," Rorty argued that if we follow through the consequences of Sellars's critique of the Myth of the Given and Quine's skepticism about the language–fact distinction, then the "Kantian" foundations of analytic philosophy crumble. Together, Quine and Sellars challenged the distinctions and unquestioned presuppositions that were the basis for analytic philosophy: the conceptual–empirical, analytic–synthetic, and language–fact distinctions, as well as the distinction between what is given and what is postulated.

Many non-analytic philosophers skipped the first two-thirds of the book (the detailed analytic deconstructions of analytic philosophy) and were delighted with the third part where Rorty discusses Heidegger, Gadamer, Habermas, Sartre, Derrida, and Foucault (though many were unhappy with his readings of these Continental philosophers). *Philosophy and the Mirror of Nature* became the most widely discussed philosophy book of the second half of the twentieth century, not only by philosophers but by nonphilosophers in the range of the humanistic disciplines and the social sciences; it has now been translated into more than 20 languages. Pragmatism does not explicitly figure prominently in the book, although in his introduction Rorty tells us that Dewey, Heidegger, and Wittgenstein are "the three most important philosophers of our century" (Rorty 1979, p. 5). Even more revealing, especially in light of his early "fourth" option of the six possibilities for the future of philosophy that he outlined in *The Linguistic Turn*, are his concluding remarks to his introduction:

> Dewey, ... though he had neither Wittgenstein's dialectical acuity nor Heidegger's historical learning, wrote his polemics against traditional mirror-imagery out of a vision of a new kind of society. In his ideal society, culture is no longer dominated by the ideal of objective cognition but by that of aesthetic enhancement. In that culture, as he said, the arts and the sciences would be "the unforced flowers of life." I would hope that we are now in a position to see the charges of "relativism" and "irrationalism" once leveled against Dewey as merely the mindless defensive reflexes of the philosophical tradition which he attacked. (Rorty 1979, p. 13)

And, in the final sentence of his introduction, Rorty expresses the hope that his book "will help pierce through that crust of philosophical convention which Dewey vainly hoped to shatter" (ibid.).

For all the deconstructive brilliance of *Philosophy and the Mirror of Nature*, Rorty left us with little guidance about his own positive intellectual stance – what happens after the "end" of Philosophy with a capital P.[4] In his concluding sentence, Rorty wrote: "The only point on which I would insist is that philosophers' moral concern should be with continuing the conversation of the West, rather than with insisting upon a place for the traditional problems of modern philosophy within that conversation" (Rorty 1979, p. 394). But it wasn't at all clear what was supposed to be the content of this "conversation of the West" or what was the "useful kibitzing" that philosophers can provide.

Rorty was much more explicit and succinct in his 1979 presidential address. Rorty clearly identified himself with the pragmatism of James and Dewey. He tells us that pragmatism "names the chief glory of our country's intellectual tradition. No other American writers have offered so radical a suggestion for making our future different from our past, as have James and Dewey" (Rorty 1982, p. 160). But Rorty's characterization of pragmatism was idiosyncratic and controversial. He now denigrates the importance of Peirce and tells us that "his contribution to pragmatism was merely to have given it a name, and to have stimulated James" (Rorty 1982, p. 161). According to Rorty, James and Dewey were reacting against Peirce's Kantianism – the misguided belief that "philosophy gave us an all-embracing ahistorical context in which every other species of discourse could be assigned its proper place and rank" (ibid.). In this respect, James and Dewey begin to look like a domesticated version of Nietzsche and Heidegger. But, unlike Nietzsche and Heidegger, James and Dewey wrote in a spirit of "social hope" and liberation. Pragmatism, according to Rorty, is "the doctrine that there are no constraints on inquiry save conversational ones – no wholesale constraints derived from the nature of the objects, the mind, or the language, but only those retail constraints provided by the remarks of our fellow-inquirers: (Rorty 1982, p. 165).

From that time until the end of his life, Rorty fiercely challenged any and all attempts to argue that there are any constraints upon us – except those that come from our fellow human beings. This is the key to his claim that solidarity should replace the philosophical worry about objectivity. Increasingly, he came to believe – like Nietzsche – that the obsession with philosophical theories of truth, objectivity, and reality was little more than a form of idolatry – a philosophical substitute for the religious belief in a transcendent God. In the collection of his essays spanning the period from 1972 to 1980, *Consequences of Pragmatism*, he announced that he was writing a book on Heidegger.

(Rorty discusses Heidegger in many of his subsequent writings, but he never published a book on him.) Friends and critics thought that Rorty was simply using the term 'pragmatism' as a cover for his postmodern turn.[5]

Public Liberalism and Private Irony

When *Contingency, Irony, and Solidarity* was published in 1989, many philosophers thought that Rorty had simply given up on philosophy. In analytic circles it became fashionable to dismiss Rorty – one no longer needed to take him seriously. He seemed to be writing for "literary types." Whatever one's final opinion of *Philosophy and the Mirror of Nature*, it was packed with complex arguments – the type of arguments that philosophers recognize, admire, and attack. But in *Contingency* Rorty mocked philosophical argument and favored the romantic invention of new and original vocabularies. Although he had long denied the charge of relativism, his characterization of the ironist as someone who realizes "that anything can be made to look good or bad by being redescribed" (Rorty 1989, p. 73) looked like a "highfalutin" relativism. No one was happy with the way in which he drew a sharp distinction between our public and private lives, or with his suggestion that some philosophers should be read as we read good novelists like Proust and Nabokov – for private enjoyment.[6] Everybody was attacking Rorty, and he seemed to delight in all the attention he was receiving. But there was one line of criticism that really stung him: "I am sometimes told, by exasperated people on both sides, that my views are so weird as to be merely frivolous. They suspect that I will say anything to get a gasp, that I am just amusing myself by contradicting everybody else. This hurts" (Rorty 1999, p. 5). Rorty was right. This is precisely what many of his critics thought, regardless of their political or philosophical orientation. This type of criticism – that he was morally and politically insensitive – prompted him to write his autobiographical sketch, "Trotsky and the Wild Orchids," an essay in which he sought to explain how he came to his current views.

Many of Rorty's relatives had been active in progressive circles, and John Dewey was their intellectual hero. His father, James Rorty, a poet and a journalist, had broken with the Communist Party in 1932.

Rorty tells us that he grew up "knowing that all decent people were, if not Trotskyites, at least socialists" (Rorty 1999, p. 6). "Trotsky" became a symbol for "social justice" and for diminishing the inequality between the rich and the poor. But Rorty, whose family divided its time between New York City and a remote little village on the Delaware River in New Jersey, describes himself as also having "private, weird, snobbish, incommunicable interests" (ibid.). He developed a passion for the wild orchids in New Jersey. He prided himself on knowing where they grew, their Latin names, and their blooming times. Wild orchids became a symbol for private interests and pleasures.

When Rorty first discovered philosophy at the University of Chicago, he was initially attracted by the Platonic idea of holding "reality and justice in a single vision" (Rorty 1999, p. 9). He thought that reaching the top of Plato's divided line – the place "beyond hypotheses" – would enable him to find a grand synthesis of public justice and private pleasures. But by the time he left Chicago, Rorty no longer believed that the study of philosophy would make one genuinely wise and virtuous. "Since [my] initial disillusion (which climaxed about the time I left Chicago to get a PhD in philosophy at Yale), I have spent 40 years looking for a coherent and convincing way of formulating my worries about what, if anything, philosophy is good for" (Rorty 1999, pp. 10–11). Eventually, he came to the conclusion that the project of seeking a synthesis between public justice and private interests is a misguided endeavor – one that had Plato led astray. He describes *Contingency, Irony, and Solidarity* as the book that "argues that there is no need to weave one's personal equivalent of Trotsky and one's personal equivalent of my wild orchids together" (Rorty 1999, p. 13). He concludes his essay by once again identifying himself with what he takes to be Dewey's alternative vision – a vision of a democratic community "in which everybody thinks that it is human solidarity, rather than knowledge of something not merely human, that really matters" (Rorty 1999, p. 20).

Despite the harsh (and sometimes vicious) criticisms of *Contingency*, many of Rorty's characteristic themes are evident: the emphasis on radical historical contingency, his groundless sense of irony and social hope, the need to extend human sympathy and solidarity, and his belief that literature may be more effective in fostering this than philosophical argumentation. In addition, we find a vehement rejection of all forms of epistemological and semantic representationalism. There is an explicit identification with romanticism, a stress on imagination rather than reason, and a call for the project of self-creation. Rorty's liberal is a figure who thinks "that cruelty is the worst thing we do" (Rorty 1989, p. xv). And the ironist is someone who faces up to the contingency of his or her own most central beliefs and desires: "Liberal ironists are people who include among these ungroundable desires their hope that suffering will be diminished, that humiliation of human beings by other human beings may cease" (ibid.).

But the political implications of Rorty's views were not yet fully clear. This is why Rorty was such an easy target to attack for both political conservatives, who accused him of being "cynical and nihilistic," and political leftists, who felt that he was simply defending status quo bourgeois liberal individualism. Rorty was accused of glossing over the racism, sexism, consumerism, and violence that are so much a part of the United States. During the 1990s, Rorty became much more explicit and forthright about his political views; he engaged in what he called "cultural politics." He strongly identified with the progressive leftist anti-Communist politics of his parents. He set forth his political credo in *Achieving Our Country: Leftist Thought in Twentieth-Century America*, in which explained how he was "a red diaper anticommunist baby" who became "a teenage Cold War liberal" (Rorty 1998a, p. 58). But Rorty was never tempted by conservatism or neo-conservatism. He always saw Emerson, Whitman, and Dewey as the poets and prophets of a progressive liberal democratic society. He chided some of the excesses of the New Left, especially the legacy of a Cultural Left that disdained anything resembling "real politics" and dealing concretely with "real" economic injustices. But he praised the New Left for fostering the cultural politics of feminist, gay, and lesbian movements. He called for a reconciliation of the reformist Old Left, with its primary emphasis on economic injustice and inequality, with the best of the legacy of the New Left: "[A]ll of us should take pride in a country whose historians will someday honor the achievements of both of these Lefts" (Rorty 1998a, p. 71). Rorty was certainly not blind to the violence and viciousness that have been so much a part of American history. In the last decade of his life he frequently expressed his pessimism about the future of the United States.[7] Nevertheless, he always affirmed his patriotism and his "ungrounded hope" that the best of the American liberal tradition of tolerance, individual freedom, and the demand for social equality would prevail.

Rorty's Humanism

I have sketched the trajectory of how the young college student who identified himself with "the little clique of reactionary metaphysicians" became disillusioned, turned into a radical critic of the pretensions of philosophy, and eventually became a controversial public intellectual who envisioned a "liberal utopia" in which imagination and self-creation would prevail. I can now clarify what I mean by Rorty's deep humanism.

Whether Rorty is dealing with abstract metaphilosophical topics, or the hotly debated philosophical issues concerning truth, objectivity, and the nature of reality, or ethical and political issues concerning human rights, or even with the role of religion in our daily lives, there is a dominant theme that emerges repeatedly. *There is nothing that we can rely on but ourselves and our fellow human beings.* There is no outside authority to which we can appeal – whether we think of it as God, Truth, or Reality. Rorty summed up what he took to be the primary dispute in contemporary philosophy:

> As I see contemporary philosophy, the great divide is between representationalists, the people who believe that there is an intrinsic nature of non-human reality that humans have a duty to grasp, and the anti-repesentationalists. I think F. C. S. Schiller was on the right track when he said "Pragmatism ... is in reality only the application of Humanism to the theory of knowledge." I take Schiller's point to be that the humanist's claim that human beings have responsibilities only to one another entails giving up representationalism and realism. (Rorty 2007, p. 134)

In attempting to shatter the "crust of philosophical convention," he was intentionally provocative. He seemed to delight in using terms that have strong negative connotations, and in turning them against his opponents. He described his understanding of human sympathy and solidarity as ethnocentric. When Jeffrey Stout, a friendly critic, characterized his version of pragmatism as a type of "narcissism," Rorty retorted:

> What Stout calls narcissism, I would call self-reliance. As I see it, the whole point of pragmatism is to insist that we human beings are answerable only to one another. We are answerable only to those who answer to us – only to conversation partners. We are not responsible

to the atoms or to God, at least not until they start conversing with us. (Cited by Stout 2007, p. 9)

Rorty's humanism explains why he was so enthusiastic about the magnum opus of his former Princeton student Robert Brandom, *Making It Explicit*. He interprets Brandom as working out a theory of discursive social practices that vindicates Rorty's own humanistic vision. Rorty praises Brandom because he advances one of the most thoroughgoing critiques of the representationalism that has dominated much of epistemology and semantics since the eighteenth century – including contemporary analytic philosophy. But, even more important, Brandom's emphasis on the explanatory promise of pragmatics, his insistence that norms are implicit in our human social practices, his emphasis on our commitments, entitlements, and responsibilities, are themes that Rorty enthusiastically endorses. As Rorty reads Brandom, he has shown that we do not need to appeal to anything other than the discursive exchanges of human beings to account for conceptual norms: "There is no authority outside of convenience of human purposes that can be appealed to in order to legitimate the use of a vocabulary. We have no duties to anything nonhuman" (Rorty 1998b, p. 127).

There is something ironic (not in Rorty's sense) about his enthusiastic endorsement of Brandom's neo-Hegelian project – and Brandom's respectful acknowledgment of Rorty as his teacher. Brandom's goal is a *systematic* one, and he carefully works through a number of epistemological, metaphysical, semantic, and pragmatic issues that have dominated contemporary analytic philosophy. Brandom is much closer to the systematic aspirations of Sellars than he is to the insouciant dismissal of systematic philosophy and argumentation that character ize of some of Rorty's quips and rhetorical flourishes. Unlike Rorty, Brandom does think that the philosopher has the responsibility to advance a fully developed pragmatic theory of truth and objectivity. But in *Contingency*, Rorty announced, "I am not going to offer arguments against the vocabulary I want to replace. Instead I am going to try to make the vocabulary I favor look attractive by showing how it may be used to describe a variety of topics" (Rorty 1989, p. 9). And he adds, "Interesting philosophy is rarely an examination of the pros and cons of a thesis."[8] Despite his disclaimers about philosophical argumentation, Rorty remained to the end of his life a sophisticated arguer – as witnessed by his responses to such critics as Habermas,

Davidson, Quine, McDowell, Williams, Putnam, Dennett, and many others.

Some Doubts about Rorty's Humanism

Frankly, I remain ambivalent about Rorty's humanism. I admire his persistent concern for his fellow human beings and the need to extend the range of our sympathy and empathy to those who suffer from economic injustice, humiliation, and gratuitous cruelty. I agree with him, Brandom, and the classical pragmatists that we can give an adequate account of the role of norms (conceptual, moral, and political) by an appeal to social practices. I appreciate his worry that as philosophy becomes more academic, professionalized, and technical, it becomes more and more remote from, and irrelevant to, the everyday concerns of human beings. I praise his attempt to keep alive and extend the best of the American tradition of radical democracy represented by Jefferson, Emerson, Whitman, and Dewey.

William James, one of Rorty's heroes, spoke about the importance of a philosopher's vision. James tells us that "a man's vision is the great fact about him," and

> [I]f we take the whole history of philosophy, the systems reduce themselves to a few main types which, under all the technical verbiage in which the ingenious intellect of man envelops them, are just so many visions, modes of feeling the whole push, and seeing the whole drift of life, forced on one by one's total character and experience, and on the whole preferred – there is no other truthful word – as one's best working attitude. (James 1977, pp. 14–15)

Rorty shared this view and he exhibited it. He dreamed of a time when philosophers might finally give up their obsession with representation, truth, objectivity, and reality – a day when the conversation of humankind might really change, when imagination and self-creation might flourish. He kept alive the hope that we might come closer to what he took to be Dewey's ideal democratic culture – a "culture no longer dominated by the ideal of objective cognition but by that of aesthetic enhancement" (Rorty 1979, p. 13). From the early days of his disillusionment with "Platonism," he was haunted by the question, What is philosophy good for? At times he despaired of giving any sensible answer to this question. But he came to think that "philosophy as cultural politics" (the title of his final collection of papers) might still play a modest role in furthering human happiness and our hopes for a liberal utopia.

Over the years, I have been asked many times, what is the difference that makes a difference between you and Rorty? And the answer I give is that I began my philosophical career convinced by Dewey's critique of the quest for certainty and his call for a reconstruction of philosophy. I never experienced the type of disillusionment that Rorty experienced. I never thought that one had to critique representationalism, traditional epistemology, and foundationalism over and over again. The task, as Dewey had indicated, was to reconstruct philosophy. I did not see Plato as the "Platonist" that Rorty caricatures, but rather as the great defender of the ongoing, unending dialogue that Rorty came to advocate. Rorty suffered from the "God that failed" syndrome. When he first became enthralled with philosophy, he really did think that he could move up Plato's divided line to the realm "beyond hypotheses" where knowledge and virtue are identical. And even when he turned to analytic philosophy, he initially half-believed that he had discovered the right way to be a philosopher. I don't think that he ever fully overcame his disillusionment, and he wavered between playing the role of the philosophical therapist and that of the prophet.[9] Rorty paid a heavy price for this disillusionment. He lost his faith in, and patience with, philosophical argument. Consider some of the philosophers that he most admired: Sellars, Davidson, Brandom, and Habermas. For all their differences, these philosophers are distinguished by the finesse, ingenuity, and detail with which they worked out their positions – the subtlety of their philosophical arguments. But after *Philosophy and the Mirror of Nature*, Rorty lost his patience with careful argumentation. *Redescription, no matter how imaginative, is not enough*. Even when Rorty is singing the praises of liberal democracy and affirming the importance of patriotism, he can sound more like a speechwriter for a presidential candidate than a serious social reformer. For a pragmatist who prides himself on paying attention to those practical differences that make a difference, Rorty doesn't provide us with the foggiest idea of how to achieve (or even approximate) the goals and hopes that he cherishes.[10] And for all his skepticism about traditional philosophical dichotomies and distinctions, he introduced a whole battery of facile distinctions that tended to obscure more than they illuminated: systematic versus edifying; public versus private; argument versus redescription; finding versus making. At times he wrote as if anyone who even thought there was a proper philosophical way to speak about truth, objectivity, and "getting things right" was "guilty" of idolatry – bowing down before an external authority. But Rorty protests too much. His fear that philosophers would backslide led him to give up too easily on what Jeffrey Stout lists as "three core commitments of a pragmatism that steer[ ] clear of narcissism": "(1) we inquirers have an interest in getting things right; (2) this interest needs to be understood in the context of social practices in which it is expressed; and (3) it need not be seen as implicated in a pseudo-explanatory conception of correspondence to the real" (Stout 2007, p. 19).

In one of Rorty's last articles, he returned to the issue of the analytic/continental distinction that has become so entrenched among "professional" philosophers. He felt that the distinction was a crude and misleading one, and he suggested substituting the "analytic–conversational" distinction.

> Substituting analytic–conversational for analytic-continental as a description of the most salient split among today's philosophy professors might help us resist the temptation to treat this split either as dividing those who love truth and reason from those who prefer dramatic effects and rhetorical triumphs, or as dividing the unimaginative clods from the free spirits. It is better understood as a split between two quite different ways of thinking of the human situation. ... This split has been deepening ever since Hegel challenged Kant's version of the Platonic idea that philosophy could be like mathematics – that it could offer conclusive demonstrations of truths about structural features of human life, rather than simply summaries of the way human beings have conducted their lives so far. (Rorty 2007, p. 127)

Rorty identifies himself with the "conversational" philosophers who engage in cultural politics by suggesting "changes in the uses of words and by putting new words in circulation – hoping thereby to break through impasses and to make conversation more fruitful" (Rorty 2007, p. 124). The vigorous international discussion of pragmatic themes today is largely due to Rorty's provocation; he has done more than anyone else of his generation to get philosophers (and nonphilosophers) to take pragmatism seriously. Recall that he concluded

Philosophy and the Mirror of Nature by affirming that "[t]he only point on which I would insist is that philosophers' moral concern should be with continuing the conversation of the West" (Rorty 1979, p. 394). Even Rorty's severest critics would admit that no other philosopher of the past half-century has stimulated as much lively conversation as Richard Rorty.

Notes

Prologue

1   James's address was originally published in *The University Chronicle* (Berkeley, California), September 1898. It was reprinted with revisions in the *Journal of Philosophy, Psychology and Scientific Methods*, 1904.
2   I speak of this as the first – the founding narrative – account of pragmatism because the story of pragmatism right up to the present can be told as a story of conflicting narratives of the history of pragmatism. See Bernstein 1995a.
3   In 1907, in a manuscript that Peirce never published, he writes: "It was in the earliest seventies that a knot of us young men in Old Cambridge, calling ourselves half-ironically, half-defiantly, 'The Metaphysical Club,' – for agnosticism was then riding high horse, and was frowning superbly upon all metaphysics – used to meet, sometimes in my study, sometimes in that of William James." MS 318 is reprinted in Peirce 1998, p. 399. For a description of the Metaphysical Club and its participants, see Menand 2001.
4   James is referring to the following passage in Peirce's article: "And what, then, is belief? It is the demi-cadence which closes a musical phrase in the symphony of our intellectual life" (Peirce 1992, p. 129).
5   In the same essay, Peirce explains why he originally adopted the term "pragmatism."

> Endeavoring, as a man of that type [experimentalist – RJB] naturally would, to formulate what he so approved, he framed the theory of conception, that is, the rational purport of a word or other expression, lies exclusively in its conceivable bearing upon the conduct of life; so that, since obviously nothing that might not result from experiment can have

any direct bearing upon conduct, if one can define accurately all the conceivable experimental phenomena which the affirmation or the denial of a concept could imply, one will have therein a complete definition of the concept, and there is absolutely nothing more to it. For this doctrine he invented the name pragmatism. Some of his friends wished him to call it practicism or practicalism. ... But for one who had learned philosophy out of Kant, as the writer, along with nineteen out of every twenty experimentalists who have turned to philosophy, had done, and who still thought in Kantian terms most readily *practisch* and *pragmatisch* were as far apart as two poles, the former belonging to the region of thought where no mind of the experimentalist type can ever make use of solid ground under his feet, the most striking feature of the new theory was its recognition of an inseparable connection between rational cognition and rational purpose, and that consideration it was which determined the preference for the name pragmatism. (Peirce 1998, p. 332)

6   See also Dewey's autobiographical sketch for an account of his early Hegelianism and how he "drifted away" from Hegel, in "From Absolutism to Experimentalism" (Dewey 1981, pp. 1–13).

7   Although Royce is typically considered to be a neo-Hegelian who defended a Christian version of absolute idealism, he displayed a subtle understanding of the significance of Peirce's work, especially Peirce's theory of signs and interpretation. Royce broadened and deepened pragmatism with his conception of the "community of interpreters." See Kuklick 2001.

8   In speaking of the "classical" period, I am referring to the thinkers associated with pragmatism during the last decades of the nineteenth century and the early decades of the twentieth century. I follow the convention of using the phrase "classical American pragmatists" to designate the triumvirate of Peirce, James, and Dewey. But I believe that the expression is seriously misleading, because it neglects the work of many others who made substantive contributions to the pragmatic movement, including George Herbert Mead and Josiah Royce. Furthermore, to limit pragmatism to Peirce, James, and Dewey excludes the contributions of some notable women, e.g. Jane Addams, and African-Americans, e.g. Alain Locke.

9   In 1910, John Dewey published an important essay entitled "The Influence of Darwin on Philosophy" (Dewey 1981, pp. 31–41). In a recent unpublished lecture, "The Importance of Darwin for Philosophy," Philip Kitcher describes Dewey's essay as "the single best philosophical response to Darwin published in the first century after the appearance of the *Origin*."

10   For discussions of James's relation to phenomenology, see Wilshire 1968, Wild 1969, and Edie 1987.

11   See Rucker 1969 for a history of this movement.

12   In "From Absolutism to Experimentalism" Dewey describes the objective biological strain in the *Principles of Psychology* as "having its roots in

a return to the earlier biological conception of the psyche, but a return possessed of a new force and value due to the immense progress made by biology since the time of Aristotle. I doubt if we have as yet begun to realize all that is due to William James for the introduction and use of this idea. ... Anyway, it worked its way more and more into all my ideas and acted as a ferment to transform old beliefs" (Dewey 1981, p. 11).

13 See especially Dewey's important and influential article "The Reflex Arc Concept in Psychology," in Dewey 1981, pp. 136–48. I discuss the significance of this article for understanding Dewey's intellectual development in Bernstein 1966a, pp. 15–21.

14 See Dewey's "The Influence of Darwinism on Philosophy," in Dewey 1981, pp. 31–41.

15 Commenting on the use of "instrumental" to charactcrize his conception of knowledge, Dewey wrote: "I have from time to time set forth a conception of knowledge as being 'instrumental.' Strange meanings have been imputed by critics to this conception. Its actual content is simple: Knowledge is instrumental to the enrichment of immediate experience through control over action it exercises" (Dewey, *LW* 10: 294).

16 As I have previously indicated, the first narrative of the meaning and origins of pragmatism is James's account in "Philosophical Conceptions and Practical Results" (1898). For Peirce's account, see "What Pragmatism Is" (1905). Dewey relates his version in "The Development of American Pragmatism" (1925). See also George H. Mead's "The Philosophies of Royce, James, and Dewey in their American Setting" (1929), repr. in Mead 1964. See my discussion of the debates about the meaning and scope of pragmatism in Bernstein 1995a.

17 This is the title of Richard Rorty's famous anthology. For a detailed analysis of the "revolution" initiated by "linguistic philosophy," see Rorty 1967, pp. 1–39.

18 See also Rorty's comparison of Heidegger and Dewey in Rorty 1982, pp. 37–59.

19 "Questions Concerning Certain Faculties Claimed for Man"; "Some Consequences of Four Incapacities"; and "Grounds of Validity of the Laws of Logic." These articles, known as the "Cognition Series" are reprinted in Peirce 1992, pp. 11–82.

20 Honneth explores the affinity between Heidegger and Dewey when examining their concepts of *praxis* as existential engagement.

21 Dreyfus (1991) claims that Heidegger radicalized "the insights already contained in the writings of such pragmatists as Nietzsche, Peirce, James, and Dewey" (p. 6). See also Haugeland 1982, where he writes: "I make Heidegger out to be less like Husserl and/or Sartre than is usual, and more like Dewey (and to a lesser extent) Sellars and the later Wittgenstein" (p. 15).

22   The pragmatic "emphasis on the primacy of practice" must be properly understood. The pragmatists are not simply reversing the traditional hierarchy of theory and practice. Rather, they are arguing for an understanding of social practices whereby theory itself emerges out of, and is dependent on, discursive social practices.

23   Much later, Rorty dismissed the importance of Peirce for pragmatism, and claimed that James and Dewey reacted against Peirce's Kantianism. Despite Rorty's own repudiation, his early article on Peirce and Wittgenstein is extraordinarily insightful. For his later "dismissal" of Peirce, see Rorty 1982, p. 161.

24   In a footnote to this passage Rorty remarks:

> In particular, Peirce and Wittgenstein complement each other especially well; one presents you with a bewildering and wonderfully abstract apparatus of categories; the other shoves you into very particular puzzles. Peirce's odd numerological categories, just because they are so abstract and so far from the clichés of the history of philosophy, are perhaps the best handles for grasping what one learns from Wittgenstein. Conversely, Wittgenstein's riddles and aphorisms, just because they are so fresh and fragmentary, let one see the point of some of Peirce's darker sayings.

25   For an illuminating exploration of the relation between William James and Wittgenstein, see Goodman 2002.

26   For this background, see Apel 1981, pp. vii–xi.

27   For additional remarks about my intellectual journey, see Bernstein 2007.

28   Oliver Wendell Holmes to Frederick J. Pollock, 15 May 1931, in Holmes and Pollock 1941, vol. 2, p. 287.

29   See Bernstein 1959, 1961, 1964b, and 1965.

30   See Richard Rorty's account of analytic philosophy in the mid-twentieth century, "Philosophy in America Today," in Rorty 1982, pp. 211–30.

31   "Realism and the New Way of Words" is the title of one of Wilfrid Sellars's early papers in Feigl and Sellars 1949.

32   See my "Myths about the Mississippi Summer Project" (Bernstein 1964a).

33   See my discussion of Arendt and Dewey in Bernstein 2005.

34   In 1948, Dewey wrote a new introduction for the reprint of *Reconstruction in Philosophy*, where he declared:

> Today Reconstruction *of* Philosophy is a more suitable title than Reconstruction *in* Philosophy. For the intervening events have sharply defined, have brought to a head, the basic postulate of the text: namely, that the distinctive office, problems and subject-matter of philosophy grow out of stresses and strains in the community life in which a given form of philosophy arises, and that, accordingly, its specific problems vary with the changes in human life that are always going on and that at times

constitute a crisis and a turning point in human history. (John Dewey, "Introduction: Reconstruction as Seen Twenty-five Years Later," in Dewey, *MW* 12: 256.

In a recent unpublished paper, "The Road Not Taken," Philip Kitcher remarks: "We need reconstruction in philosophy as much as James thought it was needed in 1907 and as much as Dewey thought it was needed in 1930. ... As it turned out, the attractions of positivist precision steered the reform movement away from the large human questions that worried James and Dewey, but, reading them again a century later, it is hard to resist the thought that they had identified the fundamental issues, issues that ought to be replaced at the center of philosophy today."

When quoting passages from *The Collected Works of John Dewey 1882–1953*, I have followed the standard procedure of listing the series, *Early Works* (*EW*), *Middle Works* (*MW*), *Later Works* (*LW*), followed by the volume and page number.

35 See my "Serious Play: The Ethical-Political Horizon of Derrida" and "An Allegory of Modernity/Postmodernity: Habermas and Derrida," in Bernstein 1991 and 2006a. See also Mouffe and Critchley 1996.

36 Elizabeth Goodstein called my attention to a passage by Kenneth Burke that epitomizes the open conversation characteristic of pragmatism.

> Imagine that you enter a parlor. You come late. When you arrive, others have long preceded you, and they are engaged in a heated discussion, a discussion too heated for them to pause and tell you exactly what it is about. In fact, the discussion has already begun long before any of them got there, so that no one present is qualified to retrace for you all the steps that had gone before. You listen for a while, until you decide that you have caught the tenor of the argument; then you put in your oar. Someone answers; you answer him; another comes to your defense; another aligns himself against you, to either the embarrassment or gratification of your opponent, depending upon the quality of your ally's assistance. However, the discussion is interminable. The hour grows late, you must depart. And you do depart, with the discussion still vigorously in progress. (Burke 1941, pp. 110–11)

Chapter 1   Charles S. Peirce's Critique of Cartesianism

1 See Prologue, n. 19.
2 Peirce makes this clear in his mature philosophy. See his critique of "The Fixation of Belief" in a manuscript written in 1909 (Peirce 1998, pp. 455–7).

3 It is instructive to compare Peirce's claims about prejudices with Gadamer's defense of prejudices and prejudgments in hermeneutics. Although Gadamer explicitly criticizes Cartesianism, he sharply distinguishes (in *Truth and Method*) hermeneutics from "method." He tends to identify method with the scientific method of the natural sciences. Peirce, on the other hand, argues that background prejudices are essential for understanding all inquiry, including scientific inquiry. See my discussion of Gadamer in Bernstein 1983, pp. 126–31.

4 Compare Peirce's claim that "justification will have to come to a halt somewhere" with the following passage from Wittgenstein's *Philosophical Investigations*: "If I have exhausted the justifications I have reached bedrock, and my spade is turned. Then I am inclined to say: 'This is simply what I do'" (Wittgenstein 2001, §217).

5 When I quote passages from the *Collected Papers of Charles S. Peirce*, I follow the standard procedure of giving the volume number followed by the paragraph number.

6 In "How to Make Our Ideas Clear" Peirce elaborates his critique of Descartes' (and Leibniz's) notion of clear and distinct ideas. He concludes by stating: "That much-admired 'ornament of logic' – the doctrine of clearness and distinctness – may be pretty enough, but it is high time to relegate to our cabinet of curiosities the antique *bijou*, and to wear about us something better adapted to modern uses" (Peirce 1992, p. 126).

7 The first two grades of clearness by which "our existing beliefs can be set in order" are familiarity and analyzing definitions.

8 This is also a theme developed by Karl Popper in *Conjectures and Refutations* (Popper 1963).

9 The phrase "Every unidealistic philosophy" suggests that Peirce identifies himself with idealism. In these early papers, Peirce was influenced by Kant's understanding of idealism. Throughout his career Peirce sought to combine what he took to be the "truth" implicit in idealism with a strong version of realism, especially a realism concerning universals. For helpful discussions that track Peirce's developing understanding of idealism and realism (and how it informs his pragmaticism) see Hookway 1985 and Apel 1981.

10 See my earlier discussion of Rorty's comparison of Peirce and Wittgenstein, pp. 21–2. See also the discussion of Peirce's categories in ch. 6, pp. 129–36.

11 Peirce's semiotics is not limited to language but encompasses nonverbal and natural signs.

12 Gallie's description of how a sign can function only as an element in a working system of signs provides further evidence for the similarity between Peirce and Wittgenstein.

13 Peirce made several attempts to distinguish different types of interpretant. See e.g. Peirce 1998, p. 409, where he discusses "emotional," "energetic," and "logical" interpretants.

14 Short 2004 explores the changes and development of Peirce's theory of signs.

15 See Bernstein 1965 and my discussion of Peirce's categories in ch. 6, pp. 129–36.

16 Short sees this development as correcting flaws that are present in Peirce's earliest theory of signs. He writes: "The fundamental revolution in doctrine that occurred in 1907 was to have recognized that it is habit itself, and not a concept of it, that is the interpretant (more precisely, the ultimate logical interpretant) of a concept" (Short 2004, p. 228). I am not convinced that this "was a fundamental revolution." On the contrary, I see it as a nuance that Peirce introduces to show how his mature theory of signs is related to his early claims about habits.

17 I examine McDowell's understanding of "second nature" in Bernstein 1995b.

18 I explore the similarities and differences between Peirce and McDowell in Bernstein 1995b.

19 See pp. 129–36.

20 Peirce stresses the need to appeal to the categories of Secondness and Thirdness to account for experience.

> [I]f the force of experience were mere blind compulsion, and we were utter foreigners in the world, then again we might as well think as we please ourselves; because we then never could make our thoughts conform to mere Secondness.
>
> But the saving truth is that there is a Thirdness in experience, an element of Reasonableness to which we can train our own reason to conform more and more. (5.160)

Peirce also appeals to Secondness and Thirdness to distinguish action, which is singular, from conduct, which is general. See Bernstein 1965.

21 Peirce's categories of Secondness and Thirdness do *not* correspond to the familiar distinction between causes and reasons. I explain this in ch. 6, pp. 129–36.

22 There is a further parallel between Peirce and McDowell. What McDowell characterizes as 'passivity' is close to what Peirce calls "uncontrollable operations of the mind." Peirce says that there are

> operations of the mind which are logically exactly analogous to inferences excepting only that they are unconscious and uncontrollable and there not subject to criticism. But that makes all the difference in the world; for inference is essentially deliberate, and self-controlled. ... Reasoning as deliberate is essentially critical; and it is idle to criticize as good or bad that which cannot be controlled. Reasoning essentially involved *self-control*. (5.108)

23 For a more detailed analysis of Peirce's theory of perception that takes account of all three categories in perception, see Bernstein 1964b. See also Rosenthal 2004.

24   In his Study Guide to Sellars's *Empiricism and the Philosophy of Mind*, Brandom (1997b) provides a helpful clarification of the differing senses in which Sellars affirms and denies that there are noninferential beliefs. Peirce would agree with this distinction, which shows the interplay of Secondness and Thirdness.

> For Sellars, there is no such thing as noninferential belief, if by that one means a belief one could have without grasping its inferential connection to at least some other beliefs. For to understand a sentence, to grasp a propositional content (a necessary condition of having a belief) is to place it in the species of reasons, to assign an inferential role in the game of giving and asking reasons, as entailing some other contents as being incompatible with others. A noninferential report or belief can be properly called 'noninferential' only in the sense that the reporter's commitment to an essentially articulated contents elicited noninferentially on this occasion – that is, that it is elicited as a response to some nonlinguistic, nonepistemic environing circumstance, rather than as a response to another belief or assertion. Noninferential beliefs do not form an autonomous discourse stratum: there could be no language game consisting entirely of noninferential reports. (Brandom 1997b, p. 153)

Chapter 2   The Ethical Consequences of William James's Pragmatic Pluralism

1   I discuss Popper's critique of the myth of the framework in Bernstein 1983, pp. 79–83.
2   See my discussion of engaged pluralism in Bernstein 1991, pp. 335–9.

Chapter 3   John Dewey's Vision of Radical Democracy

1   Dewey has been justly criticized for his awkward prose, but he could write vividly and with great passion. His response to Trotsky, "Means and Ends," is an example of the best of Dewey's prose.
2   J. Dewey, "Means and Ends: Their Interdependence," and "Leon Trotsky's essay on 'Their Morals and Ours'" in Dewey, *LW* 13.
3   A frequent criticism of Dewey, even by those who are sympathetic to him, has been that he lacks a profound sense of human evil and a tragic sense of life. For a refutation of this misguided view, see Hook 1974 and Glaude 2007. Glaude shows how Dewey's pragmatism – despite his neglect of the issue of racism – has the resources to illuminate the problems and opportunities that confront black Americans today. See also Bernstein 2005.

4   Some of Dewey's "left" critics, most notably Christopher Lasch, have accused him of advocating a "corporate liberalism," but as Alan Ryan notes: "Lasch sees quite correctly, that Dewey's view of industrial society criticizes it from what one might loosely call a corporatist direction, but he misunderstands the consequences; *loosely* is of the essence, for Dewey's critique has nothing at all to do with the defense of a corporatist state or with a defense of the modern business corporation. Dewey disliked the modern business corporation in almost all its manifestations – its bureaucratic and hierarchal structure, its routinized working practices on the shop floor and in the offices of the white-collar staff, its divorce of management and real labor, and its remoteness from the interface of man and nature" (Ryan 1995, p. 177).

5   For a spirited defense of the contemporary relevance of Dewey's understanding of democracy, see Stout 2004a.

6   The expression "rooted cosmopolitan" has taken on a life of its own in recent years, but I believe that Mitchell Cohen (1992) was the first to use this expression.

Chapter 4   Hegel and Pragmatism

1   British idealism bears a strange and strained relation to Hegel. Themes such as the Absolute, internal relations, and the concrete universal are appropriated from Hegel. But there is little of the passion of Hegel's *Phenomenology* or of Hegel's sweeping vision of historical conflict and political struggle.

2   Dewey writes that his earliest philosophical interest was stimulated by a course in physiology that used a text by T. H. Huxley:

> It is difficult to speak with exactitude about what happened to me intellectually so many years ago, but I have an impression that there was derived from that study a sense of the interdependence and interrelated unity that gave form to intellectual stirrings that had previously been inchoate, and created a kind of model of a view of things to which material in any field ought to conform. (Dewey 1981, p. 2)

3   See Peirce's review of Dewey's *Studies in Logical Theory* (8.188–90).

4   See my discussion of Peirce's categories, pp. 129–36.

5   See above, pp. 131–4.

6   I explore the similarities between Peirce and Sellars in Bernstein 1964b.

7   In *Praxis and Action*, I wrote:

> The opening section of the *Phenomenology*, "Consciousness," which deals with "sense certainty," "perception," and "understanding," is rarely read and discussed by contemporary philosophers. This is a pity because these sections can be read as a perceptive and incisive commentary and critique

of a dialectical development in epistemology which has been repeated in contemporary analytic philosophy. The stages in contemporary epistemological investigations which have moved from phenomenalism with its foundation in "sense data" to the emphasis on a "thing language" as an epistemological foundation, to the realization of the importance of "theoretical constructs" and finally the "new" concern with total "conceptual frameworks" or "language games" closely parallels the development that Hegel sketches for us in the opening sections of the *Phenomenology*. One can find analogues in the development of epistemology during the past fifty years for the difficulties that Hegel locates at each dialectical stage. I do not mean to suggest that Hegel was prophetic, but rather that he had a genuine insight into a dialectical progression of epistemological positions, which has repeated itself in a linguistic mode during our time. (Bernstein 1971, p. 24)

8   In his original lectures, McDowell takes Davidson as the primary representative of this coherentism, and he accuses Davidson of having a "blind spot." McDowell has been criticized for taking Davidson as a foil and for distorting him. Consequently, in the published version of the lectures, McDowell adds an afterword, "Davidson in Context," in order to show why he counts "Davidson as an ally rather than an opponent" (McDowell 1996, pp. 130–61).

9   Robert Pippin develops this Hegelian conception of nature in Pippin 2008. See especially ch. 2, "Naturalness and Mindedness: Hegel's Compatibilism."

10   For a discussion of these hurdles, and the problems that McDowell still needs to confront, see Bernstein 1995b.

11   For a fuller account of the contribution of Kant to the understanding of normativity, as well as the problems with Kant's account, see ch. 1, "Toward a Normative Pragmatics," in Brandom 1994, pp. 3–66.

12   I can illustrate what I mean, and why I disagree with Brandom's characterization of the American pragmatic tradition, with reference to a distinction he makes in *Articulating Reasons*. He distinguishes the "rationalist pragmatism" of Hegel, which "gives pride of place to reasoning in understanding what it is to say or do something" (2000a, p. 34), from "conceptual assimilationism," where the emphasis is placed on the continuities between discursive and nondiscursive creatures. But there is no reason why one cannot be *both* a rationalist pragmatist and a conceptual assimilationist. This is precisely the position that Peirce advocates. The following passage illustrates how Peirce understands the continuities and the differences between different grades of self-control, including those that Brandom takes to be characteristic of human rationality.

There are inhibitions and coordinations that entirely escape consciousness. These are, in the next place, modes of self-control which seem quite instinctive. Next, there is a kind of self-control which results from training. Next, a man can be his own training-master and thus control his self-control. When this point is reached much or all the training may be conducted in the imagination. When a man trains himself, thus controlling control, he must have some moral rule in view, however special and irrational it may be. But next he may undertake to improve this rule; that is, to exercise a control over his control of control. To do this he must have in view something higher than an irrational rule. He must have some sort of moral principle. This, in turn, may be controlled by reference to an esthetic ideal of what is fine. There are certainly more grades than I have enumerated. Perhaps their number is indefinite. The brutes are certainly capable of more than one grade of control; but it seems to me that our superiority to them is more due to our greater number of grades of self-control than it is to our versatility. (5.533)

Chapter 5   Pragmatism, Objectivity, and Truth

1   James Conant provides a perceptive elucidation of James's view of the role of temperament in philosophy:

> What a philosopher needs to learn to do is take responsibility for his temperament. Taking responsibility here requires openly acknowledging the role that temperament plays in consolidating one's philosophical convictions.... It also requires subjecting those aspects of one's temperament which blind one to when and why others recoil... from the very philosophy which so attracts one. (Conant 1997, p. 208)

2   I use the expression 'bad relativism' because, as with cholesterol, there are "good" and "bad" types of relativism. There are many positive ways to speak about the relativity of contexts, justifications, and language that are not controversial and do not entail the consequences of "bad relativism." See Fine 2007 for a helpful discussion of the types of anti-foundational relativism that are compatible with the pragmatic tradition.

3   Stout (2007) presents one of the best discussions of the conflicting strands in Rorty's thinking. Stout argues that in Rorty's exchange with B. Ramberg, he makes an important concession and modifies some of his more extreme dismissive claims about truth and objectivity. Rorty suggests the possibility of "a pragmatism that can do justice to the objective dimension of inquiry" (Stout 2007, p. 17). This is the position that Stout seeks to advance.

4   One of the primary motivations for developing a pragmatic theory of objectivity is to defend the idea that objectivity is not limited to scientific discourse, but has a legitimate role to play in moral and political discourse. This is clearly a motivation for such pragmatists as Misak, Putnam, and Stout.

5   When Dewey introduces the expression 'warranted assertion' in his *Logic: The Theory of Inquiry*, he states: "What has been said helps to explain why the term 'warranted assertion' is preferred to the terms belief and knowledge. It is free from the ambiguity of these latter terms, and it involves reference to inquiry as that which warrants assertion. When knowledge is taken as a general abstract term related to inquiry in the abstract, it means 'warranted assertibility'. The use of a term that designates a potentiality rather than an actuality involves recognition that all special conclusions of special inquiries are parts of an enterprise that is continually renewed, or is a going concern" (Dewey, *LW* 12.17).

6   "There are many uses for the word 'true,' but the only one which could not be eliminated from our linguistic practice with relative ease is the cautionary use. That is the use we make of the word when we contrast justification and truth, and say that a belief may be justified but not true. Outside of philosophy, this cautionary use is used to contrast less-informed with better-informed audiences, past audiences with future audiences. In nonphilosophical contexts, the point of contrasting truth and justification is simply to remind oneself that there may be objections (arising from newly discovered data, or more ingenious explanatory hypotheses, or a shift in the vocabulary used for describing the objects under discussion) which have not yet occurred to anyone" (Rorty 2000b, p. 4).

7   Cheryl Misak claims that Peirce is not seeking to "define" truth. His project is "to try to get us to see the difference of respectable tasks: providing an analytic definition of a concept like truth, which might be of use to someone who has never encountered the notion before, and providing a pragmatic elucidation of it – an account of the role concept plays in practical endeavors" (Misak 2007, p. 68). This pragmatic elucidation is Peirce's primary concern. Misak compares Peirce with several contemporary defenders of deflationism in order to show how, despite some important similarities, Peirce's pragmatism differs from deflationism.

8   See Misak's discussion of the distinction between consensus and convergence (Misak 1991, pp. 122–4). Putnam (1990) criticizes Peirce's "convergence" thesis. He thinks that this commits Peirce to a misguided "metaphysical realism."

9   Although Misak's reformulation avoids some of the standard objections to Peirce, it has its own problems. Are there any criteria for determining what it means to "fruitfully" inquire about an issue? Can we ever possibly know that a belief "would not be overturned by recalcitrant experience and argument"? There have been subtle changes in Misak's defense of a Peircian pragmatic conception of truth. In her recent paper she writes: "The pragmatist of the Peircian stripe will argue that once we see that truth and assertion are intimately connected – once we see that

to assert that p is true is to assert p – we can and must look to our practices of assertion and to commitments incurred in them so as to say something more substantial about truth" (Misak 2007, p. 70). When she emphasizes that there are "obligations" and "commitments" in asserting and believing, she comes very close to an understanding of the relations between assertion and truth defended by Robert Brandom. See the note about Brandom in Misak 2007, p. 71n.

10 Habermas and Putnam now reject their earlier conceptions of truth and objectivity. Nevertheless, the epistemic conceptions of truth originally proposed by Habermas and Putnam have had a widespread influence. Their self-critiques have helped to refine a more subtle pragmatic understanding of truth and objectivity. See Jeffrey Stout's summary of the critiques of truth as "idealized rational acceptance" in Stout 2004b, pp. 250–6. I examine Habermas's revised pragmatic conception of truth in ch. 8, pp. 186–193.

11 See Wellmer's critique of the attempt to specify "ideal conditions" of inquiry and justification in Wellmer 2004. Hacking (2007) and Fine (2007) are especially insightful about the historicity of real science and inquiry. In the development of real science, procedures, standards, and norms of inquiry change in novel and unanticipated ways. Consequently, these authors are dubious about stating once and for all the ahistorical "ideal conditions" for scientific justification. Peirce, a careful student of the history of science, was acutely aware of the historicity of science, and that norms of argumentation change in the course of scientific development.

12 I take this to be one of the key issues between Rorty and Habermas in their disagreement about the role of the concepts of "universal validity" and "context-transcending truth claims." Rorty thinks that any appeal to these notions is unnecessary, little more than empty talk. Habermas argues that they are indispensable necessary conditions for all communication and discursive justificatory practices. See Rorty 2000b and Habermas 2000b.

13 Rorty writes: "Brandom says that I 'strenuously resist the possibility of radical decoupling of truth from practices of justification' ... I used to resist this, until Davidson showed me how to render the decoupling harmless by making 'true' unanalyzable" (Rorty 2000a, p. 184).

14 In this chapter I have not attempted to distinguish 'intersubjective,' 'social,' and 'communal,' but I do think it is important to distinguish carefully these terms. To my knowledge, Peirce never used the term 'intersubjective,' and for good reason. The term is misleading insofar as it suggests that, primarily, there are independent or autonomous subjects, and that, secondarily, there is something that takes place among (inter) subjects. But one of Peirce's fundamental claims (shared by most pragmatists) is that what we take to be a subject is constituted

by its social interactions. This is what Dewey called the primacy of the social. Furthermore, it is important (for some purposes) to carefully distinguish the generic notion of what is social from the more specific types of society that we designate as communal. For example, John Dewey in *The Public and Its Problems* introduces a basic distinction between the social and the communal.

15   Peirce goes on to say:

> But, you will say, I am setting up this very proposition as infallible truth. Not at all, it is a mere definition. I do not say that it is infallibly true that there is any belief to which a person would come if he were to carry his inquiries far enough. I only say that that alone is what I call Truth. I cannot infallibly know that there is any Truth. (Peirce and Welby 1977, p. 73)

16   Wellmer acknowledges the affinity of his position with what Brandom says about the concept of objectivity. See Wellmer 2004, nn. 12 and 19.

17   Brandom has an extremely broad view of pragmatism and frequently speaks about Hegelian, Heideggerian, and Wittgensteinian pragmatism in addition to the pragmatism of the American pragmatists. I think, however, that Brandom has a distorted view of the American pragmatists and his relation to them. He fails to realize the extent to which his own project of developing a normative pragmatics and an inferential semantics was anticipated by Peirce, the founder of American pragmatism. See Brandom 2002 and Hilary Putnam's comment. For the most part, I agree with Putnam's sharp critique of Brandom's understanding of the classical American pragmatists.

18   Stout (2004b) provides a lucid and helpful account of Brandom's pragmatism (as well as the similarities and differences of Brandom's, Davidson's, and Rorty's understanding of truth and justification).

19   In response to the charge that his position amounts to a form of "linguistic idealism," Brandom claims that it is a "misplaced concern": "What must not be lost is an appreciation of the way in which our discursive practice is empirically and practically constrained. It is not up to us which claims are true (that is, what the facts are). It is in a sense up to us which noises and marks express which claims, and hence, in a more attenuated sense, which express true claims. But empirical and practical constraints on our arbitrary whim is a pervasive feature of our discursive practice. ... [D]iscursive practices as here conceived do not stand apart from the rest of the world" (Brandom 1994, p. 331). Here, once again, we find a strong affinity with Peirce. Peirce sought to highlight the way in which the world constrains inquiry and our discursive practices by his appeal to the category of Secondness – the brute compulsion that constrains us. But he also argues that this constraint should not be confused with justification. Justification is the result of controlled communal inquiry.

20 Jeffrey Stout presents clear analyses of Brandom's pragmatic understanding of objectivity and truth – "pragmatism untainted by narcissism." See Stout 2004b and 2007.

21 Brandom's conception of I–thou sociality is close to Peirce's understanding of the community of inquirers. Peirce does not think of the community as some privileged "reified entity" that determines what is true and real. On the contrary, Peirce also places emphasis on the dynamic interactions of the individual participants in an ongoing inquiry.

22 Brandom's reply to Rorty presents a clear statement of the main elements of his account of objectivity. For a helpful discussion of the differences between Rorty and Brandom concerning objectivity, see Stout 2004b, pp. 47–52.

23 See Brandom 1994, ch. 8, for a discussion of the *de re* and *de dicto* propositional attitudes. For a succinct statement of the role that this distinction plays in Brandom's account of objectivity, see his reply to Rorty in Brandom 1997a.

24 See Lafont 2002 for a sympathetic but sharp critique of Brandom. She argues that Brandom's perspectival account rests on a presupposition that there is *"the specific game of saying how things are in the world* – a world that is one and the same for all practitioners and, thus, independent of their respective attitudes. This minimal notion of reality is *neither perspectival nor reducible to any other kind of notion"* (p. 202). See also Richard Rorty's discussion of Brandom's treatment of objectivity, Rorty 1998b.

25 Rorty introduces this distinction in Rorty 1997b.

> The line between harmonizing old intuitions and replacing old intuitions with new ones is, of course, as fuzzy as the line between an intuition and the metaphor in which it is clothed. But sometimes it is useful to draw both lines. It has been useful to say, as Copernicus, Cantor, Darwin, Einstein, Freud, and Nietzsche did, "so much the worse for your old intuitions; start working up some new ones." My hunch is that Brandom would do well to take this latter, more arrogant tack, and to situate his philosophy of language within an immodest metaphilosophical framework, according to which philosophical reflection can reject the intuitions of the vulgar as well as the metaphors of the learned. (Rorty 1997b, p. 177)

Rorty makes a similar point in "Robert Brandom on Social Practices and Representations":

> David Lewis once said that philosophy is a matter of collating our intuitions and then finding a way to keep as many of them as possible. I think that it is a matter of treating both intuitions and accusations of paradox as the voice of the past, and as possible impediments to the creation of a better future. Of course the voice of the past must always be heeded, since rhetorical effectiveness depends upon a decent respect for the opinions of mankind. But intellectual and moral progress would

be impossible unless people can sometimes, in exceptional cases, be persuaded to turn a deaf ear to that voice. (Rorty 1998b, p. 137)

Hilary Putnam basically agrees with Rorty about the need, at times, to "jettison" some intuitions. "The task of the philosopher, as I see it, is to see *which* of our intuitions we can responsibly retain and which we must jettison in a period of enormous and unprecedented intellectual, as well as material change" (Putnam 1987, p. 30). But, of course, Putnam and Rorty disagree about which intuitions "we must jettison."

Chapter 6   Experience after the Linguistic Turn

1   Rorty writes: "The phrase 'the linguistic turn' which Bergmann uses here and which I have used as the title of this anthology is, to the best of my knowledge, Bergmann's own coinage" (Rorty 1967, p. 9).
2   See Martin Jay's discussion of the debates concerning the role of experience and the linguistic turn by historians and feminists in *Songs of Experience*, especially his analysis of Joan W. Scott's controversial critique of the appeal to experience (Jay 2005, pp. 249–55).
3   For an elucidation of what Rorty means by "vocabularies," see Brandom 2000c.
4   The word 'experience' is not even listed in the index to Robert Brandom's 741-page book, *Making It Explicit* (Brandom 1994). Even though Brandom closely identifies his pragmatic project with Hegel, he fails to see the philosophical importance of the concept of experience (*Erfahrung*), which plays such a prominent philosophical role in Hegel's *Phenomenology of Spirit*.

Martin Jay writes:

> One of the most hotly contested issues in the revival of pragmatism, as it turned out, was the centrality of 'experience' to the tradition. For Rorty was bluntly outspoken in denying it importance. ... [H]e argued against the way in which experience had functioned as a pseudo-solution, a kind of crypto-foundationalism for thinkers who lacked the courage to live without one. Changing the tune, Rorty implied, would not be enough to salvage the song of experience, which, he insisted, should be dropped from the repertory altogether. (Jay 2005, p. 302)

Jay provides an illuminating discussion of Rorty's blunt dismissal of experience and the strong reaction that he provoked by defenders of classical pragmatism. See Jay 2005, pp. 299–311.
5   Cited by Richard Rorty in "Dewey's Metaphysics" (Rorty 1982, p. 72).
6   John E. Smith, John McDermott, and Richard Shusterman, three of the best interpreters of the pragmatic tradition, have consistently stressed the centrality and the meaning of experience in the pragmatic tradi-

tion. See Smith 1963, 1970; McDermott 1976; and Shusterman 1992. Intellectual historians of the pragmatic tradition have sharply criticized Rorty's distortions of the classical American pragmatists – especially Rorty's "dismissal" of experience. See Westbrook 1991 and Kloppenberg 1986, 1998.

7　Peirce, as I have indicated, notes the close relation between his categorial scheme and that of Hegel, but he also expresses his strong differences with Hegel about qualitative presentness.

> When anything is present to the mind, what is the very first and simplest character to be noted in it, in every case, no matter how little elevated the object may be? Certainly, it is its *presentness*. So far Hegel is quite right. Immediacy is his word. To say, however, that presentness, presentness as it is present, present presentness, is *abstract*, is Pure Being, is a falsity so glaring, that one can only say that Hegel's theory that the abstract is more primitive than the concrete blinded his eyes to what stood before them. Go out under the blue dome of heaven and look at what is present as it appears to the artist's eye. The poetic mood approaches the state in which the present appears as it is present. (5.44)

8　For Peirce's explication of these definitions of a sign, see "Pragmatism," in Peirce 1998, pp. 398–433.

9　Peirce discriminates several different types of interpretant. In one of his classifications, he distinguishes the immediate, dynamic, and final interpretants. It is the final logical interpretant that Peirce identifies with habits of conduct and is most relevant for his pragmatic maxim. See Peirce 1998, pp. 430–3.

10　I am using 'epistemic' in a broad sense to include not only knowledge but anything that can be thought.

11　Peirce's understanding of realism is complex and changes over the course of his career. In "The Fixation of Belief" he writes: "There are real things, whose characters are entirely independent of our opinions about them" (Peirce 1992, p. 120). He also rejected all forms of nominalism and argued for the reality of universals. When I claim that Secondness can account for what recent philosophers call their "realist intuitions," I am limiting myself to Peirce's claim that there are external (not just "conversational") constraints upon what we can know empirically.

12　There is a common prejudice (shared by Bergmann) that the "linguistic turn" emerged with analytic philosophy in the twentieth century. Linguists, anthropologists, and film theorists have been much more perceptive about the path-breaking significance of Peirce's semiotics (his theory of signs), which is much broader and more inclusive than language. Long before Wittgenstein, Peirce wrote (1868):

> [T]here is no element whatever of man's consciousness which has not something corresponding to it in the word; and the reason is obvious. It

> is that the word or sign which man uses is the man himself. For, as the fact that every thought is a sign, and taken in conjunction with the fact that life is a train of thought, proves that man is a sign; so, that every thought is an *external* sign, proves that man is an external sign. That is to say, the man and the external sign are identical, in the same sense in which the word *homo* and *man* are identical. *Thus my language is the sum total of myself.* (Peirce 1992, p. 54; emphasis added)

13 See, e.g., the excerpts of Peirce's letters to James in Peirce 1998, pp. 492–502.

14 A major conflict that cuts through many issues is the conflict over realism and nominalism. Peirce strongly defended the thesis that universals and laws are real. He argued that his pragmaticism is about practices and conduct (which are general) and not actions (which are singular). James temperamentally and philosophically was thoroughly nominalistic.

15 Peirce was not happy with James's notion of pure experience. In a letter dated 3 October 1904 he chided James and expressed his exasperation: "what you call 'pure experience' is not experience at all and certainly ought to have a name. It is downright bad morals so to misuse words, for it prevents philosophy from becoming a science" (8.302). This occasional remark epitomizes the sharp difference in temperament between Peirce and James. Peirce hoped that philosophy would finally become a true science, and consequently required a technical terminology; this is precisely what James most feared.

16 For a selection of some of James's statements about radical empiricism, see James 1997, section III.

17 In different ways, Hilary Putnam and John McDowell, two contemporary philosophers who have made the linguistic turn, have sought to defend an understanding of perception and experience that has strong affinities with James's understanding of "pure experience" insofar as they both deny that there is any ontological or epistemological gap between what we can perceive and what "there really is." In this respect they both reject the alleged contrast (and conflict) that Wilfrid Sellars draws between the manifest and the scientific images of man. See "James's Theory of Perception," in Putnam 1990, pp. 232–51; and McDowell 1996, especially his second lecture, "The Unboundedness of the Conceptual."

18 Martin Jay discusses this aspect of James's project and notes its continuity with poststructuralist conceptions of experience. See "James and the Quest for Pure Experience" (pp. 272–86) and "The Poststructuralist Reconstitution of Experience: Bataille, Barthes, and Foucault" (pp. 361–400) in Jay 2005.

19 There are notable exceptions, especially philosophers like Alvin Plantinga and Nicholas Wolterstorff, but even these thinkers have been concerned primarily with the linguistic and epistemological issues con-

cerning religious faith and belief, rather than with the full range of religious experience.

20 David A. Hollinger speaks of James's

> anxiety about the fate of religion in an age of science that James frankly shared with most of the people who heard him lecture and bought his books during his lifetime. By taking this anxiety seriously, we can more easily discern … James's center of gravity: A radically secular, naturalistic vision of the process by which knowledge is produced, and a hope that religiously satisfying knowledge might still be forthcoming if only enough people would bring to inquiry – and place at risk in it – their religious commitments. James wished to reform the culture of inquiry by enriching it with exactly those energies that were intimidated by the agnostics and positivists who announced themselves to be the true representatives of "science." He sought to promote this reform exactly while developing the philosophical arguments we know as "radical empiricism," "pluralism," and "pragmatism." (Hollinger 1985, pp. 3–4)

21 There is an extensive secondary literature dealing with *The Varieties of Religious Experience*, and more generally, with James's reflections on religious experience. For a succinct account see Jay 2005, pp. 102–10. See also Taylor 2002 and Proudfoot (ed.) 2004.

22 See "The Influence of Darwinism and Philosophy," in Dewey 1981.

23 See my discussion of "The Reflex Arc Concept in Psychology" in Bernstein 1966a, pp. 14–21.

24 For Dewey's fully developed critique of the empiricist conception of experience, see "The Need for a Recovery of Philosophy," in Dewey 1981, pp. 58–97. See also my discussion of this critique in Bernstein 1971, pp. 200–13.

25 Dewey makes it clear that there may be some reflection or inference in anything that we single out as a human experience. "All this is not to deny that some element of reflection or inference may be required in any situation to which the term 'experience' is applicable in any way which contrasts with, say, the 'experience' of an oyster or a growing bean vine. Men experience illness. What they experience is certainly something very different from an object of apprehension, yet it is quite possible that what makes an illness into a *conscious* experience is precisely the intellectual elements which intervene" (Dewey 2007, p. 5).

26 See Dewey's essays "Peirce's Theory of Quality" and "Qualitative Thought," in Dewey 1960, pp. 199–210, 176–98.

27 See "The Pattern of Inquiry," in Dewey 1981, pp. 223–39.

28 In my book, *John Dewey*, I discuss the centrality of the aesthetic dimension of experience for Dewey. See ch. 11, "The Artistic, The Esthetic and the Religious," of Bernstein 1966a. See also Shusterman 1992; and Alexander 1987.

29 In *A Common Faith* Dewey examines the religious quality of experience. "Any activity pursued in behalf of an ideal end against obstacles and in

spite of threats of personal loss because of its general and enduring value is religious in quality" (Dewey 1998, p. 410). For a discussion of Dewey's (and other pragmatic) reflections on religion, see Bernstein 2005.

30   Martin Jay points out that although Dewey's account of the classical Greek conception of experience is simplified, "it is still hard to deny a certain truth to Dewey's characterization of the relatively modest role played by experience, however defined, in mainstream classical thought. ... The legacy of Plato and Aristotle, with varying coherence and often eclectically combined with elements of non-Greek thought, dominated medieval philosophy" (Jay 2005, p. 17).

31   Dewey develops both of these points about the new experimental concept of experience in "The Need for a Recovery of Philosophy," in Dewey 1981.

32   See Lafont 1999; and Jürgen Habermas, "Hermeneutic and Analytic Philosophy: Two Complementary Versions of the Linguistic Turn," in Habermas 2003, pp. 51–82.

33   "[T]he pragmatic approach to language [*Sprachpragmatik*] helped me to develop a theory of communicative action and of rationality. It was the foundation for a critical theory of society and paved the way for a discourse-theoretic conception of morality, law, and democracy" (Habermas 2003, p. 1).

34   See Habermas, 1987b; and "Individuation through Socialization: On George Herbert Mead's Theory of Subjectivity," in Habermas 1992, pp. 149–204; Tugendhat 1989; Joas 1985; Honneth 1996 and Aboulafia (ed.) 1991.

Chapter 7   Hilary Putnam: The Entanglement of Fact and Value

1   See James Conant's excellent introductions to Putnam 1990 and 1994 for an overview of Putnam's philosophical development.

2   See Putnam's discussion of the history of the is–ought and the fact–value distinctions (Putnam 2002a, ch. 1).

3   He shows this in detail and with specific reference to economics in Putnam 2002a.

4   Putnam frequently does not make a systematic distinction between values and norms, although he speaks of norms when he wants to emphasize standards of correctness and standards of what ought to be. Not all values are norms. One of his major disagreements with Habermas concerns what Putnam takes to be Habermas's rigid dichotomy between values and norms. Putnam also does not accept the dichotomy that Habermas introduces between morality and ethics.

5   For an explanation of what he means by "indispensability arguments" see Putnam 1994, pp. 153–60.

6   Putnam claims that James is more helpful in thinking about ethical decisions and Dewey is more illuminating in dealing with political decisions. Nevertheless, Putnam rejects a dichotomy between ethics and politics. Ethics requires an ethical community, and the cultivation of the practices required for such a community is a political project.

7   For Putnam's multifaceted critique of Williams's dichotomy of science and ethics, see Putnam 1990, pp. 165–78, and Putnam 1994, pp. 188–92 and 217–18.

8   Despite the many disagreements between Rorty and Putnam, Rorty would completely endorse *this* central thesis.

9   This is a statement that Putnam made in his concluding remarks at a conference dedicated to his pragmatism that was held at the University of Münster in 2000.

10 Putnam rejects the idea that there is a single "scientific method." But he also thinks that this is not what Dewey meant when he appeals to scientific method in solving ethical problems. Rather, Dewey is appealing to experimentation, imaginative construction of alternative hypotheses, open discussion, debate, and ongoing self-corrective communal criticism.

Chapter 8   Jürgen Habermas's Kantian Pragmatism

1   Writing about his college years, Peirce says: "The C.d.r.V. [*Critique of Pure Reason*] chiefly occupied my mind for three years; and it was several years more before I began to see that it was mistaken. Before I left college, I almost knew the book by heart; and certainly no day passed without my spending two or three hours in hard thinking about it" (cited in Ketner 1998, p. 139).

2   Habermas's remarks about his "weak naturalism" are extremely sketchy. He never spells out in detail the precise meaning of this "background assumption"; nor does he provide arguments to show that his "weak naturalism" can be defended against the claims of "strong (reductive) naturalists." But his naturalism is similar to the naturalism of the American pragmatists. He claims that distinguishing the methodological distinction between a participant's perspective (second person) and an observational perspective (third person) is "ontologically neutral."

> This blanket assumption of an evolutionary continuity that permeates culture, as it were, refrains from making any philosophical assumptions about the relationship of mind and body (in the sense of eliminative or reductive materialism, for example); on the contrary, it keeps us from

reifying a difference between methodological approaches that are themselves ontologically neutral. As long as we cast the issue in transcendental terms, we have to distinguish sharply between the hermeneutic approach of a rational reconstruction of the structures of the lifeworld, which we undertake from the perspective of participants, and the observation-based causal analysis of how these structures naturally evolve. (Habermas 2003, p. 28)

3 In his article "From Kant's 'Ideas' of Pure Reason to 'Idealizing' Presuppositions of Communicative Action: Reflections on the Detranscendentalized 'Use of Reason' " (in Habermas 2003, pp. 83–130) Habermas explains in detail what he means by the "idealizing presuppositions of communicative action" and develops a genealogical account of them – showing how they can be related to Kant's Ideas of Reason. His reconstruction indicates how indebted he is to a pragmatically "detranscendentalized" Kant.

4 Habermas has always engaged in discussion with his critics and has modified his views in response to what he takes to be valid in these criticisms. His revision of his epistemic theory of truth exemplifies his deep fallibilistic commitment.

5 Much of the confusion and criticism of Habermas's understanding of truth has its source in Habermas 1973. Although he rejected both correspondence and coherence theories of truth, he nevertheless coined the unfortunate phrase a "consensus theory of truth." He now acknowledges that his primary concern had been an *epistemic* understanding of truth – *justifying* true claims about the world. The objections raised against his earlier discussion have prompted him "to revise the discursive conception of rational acceptability by *relating* it to a pragmatically conceived, nonepistemic concept of truth, but without thereby assimilating 'truth' to 'ideal assertibility'."

> Despite this revision, the concept of rational discourse retains its status as a privileged form of communication that forces those participating in it to continue decentering their cognitive perspectives. The normatively exacting and unavoidable communicative presuppositions of the practice of argumentation now as then imply that impartial judgment formation is structurally necessary. Argumentation remains the only *available* medium of ascertaining truth since truth claims that have been problematized cannot be tested in any other way. There is no unmediated, discursively unfiltered access to the truth conditions of empirical beliefs. (Habermas 2003, p. 38)

It is frequently claimed (by Habermas, Putnam, McDowell, and many others) that the pragmatic "consensus theory of truth" originated with Peirce. The passage frequently cited is Peirce's early (1878) statement from "How to Make Our Ideas Clear": "The opinion which is fated to be agreed to by all who investigate, is what we mean by the truth, and the object represented in this opinion is the real" (Peirce 1992, p. 139). But Cheryl Misak has shown that this early statement does not do justice to Peirce's reflections on 'truth':

> C. S. Peirce, the founder of pragmatism, argued that a belief is true if it would be 'indefeasible', or would not be improved upon, or would never lead to disappointment, no matter how far we were to pursue our inquiries. Although he occasionally articulated this view of truth in terms of a belief's being fated to be believed at the end of inquiry, on the whole he tried to stay away from unhelpful ideas such as the final end of inquiry, perfect evidence, and the like. (Misak 2007, p. 68)

See also Misak 1991.

6   For the reasons why Habermas speaks of the world as the totality of *things, not facts*, see Habermas 2003, pp. 30–6. He wants to avoid the type of representationalism that reifies facts. He wants to defend epistemic realism, but not metaphysical realism.

7   For Habermas's critique of Rorty and Rorty's response, see their exchanges in Brandom (ed.) 2000.

8   Brandom has defended himself against the criticism that he "obliterates the distinction between the intersubjectively shared lifeworld and the objective world." See the exchange between Habermas and Brandom in the *European Journal of Philosophy* (Habermas 2000a and Brandom 2000b).

9   Doubts may be raised about whether Habermas's understanding of realism and the objectivity of the world is really compatible with Putnam's understanding of conceptual relativity and conceptual pluralism. For an explication and defense of these views, as well as Putnam's "obituary" for ontology, see Putnam 2004.

10   When Habermas initially developed his discourse theory of ethics, he had not yet fully articulated his important distinction between ethics and morality. He worked out this distinction in his essay "On the Pragmatic, the Ethical, and the Moral Employments of Practical Reason." Habermas explains how practical reason may be employed in three very different ways – and why it is essential to distinguish these three ways. In his preface to *Justification and Application* he writes: "Since then it would be more accurate to speak of a 'discourse theory of morality,' but I retain the term 'discourse ethics,' which has become established usage" (Habermas 1993, p. vii).

11   Habermas makes it clear that "discourse ethics situates itself squarely in the Kantian tradition. ... Admittedly, it adopts a narrowly circumscribed conception of morality that focuses on questions of justice" (Habermas 1993, pp. 1–2).

12   In his critique of Putnam, Habermas writes: "Whereas in metaphysics and epistemology [Putnam] proceeds along the lines of a linguistic Kantianism, in practical philosophy, he takes a pragmatist reading of

Aristotle as his point of reference. Here, *eudaimonia* – human flourishing – has the last word. Putnam understands autonomy in the classical sense of leading a reflective life rather than in the Kantian sense of rational moral self-legislation. By putting my description of Putnam's philosophy in these terms, I am implicitly raising the question of how high the price of this split loyalty is. Would Putnam the pragmatist not be better off if he remained a Kantian all the way?" (Habermas 2003, p. 214). For the dispute between Putnam and Habermas concerning values and norms, see Putnam's "Values and Norms," in Putnam 2002a, pp. 111–34, and Habermas's reply, "Norms and Values: On Hilary Putnam's Kantian Pragmatism," in Habermas 2003, pp. 213–36.

13   According to the three different employments of practical reason that Habermas discusses in "On the Pragmatic, the Ethical, and the Moral Employments of Practical Reason," the reasoning involved in figuring out how to get to my office is "pragmatic." Pragmatic reasoning is required in those cases where "we look for reasons for a rational choice between different available courses of action in the light of a task that we *must* accomplish if we *want* to achieve a certain goal" (Habermas 1993, p. 2).

14   Habermas prefers to speak about "discourse" rather than "inquiry," because he thinks that "inquiry" can be monological and doesn't fully bring out the participants' second-person perspective in communication and discourse. But pragmatists, from the time of Peirce, have always emphasized that inquiry is essentially a social process involving a "community of inquirers," and consequently encompasses a second-person perspective.

15   Although I am drawing on Rorty for some of my critiques of Habermas, I want to make it clear that I do *not* accept his extreme contextualism. I do *not* agree with his claim that the appeal to "good reasons" amounts to little more than an appeal to what some sociological group contingently accepts as good reasons.

16   See pp. 131–6 for my discussion of Secondness in Peirce. See also Steven Levine's perceptive criticism of Habermas's "Janus-faced" theory of truth (Levine, forthcoming).

17   Following Habermas, I have characterized his view of morality as constructivist. But, of course, there are many varieties of moral constructivism, including John Rawls's version. Maeve Cooke notes that Habermas's moral construction *"defines* justice as an argumentatively achieved consensus." "[A] consensus achieved under ideal justificatory conditions *guarantees* validity." She argues that this strong version leads to all sorts of problems, and that Habermas should adopt a weaker version – one where intersubjective agreement is a *necessary* but not a *sufficient* condition to justify the validity of moral norms (Cooke 2003, p. 288).

18   In fairness to Putnam, it should be noted that he also rejects this picture (caricature) of moral realism. See his "Values and Norms," in Putnam 2002a, pp. 111–34.

19   I have developed this criticism of Habermas's dichotomy between ethics and morality in Bernstein 1996.

20   One may seriously wonder – given the complex global world in which we live, with its conflicting claims about how to even frame moral issues and questions of justice – whether a formulation such as the following has any real *normative* force: "Only a maxim that can be generalized from the perspective of all affected counts as a norm that can command general assent and to that extent is worthy of recognition, or, in other words, is morally binding" (Habermas 1993, p. 8).

21   There are some persons who think that torture is 'justified' or, at least, permissible in extreme situations where we have good reasons to believe that it will extract information that will help save lives.

22   Habermas is certainly aware of the distinction between *justifying* a moral norm and *applying* it. But he thinks that these call for two different types of argumentation.

> [E]very justification of a norm is necessarily subject to the normal limitations of a finite, historically situated outlook that is provincial in regard to the future. Hence *a forteriori* it cannot already explicitly allow for all of the salient features that at some time in the future will characterize the constellations of unforeseen individual cases. For this reason, the *application* of norms calls for argumentative clarification in its own right. In this case, the impartiality of judgment cannot again be secured through a principle of universalization; rather, in addressing questions of context-sensitive application, practical reason must be informed by a principle of appropriateness [*Angemessenheit*]. What must be determined here is which of the norms already accepted as valid is appropriate in a given case in the light of all the relevant features of the situation conceived as exhaustively as possible. (Habermas 2003, pp. 13–14)

> But Habermas fails to emphasize the intricate dialectical relationship between justification and application. The very *meaning* of a moral norm is determined by what we take to be its range of application. We cannot fully anticipate unexpected applications and their consequences. Since the time when Peirce first proposed his "pragmatic maxim," pragmatists have always emphasized how consequences affect the meaning of a concept.

23   Putnam also questions Habermas's limited conception of objectivity. See my discussion of Putnam, pp. 161–7.

24   I mention Mead here for two reasons. First, Mead plays a fundamental role in the development of Habermas's *Theory of Communicative Action*. Second, in his critique of Putnam, Habermas cites Mead as a pragmatist who gives a constructivist account of the moral point of view.

> Mead's intersubjectivist reading of the categorical imperative emphasizes the necessity of decentering one's given ego or ethnocentrically limited interpreted perspectives. Reciprocal perspective-taking makes one's own

position dependent on the consideration of the polycentric structure of how all other parties understand themselves in the world. In this process, the normative validity of binding norms is understood in the sense of worthiness of universal recognition. ... For the gentle force of inclusive reciprocal perspective-taking is embedded in the pragmatic presuppositions of discursive practice, on which justification of *all* beliefs – be they empirical or mathematical, evaluative or moral – depends. Of course the need to decentralize becomes particularly significant with regard to questions of justice. (Habermas 2003, pp. 234–5)

I agree with what Habermas says about Mead, but I also think it important to call attention to what Habermas does *not* say. Mead's analysis of the "generalized other" begins with situated *local* communities. In Mead (as in Dewey) there is no sharp distinction between local "ethical" communities and a more universal "moral" community. By extending the boundaries of local communities, we *strive* to achieve greater inclusiveness and universality. Neither Dewey nor Mead would accept a sharp distinction between ethics and morality. Both seek to do justice to the local (particular) and universal dimensions of communal ethical life.

Chapter 9   Richard Rorty's Deep Humanism

1   Rorty continues: "This essay is one more attempt to restate my philosophical views in a form that may be a bit less vulnerable to Bernstein's objections" (Rorty 2004, p. 3).
2   See Robert Brandom's excellent discussion of the meaning and consequences of Rorty's conception of a "vocabulary" in Brandom 2000c.
3   For an early statement of Rorty's understanding of metaphilosophy, see Rorty 1961b.
4   See my critical discussion of *Philosophy and the Mirror of Nature*, Bernstein 1980.
5   For my critique of Rorty's "postmodern" turn, see Bernstein 1987. See Rorty's reply, Rorty 1987.
6   See my critical discussion of *Contingency, Irony, and Solidarity*, "Rorty's Liberal Utopia," in Bernstein 1991, pp. 258–92.
7   See Richard Rorty, "Looking Backwards from the Year 2096," in Rorty 1999, pp. 243–51.
8   Consider what Rorty says about philosophical arguments:

On the view of philosophy which I am offering, philosophers should not be asked for arguments against, for example, the correspondence theory of truth or the idea of the "intrinsic nature of reality." The trouble with arguments against the use of a familiar and time-honored vocabulary is that they are expected to be phrased in that very vocabulary. They are expected to show that central arguments are "inconsistent in their own terms" or that they "deconstruct themselves." But that can never be shown. Any argument to the effect that our familiar use of a familiar term is incoherent, or empty, or confused, or vague, or "merely metaphorical" is bound to be inconclusive and question-begging. (Rorty 1989, p. 8)

9 See Jeffrey Stout's (2007) perceptive discussion of these competing voices in Rorty.

10 For my critique of Rorty's version of liberalism, see Bernstein 2003.

References

Aboulafia, M. (ed.) (1991) *Philosophy, Social Theory and the Thought of George Herbert Mead*. SUNY Press, Albany.

Alexander, T. (1987) *John Dewey's Theory of Art, Experience, and Nature: The Horizons of Feeling*. SUNY Press, Albany.

Apel, K.-O. (1981) *Charles S. Peirce: From Pragmatism to Pragmaticism*, trans. J. M. Krois. University of Massachusetts Press, Amherst.

Bergmann, G. (1953) Logical Positivism, Language, and the Reconstruction of Metaphysics. Repr. in Rorty (ed.) 1967, pp. 63–71.

—— (1964) *Logic and Reality*. University of Wisconsin Press, Madison.

Bernstein, R. J. (1959) Knowledge, Value, Freedom. In C. W. Hendel (ed.), *John Dewey and the Experimental Spirit in Philosophy*, pp. 63–92. Liberal Arts Press, New York.

—— (1961) John Dewey's Metaphysics of Experience. *Journal of Philosophy* 58, pp. 5–14.

—— (1964a) Myths about the Mississippi Summer Project. *The Nation* 28 (December).

—— (1964b) Peirce's Theory of Perception. In E. C. Moore and R. Robin (eds), *Studies in the Philosophy of Charles Sanders Peirce: Second Series*, pp. 165–84. University of Massachusetts Press, Amherst.

—— (1965) Action, Conduct, and Self-control. In Bernstein (ed.) 1965, pp. 66–91.

—— (1966a) *John Dewey*. Washington Square Press, New York.

—— (1966b) Sellars' Vision of Man-in-the-universe. *Review of Metaphysics* 20/1, pp. 113–43; and 20/2, pp. 290–316.

—— (1971) *Praxis and Action*. University of Pennsylvania Press, Philadelphia.

—— (1976) *The Restructuring of Social and Political Theory*. Harcourt, Brace, Jovanovich, New York.

—— (1977) Hannah Arendt: The Ambiguities of Theory and Practice. In T. Ball (ed.), *Political Theory and Praxis: New Perspectives*, pp. 141–58. University of Minnesota Press, Minneapolis.

—— (1980) Philosophy and the Conversation of Mankind. *Review of Metaphysics* 33/4, pp. 725–75.

—— (1981) Introduction to Apel 1981.

—— (1983) *Beyond Objectivism and Relativism: Science, Hermenentics, and Praxis.* University of Pennsylvania Press, Philadelphia.

—— (1987) One Step Forward, Two Steps Backward: Rorty on Liberal Democracy and Philosophy. *Political Theory* 15/4, pp. 538–63.

—— (1991) *The New Constellation: The Ethical-Political Horizons of Modernity/ Postmodernity.* Polity, Cambridge.

—— (1995a) American Pragmatism: The Conflict of Narratives. In H. J. Saatkamp, Jr (ed.), *Rorty and Pragmatism*, pp. 54–67. Vanderbilt University Press, Nashville, Tenn.

—— (1995b) Whatever Happened to Naturalism? *Proceedings and Addresses of the American Philosophical Association* 69/2, pp. 57–76.

—— (1996) The Retrieval of the Democratic Ethos. *Cardoza Law Review* 17/4-5, pp. 1127–46.

—— (2003) Rorty's Inspirational Liberalism. In C. Guignon and D. R. Hiley (eds), *Richard Rorty*, pp. 124–38. Cambridge University Press, Cambridge.

—— (2005) *The Abuse of Evil: The Corruption of Politics and Religion since 9/11.* Polity, Cambridge.

—— (2006a) Derrida: The Aporia of Forgiveness? *Constellations* 13/3, pp. 394–406.

—— (2006b) *The Pragmatic Century: Conversations with Richard J. Bernstein*, ed. S. G. Davaney and W. G. Frisina. SUNY Press, Albany.

—— (2007) The Romance of Philosophy. John Dewey Lecture. *Proceedings and Addresses of the American Philosophical Association* 81/2, pp. 107–19.

—— (ed.) (1960) *John Dewey: On Experience, Nature, and Freedom.* Liberal Arts Press, New York.

—— (ed.) (1965) *Perspectives on Peirce.* Yale University Press, New Haven.

Bradley, F. C. (1968) *Essays on Truth and Reality.* Clarendon Press, Oxford.

Brandom, R. (1994) *Making It Explicit.* Harvard University Press, Cambridge, Mass.

—— (1997a) Replies. *Philosophy and Phenomenological Research* 57, pp. 189–204.

—— (1997b) Study Guide to Sellars 1997.

—— (2000a) *Articulating Reasons: An Introduction to Inferentialism.* Harvard University Press, Cambridge, Mass.

—— (2000b) Facts, Norms, and Normative Facts: A Reply to Habermas. *European Journal of Philosophy* 8/3, pp. 356–74.

—— (2000c) Vocabularies of Pragmatism: Synthesizing Naturalism and Historicism. In Brandom (ed.) 2000, pp. 156–83.

—— (2002a) Pragmatics and Pragmatism. In J. Conant and U. M. Zeglen (eds), *Hilary Putnam: Pragmatism and Realism*, pp. 40–59. Routledge, New York.

—— (2002b) *Tales of the Mighty Dead: Historical Essays in the Metaphysics of Intentionality*. Harvard University Press, Cambridge, Mass.

—— (ed.) (2000) *Rorty and his Critics*. Blackwell, Oxford.

Burke, K. (1941) *The Philosophy of Literary Form: Studies in Symbolic Action*. Louisiana State University Press, Baton Rouge.

Canning, K. (1994) Feminist History after the Linguistic Turn: Historicising Discourse and Experience. *Signs* 19/2, pp. 368–404.

Cohen, M. (1992) Rooted Cosmopolitanism: Thoughts on the Left, Nationalism, and Multiculturalism. *Dissent* 39/4, pp. 478–83.

Conant, J. (1997) The James/Royce Dispute and the Development of James's Solution. In R. A. Putnam (ed.), *The Cambridge Companion to William James*, pp. 186–213. Cambridge University Press, Cambridge.

Cooke, M. (2003) The Weakness of Strong Intersubjectivism: Habermas's Conception of Justice. *European Journal of Political Theory* 2/3, pp. 281–305.

Davidson, D. (1986) A Coherence Theory of Truth and Knowledge. Repr. in Lepore (ed.) 1986, pp. 307–19.

—— (2000) Truth Rehabilitated. In Brandom (ed.), 2000, pp. 65–73.

Descartes, R. (1979) *The Philosophical Works of Descartes*, ed. E. Haldane and G. R. T. Ross, 2 vols. Cambridge University Press, Cambridge.

Dewey, J. (1927) *The Public and Its Problems*. Henry Holt and Co., New York.

—— (1969–90) *The Collected Works of John Dewey 1882–1953* (*Early Works, Middle Works, and Later Works*). Southern Illinois University Press, Carbondale.

—— (1960) *On Experience, Nature, and Freedom*, ed. R. J. Bernstein. Liberal Arts Press, New York.

—— (1981) *The Philosophy of John Dewey*, ed. J. J. McDermott. University of Chicago Press, Chicago.

—— (1998) *The Essential Dewey*, vols 1 & 2. Indiana University Press, Bloomington.

—— (2007) *Essays in Experimental Logic*, ed. D. C. Hester and R. B. Talisse. Southern Illinois University Press, Carbondale.

Dickstein, M. (ed.) (1988) *The Revival of Pragmatism: New Essays in Social Thought, Law, and Culture*. Duke University Press, Raleigh, NC.

Dreyfus, H. L. (1991) *Being-in-the-World: A Commentary on Heidegger's* Being and Time*, Division I*. MIT Press, Cambridge, Mass.

Edie, J. (1987) *William James and Phenomenology*. Indiana University Press, Bloomington.

Feigl, H. and Sellars, W. (eds) (1949) *Readings in Philosophical Analysis*. Appleton-Century-Crofts, New York.

Fine, A. (2007) Relativism, Pragmatism, and the Practice of Science. In Misak (ed.) 2007, pp. 50–67.

Fodor, J. (1994) Concepts: A Potboiler. *Cognition* 50, pp. 95–113.

Fultner, B. (2003) Introduction to Habermas 2003.

Gadamer, H.-G. (1989) *Truth and Method*, trans. J. Weinsheimer and D. G. Marshall, 2nd rev. edn. Crossroad, New York.

Gallie, W. B. (1952) *Peirce and Pragmatism*. Penguin, New York.

Glaude, Jr., E. S. (2007) *In a Shade of Blue: Pragmatism and the Politics of Black America*. University of Chicago Press, Chicago.

Goodman, R. G. (2002) *Wittgenstein and William James*. Cambridge University Press, Cambridge.

Gross, N. (2008) *Richard Rorty: The Making of an American Philosopher.* University of Chicago Press, Chicago.

Habermas, J. (1971) *Knowledge and Human Interests*. Beacon Press, Cambridge, Mass.

—— (1973) Wahrheitstheorien. In H. Fahrenbach (ed.), *Wirklichkeit und Reflexion: Walter Schulz zum 60. Geburtstag*, pp. 211–65. Pfullingen, Neske.

—— (1987a) *The Philosophical Discourse of Modernity*. MIT Press, Cambridge, Mass.

—— (1987b) *The Theory of Communicative Action*, 2 vols. Polity, Cambridge.

—— (1992) *Postmetaphysical Thinking: Philosophical Essays*. Polity, Cambridge.

—— (1993) *Justification and Application*. MIT Press, Cambridge, Mass.

—— (2000a) From Kant to Hegel: On Robert Brandom's Pragmatic Philosophy of Language. *European Journal of Philosophy* 8/3, pp. 322–55.

—— (2000b) Richard Rorty's Pragmatic Turn. In Brandom (ed.) 2000, pp. 31–55.

—— (2002) Postscript: Some Concluding Remarks. In M. Aboulafia, M. Bookman, and C. Kemp (eds), *Habermas and Pragmatism*, pp. 223–33. Routledge, New York.

—— (2003) *Truth and Justification*, trans. and ed., B. Fultner. MIT Press, Cambridge, Mass.

Hacking, I. (2007) On Not Being a Pragmatist: Eight Reasons and a Cause. In Misak (ed.), 2000, pp. 32–49.

Harris, W. T. (1867) The Speculative. *Journal of Speculative Philosophy* 1, pp. 6–22.

Haugeland, J. (1982) Heidegger on Being a Person. *Nous* 16/1, pp. 15–26.

Hollinger, D. A. (1985) *The American Province*. Johns Hopkins University Press, Baltimore.

Holmes, O. W. and Pollock, F. J. (1941) *The Correspondence of Mr. Justice Holmes and Sir Frederick Pollock 1874–1932*, ed. M. D. Howe, 2 vols. Harvard University Press, Cambridge, Mass.

Honneth, A. (1997) *The Struggle for Recognition: The Moral Grammar of Social Conflicts*, trans. J. Anderson. MIT Press, Cambridge, Mass.

—— (1998) Democracy as Reflexive Cooperation: John Dewey and the Theory of Democracy Today. *Political Theory* 26, pp. 763–83.

—— (2008) *Reification: A New Look at an Old Idea*. Oxford University Press, Oxford.

Hook, S. (1974) *Pragmatism and the Tragic Sense of Life*. Basic Books, New York.

Hookway, C. (1985) *Peirce*. Routledge & Kegan Paul, London.

Hume, D. (1978) *A Treatise of Human Nature*. Clarendon Press, Oxford.

James, W. (1920) *The Letters of William James*, ed. H. James, 2 vols. Atlantic Monthly Press, Boston.

—— (1975a) *Pragmatism*. Harvard University Press, Cambridge, Mass.

—— (1975b) *The Will to Believe*. Harvard University Press, Cambridge, Mass.

—— (1977) *A Pluralistic Universe*. Harvard University Press, Cambridge, Mass.

—— (1981) *Principles of Psychology*, 2 vols. Harvard University Press, Cambridge, Mass.

—— (1987) *Essays, Comments, and Reviews: The Works of William James*, ed. F. Burkhardt. Harvard University Press, Cambridge, Mass.

—— (1997) *The Writings of William James*, ed. J. J. McDermott. University of Chicago Press, Chicago.

Jay, M. (2005) *Songs of Experience: Modern American and European Variations on a Universal Theme*. University of California Press, Berkeley.

Joas, H. (1985) *G. H. Mead: A Contemporary Re-examination of his Thought*. Polity, Cambridge.

—— (1996) *The Creativity of Action*. Polity, Cambridge.

Kallen, H. M. (1956) *Cultural Pluralism and the American Idea: An Essay in Social Philosophy*. University of Pennsylvania Press, Philadelphia.

—— (1996) Democracy versus the Melting-pot: A Study of American Nationality (1915). In W. Sollors (ed.), *Theories of Ethnicity: A Classical Reader*, pp. 67–92. New York University Press, New York.

Ketner, K. L. (1998) *His Glassy Essence: An Autobiography of Charles Sanders Peirce*. Vanderbilt University Press, Nashville, Tenn.

Kloppenberg, J. (1986) *Uncertain Victory: Social Democracy and Progressivism in Europe and American Thought 1870–1920*. Oxford University Press, New York.

Kloppenberg, J. (1998) Pragmatism: An Old Name for Some New Ways of Thinking. Repr. in Dickstein (ed.) 1998, pp. 83–127.

Kuklick, B. (2001) *A History of Philosophy in America: 1720–2000*. Clarendon Press, Oxford.

Lafont, C. (1999) *The Linguistic Turn in Hermeneutic Philosophy*. MIT Press, Cambridge, Mass.

—— (2002) Is Objectivity Perspectival? Reflections on Brandom's and Habermas's Pragmatist Conceptions of Objectivity. In M. Aboulafia, M. Bookman, and C. Kemp (eds), *Habermas and Pragmatism*, pp. 185–209. Routledge, London.

Lepore, E. (ed.) (1986) *Truth and Interpretation: Perspectives on the Philosophy of Donald Davidson*. Blackwell, Oxford.

Levine, S. M. (forthcoming) Habermas, Kantian Pragmatism, and Truth. *Philosophy and Social Criticism*.

Locke, A. (1925) *The New Negro: An Interpretation*. Arno Press, New York.

—— (1992) *Race Contacts and Interracial Relations*. Howard University Press, Washington, DC.

Lovejoy, A. O. (1963) *The Thirteen Pragmatisms*. Johns Hopkins University Press, Baltimore.

McDermott, J. (1976) *The Culture of Experience: Philosophical Essays in the American Grain*. New York University Press, New York.

McDowell, J. (1996) *Mind and World*. Harvard University Press, Cambridge, Mass.

—— (2000) Towards Rehabilitating Objectivity. In Brandom (ed.) 2000, pp. 109–22.

Mead, G. H. (1964) *George Herbert Mead: Selected Writings*, ed. A. J. Reck. Bobbs-Merrill Co., New York.

Menand, L. (2001) *The Metaphysical Club: A Story of Ideas in America*. Farrar, Straus, and Giroux, New York.

Misak, C. (1991) *Truth and the End of Inquiry: A Peircian Account of Truth*. Clarendon Press, Oxford.

—— (2007) Pragmatism and Deflationism. In Misak (ed.) 2007, pp. 68–90.

—— (ed.) (2007) *New Pragmatists*. Oxford University Press, Oxford.

Mouffe, C. and Critchley, S. (eds) (1996) *Deconstruction and Pragmatism*. Routledge, London.

Murphy, J. P. (1990) *Pragmatism: From Peirce to Davidson*. Westview Press, Boulder, Colo.

Okrent, M. (1988) *Heidegger's Pragmatism*. Cornell University Press, Ithaca, NY.

Peirce, C. S. (1931–5). *Collected Papers*, vols 1–5, ed. C. Hartshorne and P. Weiss. Harvard University Press, Cambridge, Mass.

—— (1958). *Collected Papers*, vols 7–8, ed. A. W. Burks. Harvard University Press, Cambridge, Mass.

—— (1984) *Writings of Charles S. Peirce: A Chronological Edition*, vol. 1. Indiana University Press, Bloomington.

—— (1992) *The Essential Peirce: Selected Philosophical Writings*, vol. 1: *1867–1893*, ed. N. Houser and C. Kloesel. Indiana University Press, Bloomington.

—— (1998) *The Essential Peirce: Selected Philosophical Writings*, vol. 2: *1893–1913*. The Peirce Edition Project. Indiana University Press, Bloomington.

—— and Lady Welby (1997) *Semiotic and Significs: The Correspondence between Charles S. Peirce and Victoria Lady Welby*, ed. C. S. Hardwick. Indiana University Press, Bloomington.

Perry, R. B. (1948) *The Thought and Character of William James*, 2 vols. Harvard University Press, Cambridge, Mass.

Pippin, R. (2008) *Hegel's Practical Philosophy: Rational Agency as Ethical Life*. Cambridge University Press, Cambridge.

Pitkin, H. and Shumer, S. (1982) On Participation. *Democracy* 2, pp. 43–54.

Popper, K. (1959) *The Logic of Scientific Discovery*. Basic Books, New York.

—— (1963) *Conjectures and Refutations: The Growth of Scientific Knowledge*. Routledge & Kegan Paul, London.

—— (1974) Normal Science and its Dangers. In I. Lakatos and A. Musgrave (eds), *Criticism and the Growth of Knowledge*, pp. 51–8. Cambridge University Press, Cambridge.

Proudfoot, W. (ed.) (2004) *William James and a Science of Religion: Reexperiencing the Varieties of Religion*. Columbia University Press, New York.

Putnam, H. (1987) *The Many Faces of Realism*. Open Court, La Salle, Ill.

—— (1990) *Realism with a Human Face*, ed. J. Conant. Harvard University Press, Cambridge, Mass.

—— (1991). A Reconsideration of Deweyan Democracy. In M. Brint and W. Weavers (eds), *Pragmatism in Law and Society*, pp. 217–42. Westview Press, Boulder, Colo.

—— (1994) *Words and Life*. Harvard University Press, Cambridge, Mass.

250 *References*

—— (1995) *Pragmatism: An Open Question*. Blackwell, Oxford.
—— (1997) Interview with Hilary Putnam. *Cogito* 314, pp. 44–53.
—— (2002a) *The Collapse of the Fact/Value Dichotomy*. Harvard University Press, Cambridge, Mass.
—— (2002b) Comment on Robert Brandom's Paper. In J. Conant and U. M. Zeglen (eds), *Hilary Putnam: Pragmatism and Realism*, pp. 59–65. Routledge, New York.
—— (2004) *Ethics without Ontology*. Harvard University Press, Cambridge, Mass.
Rorty, R. (1956) The Concept of Potentiality. Ph.D. dissertation, Yale University, New Haven.
—— (1961a) Pragmatism, Categories, and Language. *Philosophical Review* 70, pp. 197–223.
—— (1961b) Recent Metaphilosophy. *Review of Metaphysics* 15/2, pp. 299–318.
—— (1965) Mind–Body Identity, Privacy, and Categories. *Review of Metaphysics* 19/1, pp. 24–54.
—— (1967) Metaphilosophical Difficulties of Linguistic Philosophy. In Rorty (ed.) 1967, pp. 1–39.
—— (1977) Dewey's Metaphysics. Repr. in Rorty 1982, pp. 72–89.
—— (1979) *Philosophy and the Mirror of Nature*. Princeton University Press, Princeton.
—— (1982) *Consequences of Pragmatism*. University of Minnesota Press, Minneapolis.
—— (1987) Thugs and Terrorists: A Reply to Bernstein. *Political Theory* 15/4, pp. 564–80.
—— (1989) *Contingency, Irony, and Solidarity*. Cambridge University Press, Cambridge.
—— (1990) Introduction to Murphy 1990.
—— (1997a) Introduction to Sellars 1997.
—— (1997b) What Do You Do When They Call You a 'Relativist'? *Philosophy and Phenomenological Research* 57, pp. 173–7.
—— (1998a) *Achieving Our Country: Leftist Thought in Twentieth-Century America*. Harvard University Press, Cambridge, Mass.
—— (1998b) *Philosophical Papers*, vol. 3: *Truth and Progress*. Cambridge University Press, Cambridge.
—— (1999) *Philosophy and Social Hope*. Penguin, New York.
—— (2000a) Response to Brandom. In Brandom (ed.) 2000, pp. 183–90.
—— (2000b) Universality and Truth. In Brandom (ed.), 2000, pp. 1–30.
—— (2003) Comments on Jeffrey Stout's *Democracy and Tradition*. Paper read at American Academy of Religion Annual Meeting, Atlanta, Ga. 23 November.
—— (2004) Philosophy as a Transitional Genre. In S. Benhabib and N. Fraser (eds), *Pragmatism, Critique, Judgment: Essays for Richard J. Bernstein*, pp. 3–28. MIT Press, Cambridge, Mass.
—— (2007) *Philosophical Papers*, vol. 4: *Philosophy as Cultural Politics*. Cambridge University Press, Cambridge.
—— (ed.) (1967) *The Linguistic Turn: Recent Essays in Philosophical Method*. University of Chicago Press, Chicago.

Rosenthal, S. (2004) Peirce's Pragmatic Account of Perception: Issues and Implications. In C. Misak (ed.), *The Cambridge Companion to Peirce*, pp. 193–213. Cambridge University Press, Cambridge.

Rucker, D. (1969) *The Chicago Pragmatists*. University of Minnesota Press, Minneapolis.

Russell, B. (1910–11) Knowledge by Acquaintance and Knowledge by Description. *Proceedings of the Aristotelian Society* 11, pp. 108–28.

—— (1949) *The Analysis of Mind*. Allen & Unwin, London.

Ryan, A. (1995) *John Dewey and the High Tide of American Liberalism*. Norton, New York.

Sandel, M. J. (1982) *Liberalism and the Limits of Justice*. Cambridge University Press, Cambridge.

Sellars, W. (1949) Realism and the New Way of Words. In Feigl and Sellars 1949, pp. 424–56.

—— (1963) *Science, Perception, and Reality*. Routledge, London.

—— (1997) *Empiricism and the Philosophy of Mind*. Harvard University Press, Cambridge, Mass.

Short, T. L. (2004) The Development of Peirce's Theory of Signs. In C. Misak (ed.), *The Cambridge Companion to Peirce*, pp. 214–40. Cambridge University Press, Cambridge.

Shusterman, R. (1992) *Pragmatist Aesthetics: Living Beauty, Rethinking Art*. Blackwell, Oxford.

Smith, J. E. (1963) *The Spirit of American Philosophy*. Oxford University Press, New York.

—— (1970) *Themes in American Philosophy*. Harper & Row, New York.

Stewart, J. C. (1992) Introduction to Locke 1992.

Stout, J. (2004a) *Democracy and Tradition*. Princeton University Press, Princeton.

—— (2004b) Radical Interpretation and Pragmatism: Davidson, Rorty, and Brandom on Truth. In N. Frankenberry (ed.), *Radical Interpretation in Religion*, pp. 25–52. Cambridge University Press, Cambridge.

—— (2007) On Our Interest in Getting Things Right: Pragmatism without Narcissism. In Misak (ed.) 2007, pp. 7–31.

Taylor, C. (2002) *Varieties of Religion Today: William James Revisited*. Harvard University Press, Cambridge, Mass.

Tugendhat, E. (1989) *Self-Consciousness and Self-Determination*. MIT Press, Cambridge, Mass.

Wellmer, A. (2004) The Debate about Truth: Pragmatism without Regulative Ideas, trans. W. Egginton. In W. Egginton and M. Sandbothe (eds), *The Pragmatic Turn in Philosophy: Contemporary Engagements between Analytic and Continental Thought*, pp. 93–114. State University of New York Press, Albany.

Wenley, M. (1917) *The Life of George Sylvester Morris*. Macmillan, New York.

Westbrook, R. B. (1991) *John Dewey and American Democracy*. Cornell University Press, Ithaca, NY.

Whitehead, A. N. (1959) *Science and the Modern World*. Mentor Books, New York.

Wild, J. (1969) *The Radical Empiricism of William James*. Doubleday, Garden City, NY.

Wilshire, B. (1968) *William James and Phenomenology*. Indiana University Press, Bloomington.

Wittgenstein, L. (2001) *Philosophical Investigations*, trans. G. E. M. Anscombe, 3rd edn. Blackwell, Oxford.

Name Index

Subject Index

children, and intuitive
  self-consciousness 42
Christianized absolute
  idealism 58–9
Civil Rights movement 27
clarity, and Cartesianism 35
cognition
  and inferential processes 39
  intuitive 40
cognitive values 157–8
coherence, and cognitive
  values 157–8
communication, and the linguistic
  turn 151–2
communicative action/reason 24,
  43, 126, 151, 170, 171–2
  truth and normative
  rightness 172–3, 178
communicative freedom 24
communitarianism 81–2
community, and objectivity 111,
  164–5
community of inquirers 36, 112,
  116–17
conceptual analysis 26
conceptual determination 41
conflict
  in democratic politics 83–5
  and experience 92
consciousness
  and empiricism 56–8
  and the linguistic turn 170
  and pure experience 138
  and Secondness 132
constraint, and epistemic
  authority 50
constructivism 185–6, 192–3, 194
consummatory phase of
  experience 147–8
contextualism 176, 177, 179
Continental philosophy ix, x, 22,
  26, 104, 105, 215
conventionalism 115, 124

correspondence theories of
  truth 107–10, 114–15
counterfactuals 26
creative democracy x, 75–6, 86–7,
  88
critical commonsensism 33–4
cultural anthropology 127
cultural context of
  pragmatism 5–10
cultural politics 210, 214, 215

Darwinian naturalism 128, 144–5,
  148, 150
deconstruction 29–30, 126
deep humanism 201, 211–16
deliberative democracy 85
democracy 8, 70–88
  and communitarianism 81–2
  conflict in democratic
  politics 83–5
  creative x, 75–6, 86–7, 88
  deliberative 85
  epistemological justification
  of 163–4
  and ethical communities
  165–5
  ethics of 71–5
  failures of 79–81
  and liberalism 81–3
  negative connotations of 70
  radical 24–5, 27, 77–88, 152,
  213
  and social cooperation 85–7
democratic *ethos* 74, 76–7, 79
democratic realism 74–5
democratic sovereignty 72–3
descriptive statements, and moral
  judgements 180–1
determinism 142
discourse, and action 181–5,
  186–92
discourse theory 126
  of ethics 126, 178–9

race, and pluralism   64, 65–9
radical democracy   24–5, 27, 77–88
  and humanism   213
  and the linguistic turn   152
radical empiricism, and
    experience   137, 138–41
rational constraint   48–9
rationalist pragmatism   103
rationality, and the "Pittsburgh
    Hegelians"   103
readiness-to-hand   20
realism
  democratic   74–5
  epistemological   171, 185–6,
    198–9
  metaphysical   114, 161–2, 163
  moral   163–7
  pragmatic   161, 162
realistic intuitions   123–4, 136,
    176, 184, 192, 193, 197–8
reality, and objectivity   111, 114
reductionism   21, 26
reductive materialism   142
reductive naturalism   23
regulative ideals, truth and
    justification with   116–19
relativism   23, 29, 53–5, 120
  bad relativism   109–10, 115, 124
  ethical/cultural   159–60
  and pluralism   162
religious experience   137, 141–3
religious intolerance   65
representation, and the linguistic
    turn   151
representational theories of
    mind   140
representationalism   114
republicanism, and democracy   86
rightness, and truth   180–1, 181–5

scholasticism, and Cartesianism
    17–18, 32, 40
science

and cognitive values   157–8
  and ethics   166
  scientific objectivity   162, 163
scientism   23, 142
Secondness   49, 50, 51, 93, 129,
    130, 131–2, 135–6, 152, 192,
    199
semantics   119–20, 134
  inferential   16, 103, 177–8
semeiotics   44–6
signs
  and inferential processes   39
  and the linguistic turn   151
  and Thirdness   133–4, 136
  and thoughts   18, 19, 44–6
simplicity, and cognitive
    values   157–8
situatedness (*Befindlichkeit*)   20
skepticism
  epistemological   18, 37
  ethical   166
Social Contract theory, and
    democracy   72
social cooperation, and
    democracy   85–7
social Darwinism   84
social justification, and
    truth   176–7
social practices   9, 16, 104
  and objectivity   110, 120, 164–5
social reform, and pragmatism   8
soft objectivity   123
solidarity   176, 207, 209, 211
sovereignty, democratic   72–3
Soviet Union (former), and
    democracy   70–1, 78–9
Spanish–American war
    (1898)   63–4
spectator theory of knowledge   x,
    9, 19
stream of experience   137
subjective individualism   18
subjectivism   36